worship:

a
   s:

spirituality
and liturgy

Michael downey

The Pastoral Press

Washington, DC

ISBN: 1-56929-021-0

Copyright © The Pastoral Press, 1994

The Pastoral Press
225 Sheridan Street, N.W.
Washington, D.C. 20011
(202) 723-1254

The Pastoral Press is the publications division of the National Association of Pastoral Musicians, a membership organization of musicians and clergy dedicated to fostering the art of musical liturgy.

Printed in the United States of America

Dedicated
to

Isabelle Keiss, R.S.M.
(1931-1994)

in whose life I have known
the abundance of mercy

and
to

Richard Byrne, O.C.S.O.
(1942-1992)

who urged me to see
the contemplative dimension of everyday living

Acknowledgments

Acknowledgment is gratefully made to the publishers for granting permission to use again, sometimes in edited form, the following: "Region of Wound and Wisdom: The Heart in the Spirituality of Jean Vanier and l'Arche," *Spiritualities of the Heart: Approaches to Personal Wholeness in Christian Tradition*, ed. Annice Callahan (Mahwah, NJ/ New York: Paulist Press, 1990) pp. 186-200; "*Lex Orandi, Lex Credendi*: Taking It Seriously in Systematic Theology," *A Promise of Presence: Studies in Honor of David N. Power, O.M.I.*, ed. Michael Downey and Richard Fragomeni (Washington, DC: The Pastoral Press, 1992) pp. 3-25; "Understanding Christian Spirituality: Dress Rehearsal for a Method," *Spirituality Today* 43:3 (Fall 1991) pp. 271-280; "Christian Spirituality: Changing Currents, Perspectives, Challenges," *America* 170:11 (2 April 1994) pp. 8-10, 12; "Looking to the Last and the Least: A Spirituality of Empowerment," *That They Might Live: Power, Empowerment, and Leadership in the Church*, ed. Michael Downey (New York: Crossroad, 1991) pp. 176-192; "Trinitarian Spirituality: Participation in Communion of Persons," *Eglise et Théolgie* 24:1 (1993) pp. 109-123; "Hurdles to the Holy: Cultural Obstacles to Prayer," *Chicago Studies* 31:1 (April 1992) pp. 45-58; "Illegal Compassion: The Sanctuary Movement in the United States," *Doctrine and Life* 36:8 (October 1986) pp. 411-419; "A Balm for All Wounds: The Spiritual Legacy of Etty Hillesum," *Spirituality Today* 40:1 (Spring 1988) pp. 18-35; "Mercy within Mercy within Mercy: The Place of Vulnerability in Prayer," *Spiritual Life* 32:1 (Spring 1986) pp. 16-19; "Brief Gold," *Weavings* 8:4 (July/August 1993) pp. 17-27; "Making a Way," *Weavings* 9:4 (July/August 1994) pp. 6-16; "Widening Contexts of Sacramental Worship," *Pastoral Sciences/Sciences Pastorales* 13 (1994); "Liturgy's Form: Work of the Spirit," *Studies in Formative Spirituality* 9:1 (February 1988) pp. 17-26; "Worship Between the Holocausts," *Theology Today* 43:1 (April 1986) pp. 75-87; "Rhythms of the Word: A Spirituality of the Liturgy of the Hours," *Cistercian Studies Quarterly* 26:2 (Spring 1991) pp. 152-164; "Cry Aloud Daughter of Zion: Lament in Worship," *Today's Liturgy* 10:2 (February 1988) p. 16; "Status Inconsistency and the Politics of Worship," *Horizons* 15:1 (1988) pp. 64-76; "In the Ache of Absence: Spirituality at the Juncture of Modernity and Postmodernity," *Liturgical Ministry* 3 (Summer 1994) pp. 92-99.

Contents

Weakness Brought to Worship

Epilogue

Introduction

It is an unexpected pleasure to be given the opportunity to gather into one volume many of the articles and essays I have written since beginning teaching Christian spirituality and sacramental theology in 1982. The collection is quite diverse. The writings take up a wide range of topics with different readerships in mind. But there is an abiding concern throughout. It is my hope that if the collection is read with this concern in mind, what is gathered here will be of some use to those concerned with spirituality and liturgy at the margins of church and society.

My abiding concern during the course of my doctoral work and beyond has been to give shape to a spirituality of the weak, the wounded, the forgotten. The terms "weak," "wounded," and "forgotten" apply to persons and groups in the first place. But my concern includes the weak, wounded, and forgotten dimensions of the self as well; dimensions such as affectivity, vulnerability, and the heart, which I understand to be a region of wound and wisdom as well as the locus for discovering the true self. Put crisply: the person *is* the heart.

In *A Blessed Weakness: The Spirit of Jean Vanier and l'Arche* (San Francisco: Harper & Row, 1986), I expressed an understanding of the human person that emerges from living in community with persons who are mentally handicapped. This view of human nature recognizes that the seeds of the divine and the capacities of the human heart are found in weakness and suffering, not in power and strength. Such an understanding of the person stresses the central role of affectivity as the capacity within human beings to touch and to be touched by another, others, and God, and thereby to be in relation.

The sacredness and dignity of the human person, Jesus' cause as the cause of the oppressed, weak, and marginalized echo through the pages of *Clothed in Christ: The Sacraments and Christian Living* (New York: Crossroad, 1987). Here I attempted to describe the sacramental life of the church as expressive of an ethical horizon of communion, justice, and self-sacrificial love in which the poor, the weak, and the wounded hold pride of place. *Clothed in Christ* seems to have been helpful only if read in light of its purpose.

The present volume provides an opportunity to give further shape to a theology of the weak and forgotten by bringing together reflections on a spirituality that arises from the experience of weakness and marginalization together with reflections attempting to raise awareness of how such experiences might be brought to the fore in worship. The essays do not so much describe the liturgical life of persons and groups at the margins, but rather challenge the churches to examine how the experience of weakness and marginalization, as well as "negative" human experiences of disruption and disorientation, might be brought before God in prayer and in the corporate worship of a community.

Why this abiding concern for a spirituality of the weak and marginalized? Above all, it is because of a deeply held personal and theological conviction that the most vital signs of the work of the Holy Spirit are to be discerned in the lives of those who live at the margins of social and religious bodies, and in the marginalized dimensions of the self and God.

A second reason for consistently looking to the margins is more timely. Increasing numbers of people experience themselves as marginalized, in one way or another, from the social and religious bodies that constitute the "center" of the sociosymbolic order. For example, many women experience themselves as marginalized from the centers of authority and decision-making in the Roman Catholic Church. Single people are often marginalized in parishes where the virtues of family life are extolled as normative in sermonizing week after week. Lay people in the church often feel marginalized from the centers of power and authority comprised of male, celibate clerics. The list of those who experience themselves as marginalized in one way or another goes on and on. And this is to say nothing of those who feel themselves marginalized from their own deepest center, the "true self." The experience of marginalization is in fact so pervasive that it gives rise to the question of whether the edges, the margins, have indeed become the center.

A third reason for consistently attending to the wounded and the weak, those at the margins of church and society, is a guiding theological conviction regarding the universality and inclusivity of the redemptive mystery. Such a concern demands that experiences of the weak and the marginalized be brought to redemption. From the vantage of liturgical and sacramental theology, this entails making room for the weak and the marginalized, and allowing their experience to stand forth in our assemblies. It also requires that we find ways to "name" or voice our own marginalized and would-be-forgotten experiences, those profoundly negative experiences of loss, vulnerability, diminishment, and disorientation. But making room for such experiences in prayer and worship has vast implications. Once such experiences, persons, and groups are brought to the center of our prayer and worship, they do in fact give shape to a different understanding of redemption. Small wonder that there is resistance to the challenge posed to prevalent understandings of spirituality and liturgy by those who are last and least, wounded and weak, ignored and forgotten in both church and society.

My purpose in these pages is to attend to the Holy Spirit in the experience of weakness, discerning therein the contours of a spirituality that emerges from life at the margins.

The work is divided into five parts. In the first part I attempt to give some indication of the most formative influences in my own attempt to articulate a spirituality and theology of the weak. This requires attention to the life and work of Jean Vanier, founder of the l'Arche community for mentally handicapped persons, as well as to the thought of David N. Power, my mentor and doctoral dissertation director at The Catholic University of America. In this first part I offer a framework for understanding Christian spirituality, attentive to several features characteristic of contemporary Christian spirituality, to some of the pitfalls in this area, and to the challenges that yet await those concerned with spirituality. In part one I also attempt to articulate a spirituality rooted in the powers of the weak, and look to the mentally handicapped as a model for both human and Christian living.

In the second part of the collection, I have gathered quite disparate essays that explore very different experiences of weakness. Attention is given to the stumbling efforts we make to develop the life of prayer when faced with seemingly insurmountable obstacles posed by the culture in which we live. Then there is a description of the lives of those whose grasp on life in "the land of the free and the home of the brave" is ever so insecure. And there is also the story of a "girl" who did not know how to pray, but who finds herself gradually brought to her knees in the presence of a vulnerable God.

Part three contains three essays written in a voice that speaks of vulnerability in prayer, of our need for boundless mercy, and of the grace that heals as we suffer loss and when the world we live in crumbles.

In the fourth part I have brought together studies that in one way or another attempt to stretch prevalent understandings of sacrament and liturgy. There is a description of the ethical horizon expressed in sacramental worship, stressing the reciprocal relationship between liturgy and living, sacrament and spirituality. Then there is an essay in which I argue that normative liturgical forms must be shaped and reshaped constantly by the presence of the Holy Spirit at work in human life, history, world, and church.

In the fifth part I have gathered essays that address the importance of bringing weakness to worship. Attention is given to the critical function of the word that unsettles dominant modes of being and perceiving, and offers a new vision of a world in which the wounded and the weak, the last and the least, will hold pride of place. I have included essays that address the need for naming the negative in prayer and worship, bringing to worship those experiences and events that remind us of our vulnerability and of our wounds. The fifth part closes with an essay arguing that to welcome the wounded and weak into our assemblies, and indeed to accept our own deepest woundedness and weakness, is central to the gift and task of participating fully in the Christian mysteries.

In the epilogue I address the issues of a Christian spirituality which emerges from the experience of the absence of God at this juncture of modernity and postmodernity.

It is my hope that this volume will offer a clearer understanding of a spirituality of the weak, and provide an occasion for learning a little about spirituality and liturgy from those living at the edges of social and religious institutions by choice, calamity, or circumstance. My aim is not to advocate a place for the marginalized in church and society. It is rather to indicate that something crucial is to be learned about Christian life, spirituality, and liturgy from the experience of those engaged in the painful and lifelong struggle to accept and to celebrate marginalization as a permanent factor of their existence.

What follows is the effort of an able-bodied, white, middle-class, male Roman Catholic theologian to turn attention to the strengths of the weak. The volume is intended for those who are attempting to live the fullness of the Gospel but find themselves at the edges, pushed and shoved to the margins by those who live at the "center" of church and society. I hope that in these pages composed over the course of the last dozen years I have expressed some of what I have learned from different persons and groups who have taught me to see that human weakness, vulnerability, failure, and marginalization need not be perceived as a curse, but may be received as a blessing and as a way of participating in the very life of God.

For the invitation to gather these various essays into one volume, I am grateful to Larry Johnson and to Virgil Funk. My exchanges with Larry Johnson and with Kathleen Schaner of The Pastoral Press could not have been more congenial, making of this project a privilege rich and rare.

FOUNDATIONS FOR
A SPIRITUALITY
OF THE WEAK

1

Region of Wound and Wisdom

CHRISTIAN LIVING IS MOTIVATED BY A WAY OF VIEWING THINGS.[1] THE Spirit illumines the mind and guides the heart, enabling Christians to live by vision and hope. Christian spirituality is concerned with the ways in which the Spirit works in human life and calls forth various forms of Christian living born of different ways of viewing things and diverse approaches to making sense out of the practicalities of Christian living.

With this in mind, we may speak of the life of Jean Vanier and the communities of l'Arche in terms of a spirituality of the heart. Vanier's mode of perceiving and being is shaped in great measure by a conviction about the priority of the heart in human and Christian living. The precise nature of the heart, whose centrality gives rise to a particular way of perceiving and being at l'Arche (its spirituality), is the subject of this chapter. The following strategy will be used in explaining Vanier's understanding of the heart.

A brief biography of Vanier will be provided as well as a short introduction to the communities of l'Arche.

Since Vanier's understanding of the heart is influenced by several significant persons and events, it will be necessary to examine these. Of particular importance is Vanier's encounter with handicapped persons who have influenced his understanding of heart in a crucial way.

To appreciate Vanier's understanding of the heart, his own view must be seen in light of more traditional formulations.

Though influenced by traditional philosophical and theological insights, Vanier's view of the heart is spelled out in much simpler terms.

Vanier's way of seeing the heart leads to a unique view of the importance of friendship, justice, and contemplation in Christian life. It also provides for understanding the basis within which both action and contemplation are rooted. These elements will be highlighted.

By way of conclusion, a synopsis of Vanier's contribution to a spirituality of the heart will be offered.

VANIER AND L'ARCHE: IN BRIEF

A Canadian, born in Geneva, Switzerland, on 10 September 1928, Jean Vanier is one of five children of the late nineteenth Governor-General of Canada, Georges Philias Vanier, and his wife, Pauline Archer Vanier. Many things could be said about Jean Vanier, even in a very brief biographical sketch like this. Let it suffice to nod in several directions.

After serving in the Royal Navy as well as in the Royal Canadian Navy, Vanier resigned his commission in 1950.

Sometime after his resignation from the navy, Vanier joined l'Eau Vive, a small community of students, predominantly lay, situated in a poor neighborhood near Paris, close to the Dominican community of Le Saulchoir. Shortly after his arrival at l'Eau Vive, Vanier was asked to direct the community when ill-health forced the resignation of his friend and teacher, Dominican Thomas Philippe. Vanier directed the community under adverse circumstances for approximately six years, at which point he himself resigned from the directorship.

In 1962 Vanier successfully completed his doctoral dissertation in philosophy at l'Institut Catholique de Paris. Upon completing his dissertation, *Le Bonheur: principe et fin de la morale aristotélicienne,*[2] Vanier began teaching philosophy at Saint Michael's College in Toronto.

Shortly after beginning his career as professor of moral philosophy, Vanier moved to Trosly-Breuil, France, at the suggestion of his friend and former teacher Thomas Philippe. There he bought a small, dilapidated house, which he called l'Arche, the

Ark—Noah's Ark. After visiting a number of institutions, asylums, and psychiatric hospitals, Vanier welcomed two mentally handicapped men, Raphael and Philippe, into his home on 4 August 1964.

From the seed sown in Trosly-Breuil in August 1964, l'Arche has grown to include over one hundred communities worldwide, representing over two hundred family-like homes. Small in number, loose in structure, the communities of l'Arche are founded upon the belief in the uniqueness and sacredness of each person, whether handicapped or not. Motivated by the affirmation of the primacy of the beatitudes in Christian and human living, the gifts of each person are to be nurtured and called forth with predilection for the poorest, weakest, and most wounded in community and society. The handicapped and their "assistants" (the non-handicapped) live together in the spirit of the beatitudes.

INFLUENCES UPON JEAN VANIER

To gain a comprehensive understanding of how Vanier views the heart, it is necessary to look to several persons and events that have influenced his understanding of the human person because, for Vanier, the person *is* the heart.

Thomas Philippe

Jean Vanier claims that no individual has been more influential in his own view of the human person in relation to God than the French Dominican, Thomas Philippe.[3] It was Thomas Philippe who directed l'Eau Vive when Vanier first joined the community. It was he to whom Vanier went time and time again for counsel and direction during his early adulthood. It was during a visit with him and at his suggestion that Vanier decided to welcome two mentally handicapped men to live with him. And it is Thomas Philippe who, until his death on 4 February 1993, remained chaplain of the l'Arche community at Trosly-Breuil and Vanier's own "spiritual father."[4] At the level of Vanier's own understanding, the influence of Thomas Philippe appears mainly in five areas. First, Philippe's own Thomistic foundation is very influential in Vanier's development, especially regarding the role of the gift of wisdom as the apex of the spiritual life, and the role of the gifts of the Holy Spirit in completing and perfecting the theological virtues: faith, hope, and charity. Second, the place of the heart at the center of the person, together with the importance of the affective and the knowledge that comes through this medium, in contradistinction to rational knowledge. Third, the place given to the weak and the little in God's plan of salvation, and the notion of the evolution of the human person through stages of life. Fourth, in the understanding of the human person and all creation as mystery. Finally, Thomas Philippe's influence on Vanier is perceived in his concentration on the mystery of the divine childhood, and the agony and passion of Jesus, as well as the relationship between Jesus and Mary.

The Study of Aristotle

While living at l'Eau Vive, but after Thomas Philippe's resignation due to ill health, Vanier studied philosophy at l'Institut Catholique de Paris. The focus of his studies was Aristotle, the Greek philosopher whose influence on Vanier's own thinking he recognizes even today. Vanier's dissertation shows that he judges Aristotle's views to be incomplete in themselves. They need to be completed by Christian insights.[5] It must not be overlooked, however, that Vanier honors the merits of a purely Aristotelian ethic, even if he clearly favors a specifically Christian view. Vanier's study of Aristotle is of significance in the development of his thought because it is indicative of ideas and questions appreciated and retained. This is particularly evident since the notions of justice, friendship, and contemplation, the three highest virtues according to Aristotle, are part of the vision that continues to animate the communities of l'Arche. Such notions are nuanced considerably, however, due to the primacy Vanier attributes to love as the highest activity of God and, consequently, of the person. This affirmation also gives rise to Vanier's opinion that the philosophy of Aristotle needs to be surpassed. Happiness, for Vanier, is not to be defined as the mind's clear gaze toward unchanging, eternal reality, but rather as love's act through which we participate in the very love of God.

Georges Philias Vanier

George P. Vanier, nineteenth Governor-General of Canada, died on 5 March 1967. Jean Vanier was thirty-eight years old at the time of his father's death. Two years later Vanier published a short book on his father's life; it was entitled *In Weakness, Strength.*[6] Not a detailed biographical study, this short work attempt to illustrate the spiritual sources in the life of Georges Vanier. Vanier spells out the contours of his father's spiritual life by articulating various spiritual themes. In this domain lies the most formative influence of Georges Vanier upon his son. These include: (1) God's strength in human weakness; (2) perseverance; (3) littleness; (4) providence; (5) the role of Mary; (6) the primacy of love; and (7) unity.[7]

It is interesting to note that Vanier's book about his father is indicative of many of the attitudes and tensions that become important features later on in the work he himself does, the attitudes he adopts, and the problems he confronts. For example, the contrast between the fear that characterized Georges Vanier's religious life before his conversion to deep Christian faith in 1938 and the primacy of love in his life after that point illustrates a tension about which Jean Vanier grows increasingly aware, as evidenced in his work entitled *Be Not Afraid*, which is in large part a treatment of the dynamics of love and fear.[8] Vanier's references to his father's distaste, on the one hand, for obtuse theological discussions and, on the other hand, his desire to grow in childlikeness and simplicity, are indicative of the problems Jean Vanier himself confronts in his attempt to build communities wherein are joined persons richly endowed with intellectual ability and persons sometimes deeply wounded in terms of mental capacity. Jean Vanier's treatment of his father as one who gave himself to the primacy of love, attentive at the same time to the claims of justice, illustrates the values appreciated and retained throughout his own life and work. His exposure of his father's deep attachment to and affection for his own religious tradition, while at the same time remaining open to the truth within other religious traditions, shows Jean Vanier's own commitment to the idea of the primacy of the human person beyond religious and cultural differences. The interplay he points out between the active and contemplative dimensions of his father's life indicates the struggle Jean Vanier and l'Arche face anew each day in the communal praxis of l'Arche. Finally, the treatment Vanier gives to the theme of power and weakness as one of the foundations of his father's spiritual life, as well as to his father's increased awareness in old age of God's special predilection for the poor, is suggestive of Jean Vanier's own attitude toward what is primary and fundamental in the spiritual life.

Handicapped Persons

The decisive revelation of Vanier's vocation occurred in his encounter with the handicapped people in 1964. As a result of this meeting, Jean Vanier's understanding of the human person was clarified. Vanier writes that his life with handicapped people has taught him far more about living and about human relations than any theory or writing.[9] The decisive event, the pivot around which his life and writings turn, is the meeting of Jean Vanier, Raphael, and Philippe in 1964. We must look to this event if we are to appreciate Jean Vanier's view of the human person and of the heart.

Of the handicapped people of l'Arche, Vanier writes: "they have taught me much about human nature and the real meaning of human existence, the true value of love, of wonder, and even of contemplation."[10] What Vanier could not find in the sophisticated theory of Aristotle, he stumbled upon somewhat unexpectedly in the struggles and half-audible sounds of these two handicapped men. Vanier had learned the systems of thought that emphasize the rational and intellectual capacities of the person. Post-World War II Europe had impressed upon him the importance of efficiency and technology in national and international development. What he had not yet learned prior to the 1964 encounter is that while the person is comprised of the abilities of the intellect (head), and a great capacity for efficiency and productivity (hands), he or she is, more importantly, a being with a heart.[11] In their woundedness and affliction, while not exhibiting the capacities of the head or hands, handicapped persons do demonstrate tremendous qualities of heart: celebration, forgiveness, tenderness, and compassion. For Vanier, the person is composed of head, hands, and heart.[12] The handicapped people of l'Arche enabled Vanier to uncover insight into the third and most important of these dimensions.

Books, papers, lectures, retreats, or conferences of Jean Vanier begin or end with a note of gratitude to the handicapped people of l'Arche for, in his perception, they have taught him about being human and being Christian. In the preface to *Be Not Afraid*, Vanier writes: "I have learned more about the Gospels from handicapped people, those on the margins of our society, those who have been crushed and hurt, than I have from the wise and prudent."[13] It is to them that he looks primarily for insight into the nature of the person and the heart.

How does Vanier explain the insight into the nature of the heart that he has derived from the handicapped? According to Vanier, the handicapped person has been wounded.[14] In the mind or the body, the handicapped person bears the mark of suffering in a very visible way. The mentally handicapped person, for example, bears a wound in the brain or nervous system which causes slow, retarded, or bizarre activity or behavior. Because of this wound and the behavior and activity that result, the handicapped person is afflicted with another wound, far more painful than the first. This deeper wound is an enormous affective frustration that results from the rejection, ostracization, and alienation precisely because of the mental or physical wound.[15] Parents, family, neighbors, and society at large very often reject the handicapped person, and this brings about deep anxiety and suffering.

The wounds of the handicapped place them in a position of weakness.[16] Handicapped people, and especially mentally handicapped people, are not self-reliant. They need help and assistance in the most ordinary affairs of daily living. In contemporary western culture, with its emphasis upon technology, productivity, and competition, handicapped persons are generally viewed as a burden. From this point of view, which finds its early proponents in the Greek philosophers Plato and Aristotle, they are the weak ones who must be carried along through the provision of suitable living conditions, special schools and institutions.[17] Their quite obvious weakness and suffering is perceived as a personal as well as a corporate liability.

The handicapped person is aware of his or her wound and consequent weakness. According to Vanier: "The great suffering of the handicapped person is consciousness of his handicap, his consciousness that he is different than others and because he is different he is not loved."[18] The anguish that results from this awareness of being different from others is frequently far more severe than the anguish of the physical or mental wound itself.

Because the handicapped person is wounded in mind, or body, or both, he or she is often unable to do or accomplish much with the head or hands. As a result, the handicapped person relies much more on the third constitutive element of human nature: the heart.[19] Handicapped persons, deprived of the possibility of accomplishing great things with the head or the hands, are richly endowed with qualities of the heart: joy, celebration, forgiveness, tenderness, and compassion. It is precisely within this domain that the handicapped person is capable of making great progress.

When Vanier first began l'Arche, he understood his mission as one of providing shelter and comfort for people who were not capable of doing much or of making any significant progress.[20] But he quickly found that these handicapped persons, given a warm and loving environment of acceptance and friendship, could make great process and could quickly advance in the domain of the heart.[21] Further, as Vanier quickly learned, in its domain they are often the teachers of the clever and the robust.

Encounter with the Third World

Vanier visited India in 1970 with the hope of beginning a l'Arche community there. While in India he came into contact with the legacy of Mohandas Gandhi. Gandhi's writings and teachings had a significant impact on Vanier. The awareness of the divisions in the world, and the real obstacles to universal justice and friendship, take on increasing significance in the thought and writings of Jean Vanier, and have emerged as a prominent theme in his writings after his contact with India and the legacy of Gandhi. His contact with India enabled him to find in another person of a different religious tradition his same aspirations toward a community of justice and friendship that secures the rights and dignity of the human person, no matter how lowly or despised the person may be. The means to building this community of justice and friendship, for Vanier as for Gandhi, lies in love, gift of self, gentleness, and non-violence: the spirit of the beatitudes, or *ahimsa* in Gandhi's terms. Vanier remains nonetheless Christian throughout, and his encounter with the legacy of Gandhi intensified and deepened his experience of, and commitment to, Jesus Christ and the Gospel, as he himself testifies.[22]

The Gospel

Jean Vanier's reading of the Gospel and its influence upon him predate the foundation of l'Arche. It is difficult to determine at what point in life the Gospel became an influential factor in Vanier's development. Likewise, it is difficult to pinpoint specific scriptural texts that have influenced him. The influence of the Gospel is, rather, all-pervasive; the Gospel was Vanier's original inspiration and has remained his consistent inspiration, even as his views have evolved.

Vanier has written that he began l'Arche in the context of a Christian faith response:

> I began l'Arche in 1964, in the desire to live the Gospel and to follow Jesus Christ more closely. Each day brings me new lessons on how much Christian life must grow in commitment to life in community, and on how much that life needs faith, the love of Jesus and the presence of the Holy Spirit if it is to deepen. Everything I say about life in community . . . is inspired by my faith in Jesus.[23]

In the life of each Christian there are particular gospel themes that have an influential and formative role. The gospel themes that are found attractive and nourishing will vary, at least in part, according to the personality of each individual. Even though in the case of Jean Vanier the Gospel's influence is all-pervasive, we can nonetheless discern three gospel themes that are prominent in his life and writings: (1) the agony and passion of Jesus; (2) the hidden life of Jesus, Mary, and Joseph at Nazareth; and (3) the centrality of the beatitudes in Christian discipleship. The specifically Christian spirituality of l'Arche lies in the interplay of these three gospel themes with the Aristotelian triad of friendship, justice, and contemplation—nuanced by the primacy of love.

THE PERSON CONSTITUTED BY HEART

Vanier does not treat the notion of heart at any length in his doctoral dissertation on Aristotle. However, he does give evidence of his perception, even at the time of its writing, that Aristotle's rather singular focus on reason and intellect stands in need of a corrective.[24] Such a focus leaves out of its scope the great majority of people who could never attain human fulfillment and perfection because of lack of intellectual ability, education, or leisure.[25] Further, the priority given to the powers of intellect, especially in contemplation, leaves little room for the affective dimension.

His objections to Aristotle's vision indicate that Vanier understood the human person in a different light. His vision was even at the time of his study of Aristotle developing around the notion of the heart as the foundation or base of the human person, though this did not clearly emerge till his experience of encounter with the handicapped people of l'Arche.[26]

Vanier's experience with the handicapped enabled him to fill out what he saw as lacking in Aristotle. In Raphael and Philippe, Vanier perceived two men who, by Aristotelian standards, could never arrive at a point of fulfillment. From this perspective these men would be incapable of performing a fully human act, to say nothing of their incapacity for virtue, or the highest virtue of contemplation. Yet Vanier sensed in them something very deep, good, and worthy. Not exhibiting the ability for greatness in Aristotelian terms, they were nonetheless capable of living very simple and joyful lives with deep compassion, joy, and an ability to forgive, reconcile, and celebrate.[27] With very little intellectual ability, or ability to produce things by the work of their hands, the men—and later the women of l'Arche—taught Vanier that there is something deeper, richer, more profound and fundamental to the human person than the intellect.[28] By their very lives these men and women were living examples that it is indeed possible to live a human and happy life without the riches of the intellect. They taught Vanier that there are other values than those of the mind, and those of efficiency and productivity.[29]

Vanier then perceived in the little child, and in the very old, many of the same qualities and characteristics that he had encountered in the mentally handicapped.[30] He also noticed many of the same qualities in people in crisis and distress of all kinds. All these persons found themselves in positions of vulnerability, and therein manifested extraordinary human qualities. Situations of vulnerability, which cause one to live at the most basic level of existence, which Vanier calls the heart, can strengthen and evoke the qualities of the heart and provide the occasion for a deepening of communion.[31] Often it is only when we are stripped of all the strengths and arguments of the intelligence, and deprived of the ability to create and produce through the work of our hands, that we are able to see the essentials of human existence, that which lies deepest. Beneath the levels of intellect, and all the spheres of language, communication, and symbol, there lies the heart, which all have in common. Vanier expresses this by saying that "a person is the heart," the qualities of which must be developed by all.[32] Because all persons have the capacities of the heart, this provides the common basis and groundwork for true advancement and progress among peoples. The notions of compassion, joy, reconciliation, forgiveness, and celebration, which stem from what is deepest and most central in the person, are finally the dimensions that internally unite and vivify the human person. Furthermore, the development of the capacities of the heart make possible the unity of people desired by all.[33] What is needed, according to Vanier, by way of a solution to the massive difficulties throughout the world is a revolution of the heart, of love, of care, of forgiveness, and of compassion.[34]

The Aristotelian foundation of Vanier's view is not to be underestimated, even if this did not satisfy Jean Vanier. It is from the handicapped person that Vanier learns that there is a basis or core within the human person which he calls heart, which needs to be nurtured in the child, at the beginning of everyone's life, and with which mature adults and adolescents need to be in touch. When he turns to people in situations of crisis or distress, and those living in poverty, he brings about a type of synthesis between the Aristotelian foundation and what he has learned from the handicapped. It is precisely when their vulnerability is revealed that non-handicapped persons are most in touch with the heart, and thus that they are able to realize the virtues that Aristotle exalts, like love for truth, communion in friendship, freedom, and desire for justice. They take on a new tone in light of the Gospel, but they are fundamentally the Aristotelian virtues, given a new basis in what Vanier calls heart.

LEARNING FROM HISTORY

For Vanier, the heart is mystery and as a result constitutes the person as mystery. He writes: "The secret of the heart is so impenetrable, so extraordinary—the place where God resides in each one of us."[35] A thorough appreciation of Vanier's understanding of heart necessitates seeing his view in light of more traditional formulations because of the influence they have had upon him. The similarities between Vanier's thought on the heart and these more traditional formulations have been treated elsewhere.[36] A brief survey must suffice here.

The first element from history that helps us understand Vanier's view is the image of the heart in Christian spirituality. The heart connotes the root of diverse personal functions. It describes the origin and source of all thoughts, desires, intentions, but is more fundamental than any one or combination of them. Though in the seventeenth-century French school of spirituality the term "heart" comes to be associated with the will, and more particularly with the emotions, throughout the bulk of the history of Christian spirituality the heart is viewed as the basis and unifying foundation within the human person. It is also understood to be affective inasmuch as it is open to the pull of God's love through the indwelling of the Holy Spirit.

A second element is found in the scholastic tradition. Scholasticism distinguished between *voluntas ut natura* and *voluntas ut ratio*.[37] The former describes the natural tendency within human nature toward the good, whereas the latter refers to the deliberative pursuit of specific objectives and ends. Aquinas does not use it frequently, but the term is used in scholasticism more broadly in describing the radical, fundamental, primitive, drive toward the good within each person. This impulse is prior to thoughts and voluntary actions. *Voluntas ut natura* is an affective tension. It is to be distinguished from the quest for the good and the true which entails deliberation, judgment, and choice. This radical impulse toward the good and the true at the deepest level of the person remains operative throughout life. *Voluntas ut natura* indicates a unity prior to any distinction or separation of human operations. It is, thus, a synthetic concept. It is important in understanding human cognition and activity as well as the spiritual life. The term expresses the understanding that there is in the human person a fundamental tendency to fulfillment with which all thought, choice, and action must remain in touch.

A third factor from history that helps us appreciate Vanier's view on the heart is the Thomistic understanding of the role of the gifts of the Holy Spirit in the person, particularly the gift of wisdom. In the thought of Thomas Aquinas, God's presence resides in the soul through creation. In addition to this, there is a presence that is supernatural through the bestowal of the Holy Spirit. This bestowal is accompanied by an infusion of sanctifying grace. The theological virtues of faith, hope, and charity enable one to strive for the supernatural end as an agent endowed with the ability to perceive and to pursue the divine good. By means of the moral virtues of prudence, justice, temperance, and fortitude we are able to include in this pursuit the human enterprise elevated by grace. Both the theological and the moral virtues are supernatural. However, their principles lie within the person and, as such, the activities of these virtues are human activities.

The gifts of the Holy Spirit may be understood as permanent dispositions within the soul. By means of these dispositions the person may be moved by another, by God, from outside himself or herself. Because the grasp on the supernatural life is tenuous, the gifts are needed to complement the theological and moral virtues. In Aquinas' view of the spiritual organism, the theological virtues have priority. They unite the person to the end pursued, namely, God. This end is sought through the exercise of theological virtues, primarily charity. However, because the hold on the supernatural life is so insecure, the promptings of the Holy Spirit are necessary so that the person might move toward the supernatural end. This movement of the Holy Spirit also gives shape to the exercise of the moral virtues which allow us to act in the supernatural life according to the human mode.

The moral virtues under the influence of the gifts of the Spirit are expressed in the activity of the beatitudes.

A final point regarding the Thomistic view of the gifts is crucial for understanding Vanier's view of the person as heart. The Holy Spirit acting through the gifts, the preeminent of which is wisdom, does not prompt us to do what reason in and of itself would require. Thus, the mentally handicapped person, whose ability to reason may be seriously deficient, is capable of great acts of love when moved by God through the gift of wisdom.

By way of summary, faith, hope, and charity have pride of place in the Thomistic view of the supernatural organism. They join the person to God. The gifts, especially wisdom, complete the theological and moral virtues by disposing the person to the divine impulse or movement necessary to complement the imperfection of the human mode.

VANIER'S UNDERSTANDING OF THE HEART

In articulating his understanding of the heart, Vanier does not use philosophical or theological language. His approach is quite simple and direct. However, the philosophical and theological traditions treated above have shaped his thought, and need to be kept in view if Vanier's understanding of the human person is to be fully appreciated.

For Vanier, heart describes the most fundamental dimension of the person. He understands the person as open to attraction, to be acted up and influenced by another, and to be drawn to relationship and communion. That is to say, he views the person primarily as an affective being. This does not mean that the heart and human life are irrational. It is, rather, to say that understanding, deliberation, and choice are given direction by the affect when it is developed properly. In itself the heart is unformed, ambiguous, dubious, even disordered because of human sinfulness. When it is purified by the action of the Holy Spirit within, it becomes the basis for contemplation (communication and communion with Christ in his mysteries) and action (service of neighbor).

In the active life this attraction is formed as an openness to the weak, the wounded, and the handicapped. It requires that we be touched in our own weakness. In contemplation this love of the weak is related to Jesus in his infancy, agony, and passion as the disclosure of God.

Vanier contrasts the impurity and ambiguity of the human heart in and of itself with the heart renewed by grace. He recognizes a twofold purification of the heart. The first is by the activity of the Holy Spirit. The second occurs through participating in the life of a community in which we experience the impact of love upon ourselves.

Vanier is concerned with human needs of an affective sort. This concern helps him understand the affective dimension of human nature, and also enables him to articulate what is referred to in scholasticism by *voluntas ut natura*. But for Vanier, this is better appreciated in terms of human needs, longing, affectivity, and their fulfillment. Further, his attention to human needs helps him understand that dimension of human nature which is touched and transformed by the gifts of the Holy Spirit.

Vanier speaks of the three great needs of the human person: the need for light, life, and love. These needs might also be understood as the needs for knowledge, freedom, and love. Vanier's understanding of need is based upon experience, in which vulnerability and weakness are crucial, as is human affectivity. In speaking of the heart, Vanier is describing basic human needs, with attention to vulnerability and attraction to communion in love.

All this is related to an understanding of grace that heals and corrects the affective (*gratia sanans*). This grace also disposes one to the movements of God in the most vulnerable region of the heart. These may come directly to the person or may come through others in community. As a result, one can pursue the good through the active life, and likewise be disposed to the contemplation of God's love in the mystery of Jesus Christ.

In referring to the appeal to the heart and the instincts or promptings of the heart, Vanier is in line with Thomas' understanding of the gifts of the Holy Spirit. However, he has his own particular view, namely, that God's grace and attraction touch us at the most vulnerable region of human existence, and it is response to this action that moves us to compassion, joy, celebration, forgiveness, and similar qualities of the heart. The heart is what can be attracted, touched, moved, acted upon; the affective inasmuch as drawn, rather than moving toward of its own motion. Consequently those who act from the heart, when moved by God to compassion, become signs of God's love and tenderness.

Central to Vanier's thought on the heart is his understanding of love, which he treats in terms of compassion and openness to the wounded and the weak. Love is of preeminence for Vanier because it reflects God's very nature. Love is the highest activity of the human person. From Vanier's Christian perspective, love sublates and nuances the Aristotelian virtues of justice, friendship, and contemplation.

On the basis of this, there is a reformulation of the understanding of justice, since in efforts to bring about the common good the needs of the vulnerable and wounded should have priority. Of crucial import in the carrying out of justice is the virtue of hope, which is related to freedom. In pursuing justice we need to cultivate other cognate virtues, such as poverty, simplicity, and abandonment. Justice is the pursuit of the good for the many in obedience to the mandates of the heart transformed by grace. The exercise of justice is aimed at the establishment of an order in which *la connaissance du coeur* has an important place, and the weak, wounded, and vulnerable have a certain priority.

The goal of knowledge given in contemplation is itself based in love, since it is rooted in the heart, and looks to the weak and vulnerable, or to the mystery of Jesus in the weakness of his infancy and hidden life, as well as to his agony and passion for God's revelation. Contemplation is of the mystery of God revealed in the weak, and in the weakness of Jesus in his infancy, in his hidden life with Mary and Joseph at Nazareth, and at his agony and passion.

Friendship comes about by response to *la connaissance d'amour* as we ourselves are prompted by the attractions of grace and of the heart in another, making friendship possible between any two persons, even those who are vastly unequal in terms of human capacity. Such a view of friendship is inconceivable in strictly Aristotelian terms.

There continues to be a need for rational deliberation and prudence, as well as for the exercise of the moral virtues in efforts to realize the goals of the reign of God.

VANIER'S CONTRIBUTION TO A
SPIRITUALITY OF THE HEART

By way of conclusion we can spell out in six points the contribution of Vanier and l'Arche to an understanding of the heart in Christian spirituality.

First, Vanier has retrieved the early Christian understanding of the heart as the basis and unifying foundation within the human person. This is affective inasmuch as open to the attraction of God's love experienced directly through the prompting or impulse of the Holy Spirit, or through the attraction of love experienced with others.

Second, he has attributed positive significance to the inevitable human realities of woundedness, weakness, vulnerability, crisis, and suffering by finding therein the possibility of the revelation of the divine and the capacity of the human heart.

Third, because the inspiration of Vanier's life has been the service of the handicapped, and it has been in conjunction with his work and life with them that his thought has developed and been expressed, Vanier offers insight into an understanding of "social" spirituality of service to the weak, and of peace built on recognizing vulnerability and openness to the transcendent.

Fourth, Vanier has managed to keep in focus the primacy of personal relationship with Jesus Christ and the Gospel, thereby maintaining the quintessential value of the evangelical dimension in authentic Christian living.

Fifth, because of his focus upon significant others in human life and upon the need for community, as well as his analysis of human needs, especially affective needs, the interpersonal dimension of the spiritual life is explicated in Vanier's life and thought.

Finally, by establishing the heart as the basis and foundation within the human person, Vanier has made it possible to understand contemplation and action as unified through the gift of wisdom which resides in the deepest recesses of the one and same source.

Notes

1. Jean-Pierre de Caussade, *Lettres spirituelles*, ed. Michel Olphe-Galliard, vol. 1 (Paris: Desclée de Brouwer, 1962) 64.

2. Jean Vanier, *Le Bonheur: Principe et fin de la moral aristotélicienne* (Paris: Desclée De Brouwer, 1965).

3. Jean Vanier, personal interview held at the community of l'Arche, Trosly-Breuil, France, 15 June 1981.

4. Jean Vanier, introduction to Michael Downey, *A Blessed Weakness: The Spirit of Jean Vanier and l'Arche* (San Francisco: Harper & Row, 1986) ix.

5. See Vanier, *Le Bonheur* 420-421.

6. Jean Vanier, *In Weakness, Strength* (Toronto: Griffin House 1969, 1975).

7. For a fuller treatment of these, see Vanier, *In Weakness.*

8. Jean Vanier, *Be Not Afraid* (New York: Paulist Press, 1975).

9. Jean Vanier, *Eruption to Hope* (Toronto: Griffin House, 1971) 46.

10. Vanier, *Eruption* 39.

11. See ibid. 42, 47.

12. Vanier, *Eruption* 41, 42, 47; see also Jean Vanier, "Vivre avec le pauvre à l'école de Marie et de Joseph," *Cahiers marials* 129 (September 1981) 205-216.

13. Vanier, *Be Not Afraid* viii.

14. See Vanier, *Eruption*, Preface 1.

15. Jean Vanier, "Normalization and Changing Concepts in Residential Care" (mimeographed, 1972) 1.

16. See Vanier, *Eruption* 39-42.

17. See ibid.

18. Jean Vanier, "Spiritual Needs of the Handicapped" (mimeographed) 2; text in hand is a reprint from *Letters of l'Arche* 7 (Summer 1974) 24-27.

19. See Vanier, *Eruption* 42, 47.

20. "Jean Vanier's Account of the Evolution of His Concept of l'Arche," *Letters of l'Arche* 8 (Winter 1974/75) 10.

21. See "Jean Vanier's Account" 11.

22. See Vanier, *Eruption*, Preface 1-2.

23. Jean Vanier, *Community and Growth,* tr. Ann Shearer (New York: Paulist Press, 1979) xi; see also 35-36.

24. See Vanier, *Le Bonheur* 418-421.

25. See ibid. 419.

26. See ibid. 418-421, especially his reference to "le don de l'Esprit Saint" p. 420 and "la loi nouvelle de l'Amour" p. 421.

27. See Vanier, *Eruption* 45-46.

28. See ibid. 47.

29. See ibid. 45.

30. See Vanier, *Community* 79.

31. See Vanier, *Eruption* 42, 48.

32. See Vanier, *Be Not Afraid* 12.

33. See ibid. 12ff.

34. See Vanier, *Eruption* 102.

35. Vanier, "Spiritual Needs" 1.

36. See Michael Downey, "Jean Vanier: Recovering the Heart," *Spirituality Today* 38:4 (Winter 1986) 337-348.

37. For this treatment of the connection between the heart and the scholastic notion of *voluntas ut natura*, I am indebted to Marie-Dominique Chenu, "Les Catégories affectives dans la langue de l'école," in *Le Coeur*, Etudes carmélitaines 29 (n.p. Desclée de Brouwer and Cie, 1950) 123-128.

2

Doxological Praxis
and the Heart's Desire

It is now more commonly recognized that the Second Vatican Council encouraged and supported forces of renewal that had been at work in the church for generations. The reforms sanctioned by the council, and the renewal to which it has given rise, have brought about a "sea change" in church life and practice. Perhaps no other area of ecclesial life has been as profoundly affected by the reform and, in turn, furthered the reform and renewal, than has sacramental practice and worship.

The aim of this chapter is not to survey the developments in the sacramental life of the churches brought on by the Second Vatican Council. Nor is it to analyze, assess, or evaluate those developments. It is, rather, to spell out significant characteristics of the work of David Noel Power in such a way as to assist students and teachers of sacramental and liturgical theology in understanding some of the developments in the field during the post-conciliar period. David Power has taken liturgy seriously as a source in doing theology. It is to be hoped that in spelling out significant features in the work of this one theologian, a contribution might be made toward gaining a clearer understanding of the directions taken in sacramental and liturgical theology as a whole, as well as of the challenges that yet await us in our common work.

What many astute students and teachers of sacrament and liturgy have come to see is that the elements of a sacramental theology found in quite disparate fashion in this or that essay or monograph, the insights and snippets unearthed here and there in a given liturgiologist, historian of liturgy, or sacramental theologian, are found in a more systematic and integrated fashion in the work of David Power. This is not to say that Power simply synthesizes the work of others in such a way that the main lines of post-conciliar developments are more clearly articulated in his writings. If it is true that his work is indicative of significant turns in sacramental theology since the council, it is equally true that he has given methodological form to the study of this subject. This he has done by opening up the discourse about liturgy and sacrament to include other fields, as well as by the nature of his probings, the types of needs he addresses, the kinds of questions he engages, and the way he brings the Christian sacramental tradition to bear on the pressing needs and urgent demands of our age.

David Power is first and foremost a systematic theologian. And there may be a distinct advantage in surveying the writings of this systematic theologian in chronological order. One advantage of such a strategy is that it would provide occasion to note how his thought has developed from earlier to later stages. Having read all of David Power's work, I have opted for a different course. Rather than providing a tightly-knit survey and synthesis from the "early Power" to the "later Power," I have judged it more useful to draw attention to five *jalons de route*, signposts or indicators along the way, by which we can navigate part of the course that sacramental theology has taken in the years since the council. These are: (1) Looking to Liturgy as Source for Theology; (2) Text, Context, and the Complexity of Interpretation; (3) The Multivalence of Symbol, Language, and Culture; (4) From Liturgy to Worship: Speaking the Name of God; (5) Prayer as the Praxis of Desire. Careful attention to these indicators may provide further clarity as we navigate the course that yet awaits us at the brink the third millennium of the Christian tradition. Looking to the work of David Power can help us understand where we have traveled, as well as give some indication of the terrain that lies ahead.

LOOKING TO LITURGY
AS SOURCE FOR THEOLOGY

The work of David Power has been that of a systematic theologian who has taken with utmost seriousness the implications of the aphorism *lex orandi, lex credendi*. This entails the recognition that the prayer of the church is a vital locus for theological reflection. The church's prayer is brought to full expression in its liturgical life; hence *lex orandi, lex credendi* cannot be properly understood if untethered from a liturgical context. Though liturgy as locus for theological reflection has been a long-standing concern, it is sometimes more readily affirmed in theory than validated in practice.[1]

The Constitution on the Sacred Liturgy of the Second Vatican Council emphasized the importance of the liturgy as "source and summit of Christian life" (SC 10), and urged the reformation of liturgical rites "as soon as possible" (SC 25) so as to foster renewal and restoration based on "sound tradition" (SC 23). Accompanying this was a revitalization of interest in liturgical studies and liturgical theology, as well as significant reorientations in sacramental theology.[2] As was the case with the study of Scripture, the patristic sources, church councils, and history, new approaches to the study of liturgy and sacrament emphasized the importance of clearly articulated methods of investigation. The work of David Power may be understood not only as an effort to spell out methods for the study of liturgy and sacrament, but also to open up the discourse about this subject to include the discourse of other fields of investigation.[3]

The existence of several notable learned societies devoted to the ongoing work of liturgical studies and renewal indicates a recognition that liturgy, prayer, and spirituality are vital sources of rigorous investigation and reflection for Christian life and practice.[4] The singular importance of liturgy as a source for Christian life and reflection that is affirmed in both conciliar documents and theological positions needs to be consistently verified in the doing of systematic theology, influencing thereby systematic theology's methods, content, and conclusions.

TEXT, CONTEXT, AND THE
COMPLEXITY OF INTERPRETATION

Power's efforts have been given to probing the relationship between liturgy and culture by means of the hermeneutical repertoire of a systematic theologian. Central to this task has been the contextual interpretation and appropriation of liturgical texts and practices, both historical and contemporary. His primary task has been the mediation of worship to culture through theological thought.[5] Consequently, his work has involved different content and methods from the work of those whose primary attention has focused upon understanding the history of liturgical rites.

A systematic theological interpretation and appropriation of liturgical texts and traditions requires an awareness of the cultural settings, worldviews, ideologies, and philosophies operative in interaction between interpreter and text. Texts must be analyzed with an awareness of how language relates to meaning. This entails viewing the text within its ritual context which, in turn, must be placed within an ecclesial context of order and ministry, with particular attention to regional differences. In addition, these factors must be interfaced with theologies operative in the period(s) under consideration, particularly their explicit or implicit understanding of ritual development. Alongside these considerations, attention must be given to popular religiosity and the different meanings associated with its ritual enactment vis-à-vis predominant liturgical texts and traditions.

This work of interpretation and appropriation, in contrast to historical or doctrinal analysis pure and simple, is present even in Power's first published work. His dissertation presented for the degree of Doctor of Theology in the Liturgical Institute of San Anselmo in Rome is an attempt to interpret ordination rites as a source for theology.[6] This he does in view of the shifting perceptions and worldviews of the subject, i.e., the ordained, the needs of the community, various social factors operative in the formulation of ordination rites, and the relationship between the theologies of priesthood found in the rites to those described in other branches of theology. In his second book, *Christian Priest: Elder and Prophet*, the context for understanding ministry is widened still further, so as to include the influence of practical and even political factors in the formulation, interpretation, and appropriation of liturgical texts and practice.[7]

Interpreting the meaning of text in context entails much more than historical or doctrinal hermeneutics of the text itself. Interpretation always entails appropriation. This means that in interpreting a text there is an interaction between where we stand (our worldview) and the standpoint or worldview of the text. In this interaction, effort must be made to examine the presuppositions held by the one interpreting as well as the horizon within which the text is to be properly understood. Thus interpretation and appropriation demand that a wider view be taken so as to render account of thought forms and worldviews that influence formulation of texts and practices, and call for a self-critical consciousness of the assumptions and ideologies that underlie any interpretation. Attentive to the further implications of *lex orandi, lex credendi*, Power has been concerned throughout to demonstrate the reciprocal relationship between liturgical practice and ethics, thus attending to needs and concerns well beyond the boundaries of the text itself.[8]

Power's own standpoint or worldview cannot be understood without attention to the "option for praxis" apparent in his own interpretation and appropriation of texts and traditions. The praxis option that is already clearly evidenced in *Christian Priest: Elder and Prophet* underpins the volume of *Concilium* on *Politics and Liturgy* edited together with his mentor Herman Schmidt in 1974,[9] and continues throughout his subsequent publications. No doubt influenced by the Lonerganian schema of conversion in the task of appropriation, and by the crucial role of praxis therein, Power situates praxis at the heart of the dialectic of appropriation. Praxis forges the relationship between what is expressed in liturgy and the doing or activity of the Gospel in human life, history, world, and church. From the vantage point of the praxis option in interpretation and appropriation, liturgy does not precede praxis; one is not followed by the other. Liturgical expression and ethics are co-efficients. Liturgy is "speech-ifying" in such a way that there can be no truth in a liturgy that preaches a God of love but is not itself as large as the Gospel.

Integral to this "praxis option" is the critical function operative in reading liturgical texts and traditions.[10] In the interaction of appropriation, Power has opted for a critical stance toward the ideologies present in liturgical texts and rituals themselves. This critique calls for attention to the "Word beneath the words." We can speak of the "Word beneath the words" here if we give an analogous meaning to "Word." Power is not looking for some specific idea, metaphor, or concept; the "Word" is an address from within, as it were, that is laid bare when texts are dealt with adequately. Cognizant that such a Word is not easily discerned, it is nonetheless this which God has spoken, which beckons to ongoing conversion, and which, therefore, is to be gleaned in any interpretation and appropriation of liturgical text and tradition. Critique of ideology allows for attention to this Word, along with attention to speech that breaks open common forms of discourse. An ideology critique of prevailing meanings, plus attention to poetic and metaphoric language which "crack" words, makes it possible to hear this inner Word which questions assumptions and systems and enlarges desire that reaches beyond the precincts of language and thought. Once freed from obfuscation and untethered from ideological wraps, the Word beneath the words can then critique ideologies and worldviews antipathetic to the freedom of the Gospel.[11]

In this view of interpretation and appropriation, taking *lex orandi, lex credendi* seriously in systematic theology means that any theological understanding of the God-world relation cannot rely purely on doctrinal or scholastic descriptions. Similarly, attempts to articulate theological positions primarily in view of a Lonerganian, Rahnerian, Heideggerian, Freudian, Jungian, or Marxian framework prove deficient if account is not taken of the ways in which the perception of the God-world relation is lived out in liturgical practice and in the ethical implications of such practice. Some access to this is given through liturgical texts and practices in context. But such access is never as easy as it may first seem. Interpretation of text as well as the appropriation of its meaning is always a complex task yielding results that are necessarily incomplete and, consequently partial, tentative, and in need of further revision and refinement.

In the complex task of interpretation of text in context, even and especially when effort is made to include other data beyond the text in service of this aim, it might be thought that arriving at adequate and accurate meanings is indeed always possible.[12] Meanings gained through textual interpretation, however, may be more the result of presuppositions and convictions brought to the text in the process of appropriation than the fruit of rigorous attention to methods and data. Presuppositions and horizons play no small part in adopting this or that hermeneutical repertoire. It is crucial to be clear about what these may be.

Meanings rendered in textual interpretation may in fact conflict with tightly held convictions about precisely what a particular text is supposed to mean. Indeed, caution should be taken if they do not. And when there is conflict of interpretations, a clash between the worldview of the interpreter and the data rendered from the text, or when it becomes clear that meanings rendered do not fit into the horizon of the one appropriating text's meaning, a challenge is posed. The challenge is not primarily one of deciding which interpretation is correct and which is incorrect. It is rather more a matter of recognizing that in the clash of interpretations new questions arise, broader horizons emerge, and fresh meanings are opened up. Conflict thus plays a positive role in the work of interpretation, which may be likened to a conversation in which both interpreter and text express a process of coming to greater understanding rather than a tightly-knit worldview.[13]

Tightly-knit worldviews are attractive, providing a sense of unity, coherence, and cohesion. The High Middle Ages, a purported golden age of faith and reason, is often heralded as a high watermark of Christian history, in part because of the magisterial theological synthesis of Thomas Aquinas. But be the synthesis that of Aquinas or another, it must be accepted that such thinkers give evidence of an ongoing struggle to free themselves from ideological blinders, to wrestle with new insight from contrasting, indeed competing, worldviews, and to set aside any formal absolute synthesis, including their own, in an effort to come to deeper understanding and insight.[14]

Similarly, the work of interpretation and appropriation of text in context involves the patience and the stamina to resist rushing to incorporate fresh meanings into an already existing, often tacitly held, synthesis. Interpretation of liturgical texts and practice may yield results that do not readily cohere with what is commonly held to be authentic Christian life or doctrine. Indeed sometimes the conclusions to be drawn from the complex task of interpretation, especially when this is done in view of present need and the praxis option, may lead to the formulation of contemporary liturgical texts and practices that find no clear precedent in the Christian tradition.

THE MULTIVALENCE OF SYMBOL, LANGUAGE, AND CULTURE

David Power's earliest work is markedly influenced by the "turn to the subject," particularly as expressed in Bernard

Lonergan's appropriation of Thomas Aquinas and, to a somewhat lesser degree, Karl Rahner's. Notable influences on his
early work also include the writings of Edward Schillebeeckx,
Marie-Dominique Chenu, and Yves Congar. These influences
must be seen alongside his early interest in post-Kantian interpretation theorist Paul Ricoeur and in the definitions and distinctions of Susanne K. Langer. Attention must also be drawn to
the early influence of several historians of religion, most notably
Mircea Eliade, and the resultant sensibility to cultural and religious plurality which undergirds the bulk of Power's writings.

Power's early moves within the precincts of Transcendental
Thomism put him in touch with approaches to sacrament informed by an appreciation of symbolic causality. Both Karl Rahner
and Edward Schillebeeckx treat sacrament from the perspective
of symbolic rather than efficient causality, freed from the boundaries of the essentialist or conceptualist mode. With focus on the
self, on judgment, action, and being, rather than on essence,
Transcendental Thomists developed approaches to sacrament
and the causation of grace that eschewed clear definitions and
concepts aimed at capturing and communicating the essence of
the thing. Karl Rahner moves out of the conceptualist or essentialist understanding of sacrament. This he does by exploring
the sacraments in terms of God's self-communication in Christ
with attention to the results of this in the self. In his view of
sacrament, Rahner restores to a central position an understanding of grace as God's free and personal self-communication and
the human being's response to the divine initiative. He describes
the causation of grace in light of these categories.[15]

The early work of Edward Schillebeeckx is also an approach
untethered from an essentialist or conceptualist mode. Within the
current of Transcendental Thomism, but more properly understood as an Existential Thomist (at least during the period of his
early writings), Schillebeeckx describes the sacraments in terms of
shared meaning through personal encounter. His explanation of
the causation of grace in sacrament is set in these terms.[16]

In continuity with the insights of both Rahner and
Schillebeeckx, David Power's investigations brought him to the
question of just how such self-communication and shared meaning come about.[17] No doubt influenced by the methodological
investigations of Bernard Lonergan, he attempted to open up

the discourse about sacrament to include insights from other fields. And he turned to the exploration of language as a means of understanding how God's self-communication and shared meaning in personal encounter come about in the reality of sacrament.

In Paul Ricoeur, Power came under the influence of a theorist of interpretation with different orientations and emphases than those of the Transcendental Thomists. Though Ricoeur claims to be a philosopher, not a theologian, his attention is given to revelation, to the word, and to the nature and function of language as the key to all reality. In his work with the language of the Bible, he brings clarity to the different genres of writing in which revelation is expressed. With strong emphasis on the metaphorical as key to understanding language and meaning, and on symbol as it pertains to the bodily in self-communication, Ricoeur's investigations provided Power with a linguistic perspective from which to view sacrament and liturgy. Thus, the abiding question for Power: how do symbol and language, specifically metaphor, constitute the reality of sacramental experience? Because of his focus on language and meaning, Power's concern is not with the "essence" of things that can be pinned down in concepts and clear definitions.

Power's concern with language, specifically with metaphor as the key to understanding the nature of language, as well as his view of culture, symbol, and ritual as dimensions of language, are influenced in no small measure by the investigations of Ricoeur.[18] Language in this view does not refer primarily to the instrument of verbal communication. It may best be described as "expressivity." In this sense language both constitutes and shapes human beings and all other entities. This is to say that everything is what it is by virtue of self-expression. Being is at once given and coming to be through self-expression.

Taking these insights further, it may be useful to note that Power opts for a Gadamerian view of the linguistic character of all reality. In this he differs from the Lonerganian David Tracy and from the Existential Thomist Edward Schillebeeckx, both of whom permit the possibility of pre-linguistic or, perhaps more accurately, sub-linguistic experience. Power, following Gadamer, maintains that there is no thought without language and, consequently, no access to reality that is not linguistic. Language and symbol give rise to thought. There can be no thought aside from the thought expressed which is language, and no access to reality which is what it is by virtue of being expressed or spoken. While it may be said that thoughts and feelings exist in dialectical relation to language and are distinguishable from it, they may not *be* in their fullness without language. The line need not be drawn too sharply here between Power on the one side, and Tracy and Schillebeeckx on the other. Further investigation would likely yield greater convergence on this point than it might seem.

Human expression is mediated in and through a multiplicity of forms that together constitute what is referred to as culture. Like time, we know what culture is until we are called upon to describe it. Without prejudice to the complexity of the issue, culture may be described as that constellation of means by which humans express what is fundamentally constitutive of human being, foremost among them the family, community, society, art, literature, and ritual. Because human beings perceive and pursue the task of human expressivity in various ways, cultures differ, sometimes so greatly that they appear to be irreconcilable.

A singularly important instance of language as "expressivity" is symbol and its employment in ritual.[19] In attending to the nature and function of the symbolic, Power avoids naive understandings of both sign and symbol as realities that point beyond themselves. Symbols invite self-expression and facilitate interpersonal communication and communion. Basing his approach on studies in theology, philosophy, anthropology, and— perhaps most importantly—sociological theorists Victor Turner and Mary Douglas, Power views symbols as gestures, actions, words, or objects that

> belong within a given cultural context, bear of repetition without being rigid stereotypes, meet affective needs of meaning and belonging, express group identity even though some are more immediately related to the group and others to the individual, and are subject to the changes that come with the evolution of time, moving perspectives and changing values.[20]

In this view the symbolic is related to self-expression as public. It includes the affective as well as the cognitive in mediating human expressivity. In addition, the symbolic addresses the personal, unconscious, and the cosmic in expressing a human being's relationship to the real.

Two characteristics of the symbolic are important when considering Power's view of symbol and its employment in ritual as part of the task of human self-expression which is language. First, there is a non-identity between the symbol and the reality expressed therein. Words spoken may express the deepest longings of the human heart, but they must be distinguished from those longings in and of themselves. In this view there is a loosening of the connection between symbol or word and its referent, an emphasis on negation, on the distance between image and what is represented, so that any symbolic expression both is and is not the reality communicated. If effective "presencing" or communication of such intimate feelings to another is to occur, this distinction must be kept to the fore. Effective "presencing" or communication in and through language demands that we recognize what is not given in self-expression as well as what is.

What is given in symbolic communication is absented in the distance inherent in all communication between the self and the other. This is something common sense recognizes. When I speak to another there is space or distance between us. This is accepted as part and parcel of effective communication. Legacies of a bygone era are communicated through the distance of time and space in speech. There is, of necessity, distance and absence between narrative and reader or hearer, and this too must be accepted if communication is to occur. At an even more fundamental level, I can only know what I look like through a mirror that is at a point of some distance from myself. But I am not the mirror image of myself, no matter how identical a likeness is projected therein. Further, we cannot know or understand our own thoughts and feelings unless they are expressed in writing or speech, which is a manner of putting them at a distance from oneself. And I cannot know the heart and mind of another except through what is offered between myself and the other as the medium of our communication.[21] This is all to say that in the "presencing" rendered in and through language and symbol, absence and distance are inextricably a part of the very modality of presence. Absence is a dimension of presence.

This dimension of non-identity must be kept to the fore in understanding sacrament which, for Power, is symbolic in nature. What is expressed in sacrament is mediated in a form other than itself. For example, in the sacrament of the eucharist Christ is not present in his own form. The presence of Christ in the eucharist is a sacramental presence in and through symbol, i.e., a mediated presence which is by its very nature a presence of non-identity with Christ's own form. But this presence is not any the less real by virtue of non-identity, which is intrinsic to any and all symbolic expression. Further, it is the very nature and function of religious language and symbol to express the relation of human beings to that with which it can never claim identity: God. Consequently, this dimension of non-identity needs to be kept to the fore all the more in language and symbols of the holy.

A second characteristic of language and symbol to which Power has given considerable attention is that of polysemy or polyvalence. Specifically when it comes to language and symbols of the divine, he is critical of efforts to pin down meanings in concise concepts and precise definitions. Though it may be judged necessary to stress a singular meaning in thought and discourse about sacrament, e.g., eucharist as sacrament of the body and blood of Christ, or baptism as sacrament of incorporation into the Body through forgiveness of sin, these focal meanings can only be enriched by the rich array of meanings expressed in other language and symbols of the God-world relation. No matter how appropriate a word or symbol may be to express the holy, and no matter how adequate in conveying the human response to the divine initiative, no one symbol or constellation of symbols is capable of fully expressing the ineffable, the being beyond being, the mystery that overspills any and all attempts to speak it. The presence of the holy both *is and is not* expressed in word and sacrament, due to the surplus of meaning that is not communicated in any presencing through word and sacrament. Said another way, God both *is and is not* present in this or that sacrament, the Scripture both *is and is not* the word of God, and Jesus both *is and is not* God.

The key to understanding this view of symbol and its employment in ritual is metaphor. Metaphoric predication juxtaposes unlikes in order to find fresh meaning. The interplay of contrasting images and stories in metaphor creates new possibilities. Within the juxtaposition of images, similarities are discovered in the very differences that are yoked in the metaphor. Metaphor's first move is to break open perceptions and commonly held expectations, surprising us with the whisper that *this* both is and is not *that*, thereby keeping alive the tensive nature of all language. Similarly symbol invites beyond itself to the surplus of meanings in other, often surprising, words and symbols which are also expressive of the holy. Hence no matter how adequate it may be as a symbol, *this* sacrament is and is not *that* fullness of God's presence which overspills any and all symbolic mediation of the divine presence.

The metaphorical may also provide a key to the nature of liturgy. If liturgy is viewed as language, then liturgy may be understood as the central, world shaping act of self-expression on the part of the Christian people. Be it in the eucharistic assembly or in the province of private devotion, human beings express and receive their identity by what is said and done in the language of worship, by speaking in response to what God has spoken. But this language is always a way of "talking back" to those established wisdoms that are antipathetic to the grace and freedom of the "Word beneath the words." The metaphorical nature of liturgy, once unleashed, untethers the heart from commonly held perceptions, ideologies, and worldviews through the whisper of the promise that the freedom and grace expressed in *this* Word and sacrament *is and is not that* which the established wisdom insists is God's will and way in the world. Even further, *this* liturgy must never be confused with *that* fullness of God's presence which it expresses. Consequently, authentic liturgical praxis must attend to God's coming in ways that may indeed interrupt and break open our perceptions of what constitutes good liturgical order and ritual performance.

Hopefully, without pressing the point, I would like to suggest here that Power's entire project of mediating worship to culture through theological thought may itself be understood by a turn of this metaphorical key. Power seems to have listened and taken heed to metaphor's whisper: *"this* is not *that,"* *"it is and is not."* In our words, concepts, and images there is for Power a greater degree of dissimilarity than similarity, more unlikeness than likeness, to the mystery they stretch to evoke, to name, to express. There are two poles of a dialectical tension that undergirds all David Power's work in sacramental and liturgical theology. Though his writings evidence a sustained interest in what may be said of God *in esse*, as well as in what may be known of God through reason illumined by faith, there is also an abiding recognition that whatever claims are made about God, or the divine attributes, or God's intention for the world, these are at best partial and incomplete, and our grasp on grace quite tenuous. But rather than shunning or setting aside ontological considerations, Power invites to the doxology of the heart, the culmination of prayer, beyond words and thoughts though fostered by both.[22]

The metaphorical as key to understanding Power's work is also obvious in the attention he has given to "contrast experience" as revelatory. Power has consistently sought to include alternative voices and lesser known viewpoints in the field of investigation, with particular attention to the experience of those at the margins of social and religious institutions who are weak, voiceless, and powerless. Whether it be his sustained attention to the emergence of base Christian communities as clear expression of the Spirit's voice in the churches,[23] his continuing commitment to the development and support for lay ministries in the church,[24] his attentiveness to the emergent consciousness of women in church and society,[25] his commitment to the mission of evangelization of and by the poor,[26] or even his efforts to assure that the often facilely villainized Tridentine theology of sacrifice be given a fair hearing,[27] his concern is to give attention to those experiences and to those voices which speak a different word from what the prevailing social and ecclesial orders maintain is the way things are and must be. By looking to contrast experiences as revelatory, Power's work is at once a participation in the tensive movement of metaphor as well as an invitation beyond what *is* and *is not* to what *may* or *might be*.

In considering liturgy as the central world-shaping expressive act of the Christian people, the task is to think from what is done and said therein. Rather than bringing tightly-knit philosophical preconceptions and definitions of what sacrament is and must be, the grace of sacramental communion is given in attentiveness to the Word beneath the words, in the invitation to think from the symbol, to attend to what is known in the simple act of blessing, breaking, and sharing of a crust of bread, and in the passing of a cup hallowed by the speaking of Christ's name. Thinking from the symbol is the condition for the possibility of receiving what is given in the sign of the one who washed the feet of others, and of participating in what may be known through the giving of a cup of cold water in his name. Thinking from what is said in liturgy is an invitation to lean on hope, even and especially when there seems no plausible reason to do so, and to be enlivened by that blood poured out for those whose only strength is found in his self-emptying.

If we are to think from the symbol, then interpretive preconceptions of all sorts are to be set aside: philosophical, theological, religious, political, ethical, aesthetic, economic. Each subjective horizon of appropriation provides some access, but also some barriers, to experiencing the polyvalence of symbol. In overcoming the obstacles that thought and speech may impose, we may come to a knowledge of God through the words and symbols that unite us to God in their plurality, as well as through the multiplicity of expression that they may be given at different times and in diverse cultures.

FROM LITURGY TO WORSHIP:
SPEAKING THE NAME OF GOD

In mediating worship to culture through theological thought, much of David Power's effort has been given to promoting and advancing liturgical practice. This has necessitated the study of liturgical rites past and present, an ongoing analysis of classical and contemporary theologies of sacrament and the causality of grace, as well as a thoroughgoing appreciation of the nature and function of symbol and language. Such studies, helpful though they may be, especially when undertaken in service of liturgical renewal, do not of themselves bring about the realization of liturgy's purpose. Just as the grace of sacramental communion cannot be measured by dogged adherence to rubric, neither can it be guaranteed by efforts to assure that the prayer of the Christian people is "liturgically correct." Preoccupation with rubric on one hand, or "good," "moving" liturgical celebration (read performance) on the other, can easily lead to reductionism. The nature and work of grace cannot ultimately be explained or guaranteed by ritual study or correct performance.[28] Grace escapes human comprehension, and the best response to its presence is an attentive and receptive faith. The granting of grace and response to it is in the final analysis ineffable. And this gift and response are the aim of any and all liturgy of the Christian people.

The metaphoric is again helpful in avoiding ritual or rubrical reductionism. Power's attention to the metaphorical, or to the ineffable present in all language, even and especially in the language of the holy, serves to underscore the apophatic, the way of knowing by way of unknowing. We do not hear what God speaks or recognize how God is present unless we are able to recognize what God is not. With attention to the metaphorical key, language has the ability to carry the human being beyond preconceptions, tightly-knit world views, and firmly held convictions, into the regions of personal faith wherein we are invited to communion with the unknown God.

Liturgy is understood by Power as the central world shaping expressive act of the Christian people. In articulating the nature of Christ's presence therein, he uses the idea of opening up to mystery rather than efficacy in giving grace. Here again our attention is drawn to the apophatic. Apparent in his attention to the metaphoric, to the non-identity of symbol and symbolized, to the multiplicity and surplus of meaning in all word and symbol, to the need to consult alternative, contrasting experience as the locus of God's coming, the apophatic or aniconic again comes into play in Power's conviction that Christ's sacramental presence cannot be reduced to any type of localized imagery. Faith in Christ, even when expressed in the words, narratives, actions, gestures, and objects that together constitute the liturgy of the Christian people, is a response to an invitation into communion with the life of God in Christ, the fullness of which is outside the reach of our imagination, comprehension, and speech.

Even with the limits they impose, symbol and word are nonetheless our means of access to the real. Liturgy as "speech-act" gives way to true worship as the name of God is falteringly uttered within that space which is the very opening up to the divine presence at the limits of language and symbol. In this view worship cannot be confined within the precincts of liturgy as ritual, however much true worship may be fostered by good liturgical practice. Good liturgical form and adherence to the rubrical canon do not necessarily aid us in the articulation of the name of God, the task of true worship to be taken up again and again in different times, in various places and diverse cultures. The purpose of liturgy is to invite to true worship of the God who is in our midst as the Christ, and who is known in contemplation of the name beyond our ability to name definitively.

Here attention must be drawn to the role of narrative and memory in worship. Narrative is context for metaphoric predication. The purpose of narrative is not simply to render a past event present. Nor is it to render the present to the past. It is to tell of a presence present now in and through remembrance, so that the present presence of Christ may be known.[29] In liturgy it takes on much the character of prophetic telling, of speaking a word of hope in view of much evidence to the contrary. Narrative is the naming of that presence present to Moses (Exodus 3: 13-15) which is brought to self-expression in the name "I am Who I am" or "I will be Who I will be." It is the invitation to remembrance of the Christ in whose life and cross God comes, and to attend to God's coming in the interruptive and disorienting events of history. Narrative holds out the promise of God's presence even and especially at the limits of language and symbol. It hearkens to faith and true worship when trust in established wisdoms weakens, when confidence in creeds crumbles, and when all our efforts at good and sound liturgical practice fail. The Word beneath the words which is untethered through prophetic telling in narrative is an invitation to respond to a promise of presence. True worship beyond the precincts of ritual purity and good liturgical form is an activity of the human heart, in communion with others and with the Word beneath the words, which is brought to self-expression in the naming of God as the One who comes.

PRAYER AS THE PRAXIS OF DESIRE

Whether the subject of investigation be a liturgical rite, a theological explanation of sacramental efficacy, or the formulation of contemporary liturgical text, Power's concern is with the movement of the human heart toward God in prayer. It may be useful to offer clarification about what is meant by the terms "heart" and "prayer," and in so doing bring some of my own concerns and perspectives into conversation with David Power's contribution.

In speaking of the human heart, I am not referring to the region of "private," "individual" feelings or emotions in contradistinction to other dimensions of the self. The term "heart" describes the deepest, most fundamental center of the self, and as such is found in Hebrew and Christian Scriptures and in the history of Christian spirituality to describe the whole person.[30] Properly understood, the heart is the name for "affectivity," or the affective dimension of the person, the very openness of the human being to be touched by another, others, and God. As such, it is inclusive of communal and social realities. To have a heart is to possess the capacity to be in relation. Further, the heart describes human being's openness to relate to the real. It is the very being within human beings toward the good.[31]

In speaking of prayer I have in mind the deeply personal movement of the heart as I have described it. Thus prayer is not necessarily a private and isolated activity. It finds its fullest expression in interpersonal communion in and through communication with another, others, and God. Thus prayer cannot be properly understood if it is thought to exist in opposition to the liturgy which is the coming together of the Christian people. The public liturgy of a people is intended to foster true worship, to lift the mind and heart of this people to God in prayer. To maintain that the prayer of the heart is deeply personal is not to imply that it is a private matter.

With these clarifications to the fore, prayer may be understood as the praxis of the desire of the human heart. The openness to relation which is a constitutive dimension of human being is in itself an absence, a longing for completion and fullness. Desire is that which in the human being longs for its own increase. For Paul Ricoeur, desire is the yearning for being. Or, said another way, desire may be understood as the effort to be.[32]

Desire, then, is the basis, the root, of all self-expression. Said another way, desire is what inheres in all "speechifying," language, or expressivity. Desire seeks to participate in being by speaking itself in culture, symbol, and other elements of language systems. For Ricoeur, human being is both given and that which we desire yet to be.

As human being is brought into fuller being through self-expression, this necessarily entails another and others. It lies at the very heart of human being, then, to be in communion with another and others by virtue of this self-expression. This effort to be, that is desire, takes the form of action which may be understood as the self-articulation of human being. For our purposes it is useful to note the importance of the corporate activity that is worship, by which the church expresses and receives its identity as the Body of Christ in and through his grace. Worship, from this perspective, is the "speechifying" of this people as the Body of Christ. In and through worship the Christian people are brought into being through self-expression as Christ's Body and thereby invited into communion with Being itself. But because being is both given and achieved, prayer of the heart also finds expression in simple loving attentiveness to Being, as well as in the self-expressive action in word and sacrament. Here the corporate activity of worship and the heart's movement of loving attentiveness to Being beyond being are co-efficients in the praxis of desire.

In this view, the effort to be involves the corporate activity of worship, which is the self-expression and articulation of the Christian people as the Body of Christ. But the yearning for being and fuller self-expression entails the recognition that being is also given, a gift, the very condition for the possibility of human being seeking to participate more fully in Being.

Thus liturgy and sacrament find their purpose in fostering prayer as the praxis of desire. As the basis of all expressivity, desire is brought to articulation in what is said and done in liturgy. But it is also articulated when the human heart silently attends to the Word beneath the words, and to the symbols of the holy, recognizing therein God's fidelity to the divine promise. This is the promise of future glory in which faith stakes its claim, but it is also the promise of presence of the One who comes even now as speech stretches to make enough room for silence.

* * * * * *

In pointing to five distinctive factors in the work of David Power, I have aimed to give some indication of significant issues and concerns in the field of sacramental and liturgical studies in the post-conciliar period. These arise when liturgy is taken seriously as a source for theology.

My intention has been to give some attention to significant influences on Power's work and to take up the central concerns that have occupied him. This I have done rather than charting his development from early to later stages. The task has been undertaken in the hope that the methodological form that he has brought to the field will be instructive in the raising of fresh questions, tackling thorny issues, and probing the mystery of God's love in word and sacrament.

It may seem a bit ironic that an essay which treats the work of one in whom the critical function plays such a large role should itself not offer critique. A sharper analysis of Power's work would likely take issue with some of his interpretations or call for further clarification of his positions.[33] I do not shun critique. A thorough, careful, and constructive critical analysis of the contribution of David Power is a task that yet awaits us in our common work.

Notes

1. For a very helpful treatment of the use of the *lex orandi, lex credendi* principle, see Geoffrey Wainwright, *Doxology: The Praise of God in Worship, Doctrine, and Life* (New York: Oxford University Press, 1980) especially chapters 7 and 8.

2. For example, Raymond Vaillancourt, *Toward a Renewal of Sacramental Theology* (Collegeville: The Liturgical Press, 1979) provides a survey of such reorientations in view of the renewed anthropology, Christology, and ecclesiology articulated in the conciliar documents.

3. In consciously striving to open up the discourse about liturgy and sacrament to include discourse from other fields, Power is influenced by the methodological investigations of Bernard Lonergan.

4. Most notable among these professional societies are the North American Academy of Liturgy and the Societas Liturgica.

5. This concern is well expressed in both the title and content of the collection of his articles spanning nearly twenty years, *Worship: Culture and Theology* (Washington, D.C.: The Pastoral Press, 1990).

6. The doctoral dissertation has been published as *Ministers of Christ and His Church: The Theology of the Priesthood* (London: Geoffrey Chapman Publishing Co., 1969).

7. *Christian Priest: Elder and Prophet* (London: Sheed & Ward, 1973).

8. See, for example, D.N. Power, "Households of Faith in the Coming Church," *Worship* 57 (1983) 237-254.

9. *Politics and Liturgy,* ed. Herman Schmidt and David Power (New York: Herder and Herder, 1974); see especially Power, "The Song of the Lord in an Alien Land" 85-106.

10. The critical function of liturgy is treated at greater length in D.N. Power, *Unsearchable Riches: The Symbolic Nature of Liturgy* (New York: Pueblo Publishing Co., 1984) especially chapter seven. See also "Liturgical Praxis: A New Consciousness at the Eye of Worship," *Worship* 61 (1987) 290-305; "Unripe Grapes: The Critical Function of Liturgical Theology," *Worship* 52 (1978) 386-399; "Forum: Worship after the Holocaust," *Worship* 59 (1985) 447-455; "Sacraments: Symbolizing God's Power in the Church," *Proceedings of the Catholic Theological Society of America* 37 (1982) 50-66.

11. For a fuller treatment of this point, see Mary Catherine Hilkert, "The Word Beneath the Words" in *A Promise of Presence,* ed. Michael Downey and Richard Fragomeni (Washington, D.C.: The Pastoral Press, 1992) 49-70.

12. In the 1991 Berakah address, "When Words Fail: The Function of Systematic Theology in Liturgical Studies," Power maintains that it is an illusion to think that it is a relatively simple matter to find the meaning of a text from a past age. See the *Proceedings of the North American Academy of Liturgy,* 1991, 18-26, pp. 19-20.

13. Power, "When Words Fail."

14. Power writes "We learn more by attending to the process of thinking in the past than by retrieving ideas that have been thought. The sense of *pensée pensante* is more instructive than *pensée pensée.*" "When Words Fail" 22.

15. See Karl Rahner, *The Church and the Sacraments,* tr. W.J. O'Hara (Freiburg: Herder; London: Burns and Oates, 1963); "The Theology of Symbol," *Theological Investigations,* vol. 4, tr. K. Smyth (Baltimore: Helicon, 1966) 221-252; "What Is a Sacrament?" *Theological Investigations,* vol. 14, tr. D. Bourke 135-148; "Considerations on the Active Role of the Person in the Sacramental Event," ibid. 161-184.

16. For Schillebeeckx's early treatment of these themes, see his *Christ the Sacrament of the Encounter with God* (New York: Sheed and Ward, 1963).

17. Power does have misgivings about some of Rahner's views which he judges to be too abstract. See, for example, D.N. Power, "The Holy Spirit: Scripture, Tradition, and Interpretation," in *Keeping the Faith: Essays to Mark the Centenary of Lux Mundi,* ed. Geoffrey Wainwright (Philadelphia: Fortress, 1988) 156.

18. For an introduction to Ricoeur's work, see C.E. Reagan and D. Stewart, eds. *The Philosophy of Paul Ricoeur: An Anthology of His Work*

(Boston: Beacon Press, 1978). For Ricoeur on metaphor, see "Creativity in Language: Word, Polysemy, Metaphor," *Philosophy Today* 17 (1973) 105-112; see also his *La Metaphore Vive* (Paris: Seuil, 1975) especially "Metaphore et discussion philosophique" 325-399.

19. For Power's understanding of symbol see *Unsearchable Riches*.

20. Ibid. 62.

21. The notions of presence, absence, and distance in self-expression and communication, as well as the examples used to clarify this point, are developed in Power's *The Eucharistic Mystery: Revitalizing the Tradition* (New York: Crossroad, 1992).

22. "When Words Fail" esp. 25-26.

23. See, for example, D.N. Power, "Liturgy and Culture," *East Asian Pastoral Review* (1984/4) 348-366.

24. D.N. Power, *Gifts That Differ: Lay Ministries Established and Unestablished* (New York: Pueblo, 1980, 2d edition 1985).

25. See, for example, D.N. Power, "Liturgical Praxis: A New Consciousness at the Eye of Worship," *Worship* 61 (1987) 290-305. It may also be worthwhile noting the number of contributions by women that have been included in the volumes of *Concilium* edited or co-edited by David Power. Especially noteworthy in this regard is his collaborative work with Mary Collins. For example, see *Can We Always Celebrate the Eucharist?*, ed. Mary Collins and David Power, *Concilium* 152 (New York: Seabury, 1982).

26. It is not often taken into account that David Power is a member of the Oblates of Mary Immaculate, an international missionary congregation whose primary purpose is the evangelization of the poor.

27. D.N. Power, *The Sacrifice We Offer: The Tridentine Dogma and Its Reinterpretation* (Edinburgh: T. & T. Clark, 1987).

28. "When Words Fail" 20.

29. For Power on narrative memory, see, for example, *Unsearchable Riches* 39; 141ff.; see also "When Words Fail" 20.

30. An extensive analysis of the nature of the heart is provided in my doctoral dissertation *An Investigation of the Concept of Person in the Spirituality of l'Arche as Developed in the Writings of Jean Vanier* completed in 1982 at The Catholic University of America under the direction of David Power. A brief synthesis is also provided in Downey, *A Blessed Weakness: The Spirit of Jean Vanier and l'Arche* (San Francisco: Harper & Row, 1986) chapter 5: "The Heart Knows."

31. For parallels between this understanding of heart and more classical formulations, see Downey, "A Costly Loss of Heart: The Scholastic Notion of *voluntas ut natura*," *Philosophy and Theology* 1:3 (Spring 1987) 242-254.

32. For Ricoeur on desire, see *Fallible Man: Philosophy of Will*, tr. Charles Kelbley (Chicago: Henry Regnery, 1967) esp. 191-202. It may be instructive to note that in a more recent interview Ricoeur speaks of the singular importance of this work: "le travail auquel je suis finalement le plus attaché, c'est *L'Homme Faillible*, qui était une sorte de petite ontologie. . ."; see "Entretien avec Paul Ricoeur," *Revue des sciences philosophiques et théologiques* 74 (1990) 89.

33. For example, see Stephen Happel, "Worship as a Grammar of Social Transformation," *Proceedings of the Catholic Theological Society of America* 42 (1987) 60-87, especially 76ff.

3

Understanding Christian Spirituality

PERUSE THE SHELVES OF WALDENBOOKS, CROWN BOOKS, B. DALTON, Brentano's or another large bookseller downtown or at the nearest shopping mall. If your interest is in spirituality, the first stop will be that nook labelled "religion" or "inspiration." There will likely be "slim pickins" there. No doubt there will be a few Bibles from which to choose, a sampling of Judaica, perhaps some M. Scott Peck, and a smattering of esoteric Asian philosophy or spirituality. These days it's likely that there will be several copies of Joseph F. Girzone's *Joshua* and *The Shepherd*. From time to time there will be a few titles by Gethsemani's most celebrated son, Thomas Merton. If there is time and stamina, a closer look may yield rich fare on some other shelves. Try "history," "self-help," "women's studies," "biography," or perhaps a few of the others.

In much the same way that the bookseller is often at a loss when it comes to knowing just where to shelve books for those interested in spirituality, the meaning of the term *spirituality* is itself a bit unfocused and its referents quite scattered. For all the interest in spirituality today, there remains a lack of clarity as to what people mean when they speak of spirituality or, for our purposes, Christian spirituality. In academic circles, those who focus their energies on the study of spirituality are sometimes viewed by their peers as dabblers and dilettantes who lack the academic rigor required to do "bread and butter theology," i.e., systematic/dogmatic theology.

My purpose here is threefold. First, I would like bring a little light to the question of the precise scope and limits of what is described by that slippery term "Christian spirituality." Second, I shall point to significant trends in Christian spirituality today. Third, attention will be given to a method for understanding and studying Christian spirituality.

WHAT IS CHRISTIAN SPIRITUALITY?

"Christian spirituality" refers to both a lived experience and an academic discipline. In the first instance, the term describes the whole of the Christian's life as it is oriented to self-transcending knowledge, freedom, and love in light of the ultimate values and highest ideals perceived and pursued in the mystery of Jesus Christ through the Holy Spirit in the church, the community of disciples. That is to say, spirituality is concerned with everything that constitutes Christian experience, specifically the perception and pursuit of the highest ideal or goal of Christian life, e.g., an ever more intense union with God disclosed in Christ through life in the Spirit. At a second level, Christian spirituality is an academic discipline, increasingly interdisciplinary in nature, that attempts to study religious experience and to promote its development and maturation.

Most noteworthy among the contributors to the development of the academic discipline of Christian spirituality are Sandra Schneiders and Walter Principe.[1] It is also important to note here the contributions of several scholars who bring clarity to the discipline of Christian spirituality by making connections between systematic theology and spirituality. The work of Tad Dunne and Vernon Gregson is an example of this effort within a Lonerganian framework, while James Bacik, Annice Callahan, Harvey Egan, J. Norman King, and Robert Masson attempt to spell out in a systematic fashion the implications of the work of Karl Rahner for Christian spirituality.

In specifying just what Christian spirituality is, and in trying to give some methodological form to understanding and studying it, we can identify several noteworthy trends in spirituality today.

TRENDS IN SPIRITUALITY TODAY

The following survey of the current trends in spirituality today may provide indication of the shape or direction of spirituality on the brink of the third millennium.

1. Much of the renaissance in contemporary spirituality has been given impetus by the Second Vatican Council. As a result, many of its fundamental orientations and convictions undergird a good measure of contemporary understandings of Christian spirituality, though it must be acknowledged that there have remained all along signs of a defensive reaction to the reforms and renewal occasioned by the council.

2. Because the council stressed the reciprocal relationship between liturgy, especially the eucharist, and Christian life (SC 1 and 10), as well as the singular importance of Scripture and its formative role in the spiritual life, contemporary understandings of spirituality rest on the premise that Christian spirituality is a liturgical and scriptural spirituality. In addition, the council's universal call to holiness (LG 40-41) has dealt a fatal blow (at least in theory) to the tightly held conviction that the fullness of the Christian spiritual life is reserved for an elite (usually vowed religious and clergy). All the baptized are called to the fullness of life in the Spirit. Expressions of Christian spiritual life among the faithful cannot be understood or explained simply by extension or comparison to the paradigms of mature spirituality appropriate to clergy and religious.

3. Since the council there has been sustained attention to a more holistic understanding of spirituality. Rather than beginning with doctrinal formulations or theoretical explanations of Christian life, contemporary approaches to spirituality tend to begin by stressing the singular importance of the concrete experience of searching for God, and of finding appropriate ways to live out our response to the divine initiative. This has been coupled with attention to the importance of the specific context within which we live out our relationship with the other, others, and God, and the significance of culture as it shapes these relationships. There has been a deepening appreciation for the particular, the specific, and for differences. This is expressed, for example, in the attention given to the need to retrieve and/or

develop approaches to prayer appropriate to persons in a great variety of life forms.

4. The attention given to the experiential and the contextual has been accompanied by an effort to undercut dualisms of all sorts. Hence, there has been a sustained attempt to distinguish rather than unduly separate soul and body, spirit and flesh, church and world, sacred and profane. To this has been joined a concern to focus on the "ordinary" and the "everyday," and the opportunities therein for the baptized to be a corporate witness and sign, or sacrament, in and to the world. With the setting aside of subtle and not so subtle dualist convictions, and the embrace of a more incarnational and sacramental approach to spirituality, there has been a deeper appreciation of the value of interpersonal relationships, inclusive of intimacy and sexuality, with particular attention to the sacredness of marriage as the paradigmatic human relationship disclosing the divine. In high-lighting the relational as disclosive of the holy, great attention has been given to the significance of life in community, particu-larly communities of self- and mutual help, whether these be parish renewal groups, prayer-study groups, Marriage Encoun-ter, Cursillo, *communidades de base,* or various groups inspired by the Twelve Steps of Alcoholics Anonymous.

5. This focus on the relational, interpersonal, and communal is related to another current in contemporary spirituality which, though certainly not novel in the history of Christian spiritual-ity, has been given unique emphasis in our own day. In the perennial search for the true, authentic self, contemporary un-derstandings of spirituality reflect a reliance on interdiscipli-nary methods, drawing from biblical studies, psychology (espe-cially developmental psychology) theology, history, and pasto-ral experience. Resources often extend beyond the author's par-ticular religious tradition, reflective of the ecumenical and interreligious sensibility characteristic of religious and theologi-cal studies since the Second Vatican Council. The attempt to bring interdisciplinary and ecumenical/interreligious insights to bear on the subject of Christian spirituality might be exempli-fied in the writings of those who attempt to use personality type indicators from the investigations of Myers-Briggs or the Enneagram, which has its roots in the tradition of the Sufis, in the process of Christian growth and development. Such ap-

proaches to the quest for the true self are grounded in the conviction that human and spiritual development are not opposing, competing dynamics, but are rather interrelated and complementary. The authentic self is one which is given by nature and developed by grace and Spirit. Such development requires commitment to ongoing self-scrutiny and willingness to risk and change. But this self-scrutiny extends beyond the province of the individual to include a mature critical consciousness vis-à-vis the social-symbolic order with its dominant ideology. Without such critical consciousness there is a tendency to overlook the truth that any authentic Christian spirituality is intrinsically relational, social, and indeed political.

6. Just as much contemporary spiritual writing assumes that human and spiritual development are interrelated and complementary, so too is there a sustained conviction that prayer and action are two dimensions of the human person that are to be held together in a noble tension in an ever-deepening integration. This must be understood against the background of a long tradition that tended to separate the "active life" and the "contemplative life." Without prejudice to the complexity of the issue, it may be said that there is a deeper recognition today that prayer and action are rooted in one same source, the human person, who is called to the prayer of loving attention, gratitude and praise for the presence and action of God in human life, history, world, and church, and to the activities whereby God's reign is advanced, especially through the works of prophetic service and the promotion of peace and justice. This is to recognize the importance of praxis in Christian life and spirituality. In contemporary spiritual writing "praxis" does not refer to any and all action or practice. It is the practice of the Gospel through which persons and communities do the truth in love freely, and in so doing enable others to do the truth in love freely, thereby participating more fully in the mystery of Christ who is contemplated in Christian prayer.

7. The recognition of the demands of justice in the Christian spiritual life has drawn greater attention to the rights of women in church and society, and to the struggle to work for the equality of women in all spheres of life. Indeed the emergence of a specifically feminist spirituality is arguably one of the most significant, albeit unanticipated, results of the Second Vatican

Council. The place of women's experience and the significance of women's contributions in Christian tradition has been given a good measure of attention in contemporary spiritual writing, and is undoubtedly one of the most notable developments in the field. Similarly, the struggle for peace and justice has drawn attention to the experience of persons and groups at the margins of social and religious bodies, be they persons of color, the physically and mentally disabled, the divorced and remarried, persons in the Third World, gays and lesbians, or the economically oppressed. The experience of such persons, and of the countless women who have often been invisible and powerless in church and society, has become an increasingly important and indeed indispensable source for reflection on the nature of authentic Christian experience and praxis.

8. On the brink of the third millennium, there is ever increasing attention to the implications of authentic Christian spirituality for the protection, preservation, and care for the earth and the earth's resources. The threat of nuclear annihilation, and the destruction of the ecological balance through systematic ravaging of the earth's resources, has caused some to remind of the value and dignity of other forms of life, and to invite to a just and non-violent way of living with other species and the whole of creation upon which humans depend for their very existence.

9. Contemporary spiritual writings evidence a strong commitment to find solutions to the problems that Christians face today by retrieving the riches of the past. This requires much more than recovering insights from former epochs and applying them uncritically as solutions to current problems. Rather it demands a deep appreciation of the particular historical context within which the formulation of a given insight or truth took place, so that the fundamental orientations and motivations of a given historical age that underlie such a formulation might be brought to bear upon a very different context and set of circumstances marked by very different modes of being and perceiving.

10. There is increasing attention to specifying the precise limits and scope of spirituality as both lived experience and as an area of disciplined study. As an academic enterprise, Christian spirituality is an emergent and immature discipline. Though scholars have agreed on some common vocabulary, issues of concern, and methods of investigation, there is not as yet a

commonly recognized theory regarding the precise limits and scope of this area of study.[2]

In view of these current trends, it may be useful to offer a few reflections on how I understand the nature and scope of Christian spirituality as both lived experience and academic discipline. In so doing it is my hope to bring some methodological form to the understanding and study of Christian spirituality.

A METHOD FOR UNDERSTANDING
CHRISTIAN SPIRITUALITY

In charting the terrain of Christian spirituality it may be helpful to identify seven focal points of investigation. From this vantage point, Christian spirituality is concerned with the work of the Holy Spirit (in itself a rather slippery term) in persons: (1) within a culture; (2) in relation to a tradition; (3) in light of contemporary events, hopes, sufferings and promises; (4) in remembrance of Jesus Christ; (5) in efforts to combine elements of action and contemplation; (6) with respect to charism and community; (7) as expressed and authenticated in praxis.[3]

Such a framework can be used by those who are studying spirituality in a disciplined way, as well as by those who are simply attempting to come to a deeper understanding of spirituality, their own or others', past or present. Whether we examine a scriptural or theological text, a legend of a saint or a painting of her with eyes turned heavenward, a type of religious vesture or sacred music, a kind of church architecture or sculpture, it is useful to consider the object of study in view of these seven focal points. We might ask: what was the *culture* within which this depiction of the Last Judgment was painted? When considering a treatise on virtue, we might ask: what are the religious and theological *traditions* reflected, adhered to, departed from in this text? What are or were the significant *events, hopes, sufferings, and promises* of the age in which this score of sacred music was composed? How does it reflect, nuance, or critique them? How is the *memory of Christ* expressed, or what is the dominant image of Christ being expressed, in this bronze? What is the view of the relationship between *contemplation and action* expressed in this stained glass depiction of Mary with book-in-hand? Or with Jesus in her arms? Or with hands folded in prayer? What is the understanding of *charism and community* expressed in the uniform attire of women religious prior to the Second Vatican Council? And what understandings of charism and community are expressed in the variegated attire of women religious today? These are a few of the types of questions that might be raised in trying to uncover the specific spirituality of a person or a group, past or present.

How might one work within this framework when considering a text or life of an individual of an earlier epoch? As an example, we might focus on the life and writings of Francis of Assisi. In trying to understand Francis' spirituality, we could consider the way in which Francis remembers Christ, or try to uncover the predominant image of Christ that emerges in early Franciscan writings and devotion, e.g., the poor Christ crucified. By way of contrast we might then focus on what can be known of how Christ was remembered, or what image of Christ predominated, in the legacy of Dominic and his first followers. Whatever similarities there may be, there are significant differences in the way Christ was remembered by Dominic and the early Dominicans on the one hand, and by Francis and his followers on the other. And the praxis (the seventh focal point of the framework) of the Gospel appropriate to a Dominican, i.e., preaching, teaching, study, will be somewhat different from the praxis appropriate to a Franciscan. This is due, at least in part, to the way Christ is remembered, or which image of Christ predominates, in each tradition. Said another way, there are distinctively Dominican and Franciscan spiritualities due to the fact that the central understanding of Christ that lies at the heart of each is quite different. We might then juxtapose these insights alongside what may be gleaned from a reading of the Ignatian sources in view of the question of how Christ is portrayed therein, attentive to what have been judged appropriate forms of praxis that result from such a remembrance. The same might be done when looking to the life and writings of some contemporary figures such as Dorothy Day, Roger Schutz, Jean Vanier, or Thomas Merton.

If we were to shift attention to a contemporary text such as the United States Catholic Bishops' pastoral letter on the economy, *Economic Justice For All*, with an eye to the spirituality expressed in its pages, it might be useful to consider the understanding of culture (the first focal point) operative therein. How is the Spirit at work within a culture shaped by materialism and consumerism? Where is the work of the Spirit in economic systems that systematically impoverish one culture for the benefit of another? How is the Spirit expressed and authenticated in the praxis of the Gospel amid conflicts of impinging cultures replete with economic ambiguities?

As another example of the attempt to understand a contemporary text, person, or movement, we might consider Christian feminist spirituality and focus on the role of tradition (the second focal point) in women's spirituality. How has the Spirit been at work in Christian traditions that have rendered the voices and experiences of women inaudible and insignificant? How has the Spirit enabled women to resist, critique, and/or reject those traditions by which they have been willfully and systematically excluded?

Whether the focus be on the past or the present, using this framework enables one to attend to the crucial importance of praxis as the expression and authentication of the Spirit's work (the seventh focal point). The praxis appropriate to a person or group, past or present, will vary due to the way in which the Spirit is at work within a culture, in relation to a tradition, in response to the events, hopes, sufferings, and promises of an age, in view of different ways of remembering Jesus, in efforts to combine elements of action and contemplation, and with respect to diverse charisms and different constellations of community. Thus the praxis of the Christian life, or spirituality, appropriate to the members of an enclosed monastic community of Cistercians will be quite different from that of the members of the Catholic Worker House due, in no small measure, to different perceptions of how action and contemplation are to be integrated within a life project in response to the work of the Holy Spirit.

* * * * * *

My purpose in this chapter has been to draw attention to significant trends in the field of Christian spirituality as both lived experience and academic discipline. As lived experience, current trends in Christian spirituality give evidence of vitality, growth, and maturity on the part of those who profess faith in Christ Jesus and live by the power of the Spirit on the brink of the third millennium. As an academic discipline, spirituality is still in its adolescence. But great effort is being made on the part of students and teachers in the field to shape a firm identity by specifying its scope, precise subject, and limits. Central to this task is the work of bringing methodological form to understanding and studying spirituality so as to facilitate its fuller development and maturation.

Notes

1. My own work is greatly influenced by that of Sandra Schneiders and Walter Principe. See, for example, Sandra M. Schneiders, "Theology and Spirituality: Strangers, Rivals, or Partners," *Horizons* 13:2 (1986) 253-274; "Spirituality in the Academy," *Theological Studies* 50:4 (1989) 676-697; see also Walter Principe, "Toward Defining Spirituality," *Studies in Religion/Sciences Religieuses* 12:2 (1983) 127-141.

2. Since this essay was first written, important theological developments have influenced Christian spirituality. In light of these developments, to the trends noted I would now add the recovery of a revitalized understanding of the doctrine of the Trinity with its practical implications for Christian life and prayer; see chapter 6, "Participation in Communion of Persons," in this volume.

3. I have developed this framework more thoroughly in a book tentatively entitled "Understanding Christian Spirituality: Learning From Life at the Margins" (forthcoming).

4

Christian Spirituality: Changing Currents, Perspectives, Challenges

LIKE COMMUNITY AND EXPERIENCE, SPIRITUALITY IS ONE OF THOSE WORDS that has become central to the grammar of the post-conciliar church. As with other oft-used terms in this vocabulary, its meanings are sometimes quite hazy. Despite efforts of scholars and pastoral practitioners alike to specify just what spirituality is, there remains a lack of clarity that will likely persist for some time. Spirituality is a slippery term.

The phenomenon itself is not new. Christian spirituality is nothing other than life in Christ by the presence and power of the Spirit; being conformed to the person of Christ, and being united in communion with God and with others. Spirituality is not an aspect of Christian life, it *is* the Christian life. Different responses to the presence and activity of the Holy Spirit give rise to different forms of life, which may be recognized as different spiritualities. What is new, however, is the enormous groundswell of interest in Christian spirituality on the part of people in all walks of life.

The council's clear affirmation of the universal call to holiness (LG 40-41) has brought about changes in currents and perspectives, and so spiritual experience. This is much more diversified, no longer tethered to the notion that priests and religious are the only ones who can truly realize the call to holiness, or that married people have to somehow get over that disability in order to enter the higher regions. Now a variety of persons and groups find the Spirit awash in a great diversity of situations.

Robert Hamma's survey in *America* (vol. 169, no. 27, 27 November 1993) provides a helpful sketch of shifting patterns in the authorship and readership of books in spirituality over the last twenty-five years. In contrast to writings in spirituality twenty-five years ago, contemporary writers include priests, monks, nuns, religious, and laypersons, male and female, married and single. There continues to be an abiding interest in particular spiritualities, and there is a great deal of writing on these, e.g., spiritualities of the priesthood, religious life, married life. Hamma's thumbnail sketch cannot indicate the wide range of publications in the field, however. This includes resources and research tools for those engaged in the disciplined study of spirituality, substantial contributions in various scholarly journals, periodicals devoted to making the findings of scholarly research more accessible to an educated readership, and journals/magazines of a more popular/practical sort. Books in spirituality range from the scholarly and esoteric to the "pop," "thin," and "fluffy," from critical editions of the Christian classics and mystical treatises to self-help manuals for coping with grief or handbooks for living with integrity through separation and divorce. Even though the range of writings and topics treated is quite diverse, it is possible to note several characteristics of contemporary Christian spirituality as expressed in the various genres of writing, conference talks, workshop themes, titles of audio cassettes, and the like.

CONTEMPORARY CURRENTS

Above all, there is focus on a more integrated or holistic understanding of the human person, and on the singular importance of the experience of participation in Christ's mysteries. Great attention is now given to the contextual and relational dimensions of the Christian life, inclusive of affectivity, intimacy, and sexuality. There is stress on the liturgical and scriptural foundations of Christian spirituality, as well as attention to the universal call to holiness, thereby undercutting the notion of a spiritual elite. Writing on particular spiritualities for clergy and religious usually reflects this sensibility. As in every age, there is attention to the search for the true self, but with greater appreciation for the complementarity of authentic human and spiritual development. In this quest for the true self, self-scrutiny goes hand in hand with developing a critical social consciousness in the face of oppression and injustice. This is related to the attempt to integrate prayer and service as an expression of the faith that does justice in ways appropriate to the urgent demands of our age. Among these urgent demands is the promotion of the full equality of women in church and society, and the inclusion of those who have been marginalized. More, but still insufficient, attention is being given to the appropriate Christian response in the face of the possibility of nuclear annihilation and the probability of ecological crises of proportions heretofore unimaginable. There is a fuller recognition of both the riches and the shortcomings of the Christian tradition in answering the problems to be faced in the next century. Finally, there is a renaissance in studies of the doctrine of the Trinity. What has often been assumed to be the loftiest, most abstract and ethereal Christian doctrine, the Trinity, is after all the most practical. Taken as the point of entry and destination of Christian life, the Trinity gives rise to an understanding of a spirituality whose keynotes are participation in communion of persons both human and divine, and the perfection of these relationships in self-donation, mutuality, and reciprocity. Because it is personal, relational, and communal, Trinitarian spirituality naturally connects with the ethical demands of Christian life in the Spirit, now viewed in terms of the flourishing of persons in loving communion rather than as individual sanctification achieved by a journey inward.

NEW PERSPECTIVES

Any pre-Vatican II priest would have had on his bookshelf, alongside his *Manuale Theologiae Dogmaticae,* and his *Manuale Theologiae Moralis,* a copy of his *Manuale Theologiae Ascetico-Mysticae.* In addition, there were the standard manuals of spirituality, such as those of de Guibert, Garrigou-Lagrange, and Tanquery. But shifting currents and perspectives on the experience of the Spirit have called for new methods of reflection and integration. In the academy there has been a strong turn to the history of spirituality, to take account of the diversity of experiences and traditions and of things unnoticed. But different methods of systematic reflection are slowly emerging. Sandra Schneiders, Walter Principe, Bernard McGinn, and Joann Wolski Conn have in different ways sought to bring methodological form to the scholarly discipline of spirituality studies. Efforts like theirs notwithstanding, spirituality's place in the halls of the academy is still quite tenuous. Unlike systematics, real "bread and butter" theology, spirituality is often thought to be "fluff," its methods and subject "fuzzy." Perhaps this is because scholars in this field generally agree that however important the study of spirituality may be, living in Christ through the presence of the Spirit has both ontological and existential precedence over the study of it.

As editor-in-chief of *The New Dictionary of Catholic Spirituality* (NDCS), I set out to weave these two strands together. My aim was to put together a volume that would cover the major topics in Catholic spirituality in a way that would provide readers with occasion for holy reading, a sort of *lectio divina*, without compromising the requirements of good scholarship. If one of the features of contemporary spirituality is its holistic, integrating function, then this first-of-its-kind dictionary of Catholic spirituality in English should be at once a reliable theological and pastoral resource while moving the heart to prayer.

One of the foundational tasks in such a project is to provide a clearly articulated vision of the subject at hand so as to offer guidance to contributors, and to serve as a unifying principle by which several hundred entries might be brought together in a coherent whole. In spelling out what distinguishes this field of inquiry from other disciplines, the following features stand forth.

Spirituality is concerned with the human person in relation to God. Whereas this may be said to be the concern of any area of theology or religious studies, it is the specific concern of the discipline of spirituality to focus precisely upon the *relational* and *personal* (inclusive of the social and political) dimensions of the human person's relationship to God.

Earlier distinctions between the *credenda*, what is to be believed (the domain of dogmatic or systematic theology), and the *agenda*, what is to be done as a result of belief (the domain of moral theology), are not always as clear as they may seem. The discipline of spirituality has developed out of moral theology's concern for the agenda of Christian living. But the focus in the study of Christian spirituality is on the full spectrum of those realities that constitute the *agendum* of a Christian life in relation to God, including the *credenda*. Thus the relationship between spirituality and biblical theology, systematic theology, moral theology, pastoral theology, and liturgical studies is stressed. What differentiates spirituality from, say, systematic theology or moral theology, is the dynamic and concrete character of the relationship of the human person to God in actual life situations. Moreover, the relationship is one of *development*, of *growth* in the life of faith, and thus covers the whole of life. Spirituality concerns religious experience as such, not just concepts or obligations.

The study of spirituality in the post-conciliar period is an interdisciplinary enterprise. Scholars in the field tend to bring insights from other disciplines (e.g., sociology, history, economics, especially psychology) as any one or several of these may contribute to a fuller understanding of the subject at hand. Additionally, the fruits of ecumenical and interreligious dialogues are brought to bear on the subject where appropriate.

The warm reception with which the NDCS has been met in both academic and pastoral circles is indicative that it is possible to accomplish the task of integrating spirituality as both lived experience and disciplined study. Helpful critics have noted the provisional and transitional nature of the dictionary, dealing as it does with a discipline still in the early stages of development. Lawrence Cunningham has written that the NDCS signals our arrival on a plateau from which we may glimpse a horizon in which spirituality will be a key component in articulating a new theological vision for the century ahead.

PROBLEMS ENCOUNTERED

The widespread interest in Christian spirituality is indicative of the enduring concern for those issues ordinarily associated with spirituality, e.g., prayer, meditation, contemplation, mysticism, and asceticism. But there is growing interest in spirituality beyond recognizably Christian or Catholic circles. This seems to be a hopeful sign of an increasing awareness that there are levels of reality not immediately apparent. But as might be expected, some odd ideas have accompanied changes in currents and perspectives. On one hand, there is the tendency to let experience free-float. On the other hand, there is the effort to categorize rich and diverse spiritual experience far too neatly by reliance on tools like the Myers-Briggs personality type indicator or the Enneagram. In either case, serious reflection and discernment are avoided. Such tendencies bespeak deeper problems, problems that present tough sticking points in the area of Christian spirituality today.

The Journey Inward

Even though contemporary currents and perspectives emphasize more holistic and integrative approaches to the Christian life, the common perception is that spirituality is primarily concerned with the life of the soul, the interior life, one's "prayer life," one's "spiritual life" as a separate component of the Christian life. The tendency to equate the spiritual life with the interior life is particularly prevalent in our own day. Traditions that once provided a cohesive worldview and sense of belonging no longer do so for a growing number of people. Worship, Bible, and tradition no longer provide the sense of unity, clarity, and security they once did. And so there is a flight inward, into deeper and deeper levels of the self as outer worlds of meaning seem increasingly unreliable and on the brink of collapse. Personal identity once shaped by the shared customs and traditions of neighborhood, community, or parish, is now sought in "spirituality" by those disaffected by or indifferent to "religion." Such a tendency is found in the pious and devout who take flight to Medjugorje or inscribe in the Blue Army, as well as in those post-Christians who live by the light of a New Age. In both cases spirituality is focused on the interior world of feelings and imagination with little if any explicit attempt at integrating the humdrum, the tedium of too much work, the demands of sociopolitical responsibility, or economic accountability.

Self-Focus

Perhaps the most persistent problem in some approaches to spirituality today is its often near-narcissistic self-preoccupation. The lingo of "my spiritual life," "my prayer life" indicates this. Whether one finds the culprit in the climate of the post-Enlightenment view of the human subject, or in the specific habits of North Americans, it is helpful to recognize that Christian spirituality has been afflicted with a brand of individual self-focus with longer and deeper roots.

It may seem unbecoming to apply any criticism whatsoever to Augustine, a figure so imposing by his insight, erudition, and balance. Augustine's theology has had a deep and lasting influence on the history of western Christian spirituality. Whether Augustine intended it or not, his version of contemplation and ascent to God through descent into the self muted the relational and communitarian dimensions of the Christian life. His theological reflection on the Trinity was focused on the structure of God's "intradivine" life, that is, the relationships of Father, Son, and Holy Spirit to one another. Augustine favored images of the Trinity drawn from the psychology of the human person, understood to have the faculties of intellect, will, and memory. He believed that the structure of the individual human soul was a mirror image (vestige) of the Trinity. By knowing ourselves, we would know God.

Much contemporary reflection on Christian spiritual life is rooted in an approach to the Trinity emphasizing the intradivine life, mirrored in the inner life of the individual person. Knowing God means knowing the self in itself, in an ever deeper journey inward. There is always the danger that an unchecked pursuit of a personal spirituality will amount to nothing more than a narcissistic self-absorption and self-preoccupation. Augustine was certainly correct that the human person is a unique locus of the divine self-disclosure. And, given that we are created in the image and likeness of God, it is natural to look for the contours of that image within ourselves. However, the early chapters of Genesis suggest that God's image is to be found in the relationship between female and male, which gives the divine image in us a dimension beyond the solitary self.

Self-Fix

It appears that in recent years the therapeutic has emerged as the primary framework for understanding the spiritual life, so much so that it seems to have eclipsed the salvific as the governing category in spirituality. The typology of Myers-Briggs and the Enneagram has become virtually synonymous with spirituality in some circles. The result is that spirituality has become jingo-ridden. The language about Christ and Christ's mysteries has receded into the background as voices exhorting us about "getting in touch with anger" and the need for "quality time" and the importance of "taking care of me" hold center stage.

Without doubt one of the more hopeful developments in contemporary spirituality is the affirmation of the complementarity of human and spiritual development. The insights of psychological investigations, especially the contributions of developmental psychology, have been most helpful in understanding the dynamic of human and Christian life. However useful these may be, the hope that motivates the Christian is not sustained by deeper and deeper penetration of the unconscious, getting to the root of our "life issue." Rather it is buoyed up by looking to a promise of a future restoration, even and especially of our own woundedness and weakness, fragility and brokenness, in and through the grace of Christ.

A Useful God

The underlying problem with some of these "wrong turns" in spirituality is a view of God as useful. Friends, colleagues, and parishioners report unabashedly that their day just doesn't seem to go right if they don't take time for daily prayer. God seems to be an instrument, and prayer an exquisitely fashioned tool in service of a higher goal, that is, the cultivation of our "spiritual life." But even in approaches to spirituality that do not dabble in self-focus and self-fix, e.g., those with a strong and clear social justice orientation, there can be tightly-held convictions about God as a means of bringing about a particular sort of social program. In the face of such a distortion, the only response is to recognize the importance of believing in God because God is God.

Specialties

The history of Christian spirituality is a story of a great diversity of approaches to the Christian life, different schools or types of spirituality, e.g., Franciscan, Ignatian, the French school, and so on. In our own day there is a great flourishing of diverse spiritualities. There is a spirituality of the midlife crisis, of aging, of separation and divorce. There is a spirituality of single people and of the vows. There is spirituality for ministry and the priesthood. Then there is African American spirituality, Hispanic American spirituality, feminist spirituality, and male spirituality. There are those who insist quite passionately on spelling out the contours of a distinctively liturgical spirituality.

Cultural differences, diversity of social location and vastly different situations in life require attention to the manifold ways in which the Holy Spirit is at work in persons within a culture, in relation to different traditions, and in light of the urgent demands and exigencies of different ages. But it is not altogether clear that this proliferation of spiritualities has not overshadowed elements of a common approach to the spiritual life in which all participate by virtue of baptism, regardless of the distinctiveness of their walk of life. Put more crisply, particular spiritualities must not obfuscate that in which all are rooted and which binds them. And this, of course, is the primacy of charity.

THE CENTRALITY OF THE CROSS

One of the most significant achievements in recent studies in spirituality is the recovery of forgotten traditions, of spiritual experience gone unnoticed. Contemporary approaches stress the importance of attending to alternative experience, looking to the margins of church and society, to marginalized persons and groups as well as marginalized dimensions of the self for the self-disclosure of God. This necessitates a close relationship between Christian spirituality and systematic theology.

Systematic theologians recognize experience as the locus of revelation. Out of their theologies Karl Rahner, Edward Schillebeeckx, Gustavo Gutiérrez and other systematicians have generated spiritualities and methods of reflecting on this experience. However, as Sandra Schneiders has shrewdly cautioned, the study of spirituality cannot be forced back under the tutelage of systematic or moral theology. I agree with her view that systematic theology and spirituality are neither strangers nor rivals, but partners. But I would urge a closer alignment than she would hope for. As I see it, the task that yet awaits those in the field of Christian spirituality is to find ways of describing and integrating a vast array of spiritual experience in light of the mystery of the cross, a soteriology. And this requires a strong note of systematic retrieval. Such a retrieval presents enormous difficulites to some currents of spirituality. The strongly patriarchal soteriology of the past puts a heavy burden on feminist Catholics and Catholic feminists. The way in which the cross was and is the emblem of crusaders of different types and periods presents a whole range of obstacles not easily hurdled. But oppressive soteriological symbols are now giving way to images of the black Nazarene of non-western, non-white cultures, and of the despised and rejected Compassion of God living in solidarity with the wounded and the weak, the last and the least, unto death and into hell.

From the perspective of a specifically Christian spirituality, the cross is the vital center for reflection and discernment, and provides a check against the pitfalls noted above. One of the more pressing challenges facing scholars in the field of spirituality studies is to avoid the tendency to let spiritual experience free-float. This calls for methods of description and reflection that seek to integrate vastly different spiritual experiences into the redemptive mystery of Christ. But an equally important challenge is to find ways of discerning and describing authentic Christian spiritual experience that does not fit into inherited categories for understanding and speaking of redemption in Christ. Above all, the task of those who study and teach spirituality, as well as all who live in Christ, is to continually look for the most compelling signs of the redemptive mystery in the lives of those who have been pushed and shoved to the margins of church and society. And to marvel as the edges become the center in the redemptive mystery of Christ, including those manifestations of the Spirit that seem to be without precedent in the life of the church.

5

Looking to the Last
and the Least

THE TITLE OF THIS CHAPTER DERIVES FROM THE WRITINGS OF SALLIE McFague who views the word and work of Jesus in light of his relationship to "the last and the least."[1] His message is a word of hope to those at the margins of social and religious institutions.

This chapter proposes to provide an understanding of power and empowerment. It considers these issues by looking to the last and the least, those at the margins of the social-symbolic order. From them we can learn about the nature of power and empowerment. It must be noted from the outset that I am not attempting to chart a program for empowering the marginalized. It is rather more an issue of *learning from* the last and the least so that dominant understandings of power and empowerment, as well as those who live within such perspectives, might be transformed. From this goal, two questions follow: what can be learned about the nature of power and empowerment from those at the margins; and what might this contribute to an understanding of Christian spirituality?

My response to these questions employs the following strategy. First, it is necessary to examine the notion of margin and marginality. Second, an explanation of that ever-so-slippery term "spirituality" will be offered. Third, different understandings of power will be treated. Fourth, a hermeneutics of marginality will be described with the aim of bringing it to bear on the question of a spirituality of empowerment. Fifth, attention will be drawn to the significance of the *kenosis* of Christ and the life of Jesus as the parabolic word of God for a spirituality of empowerment. Sixth, some practical elements of the process of empowerment will be described. Finally, characteristics of a spirituality for empowerment will be offered in view of the goal of emancipatory transformation so that all might participate in the fullness of human flourishing.

LIFE AT THE MARGINS

The terms "margins" and "marginalization" are used with increased frequency to describe those at the edge of the social-symbolic order and its ideology. Said another way, those at the margins do not fit, or are not in step with, prevalent modes of being and perceiving.

"Margin" or marginalization conveys three distinct notions.

First, the margin represents the periphery, the place that does not have much importance because it is distant from the center where power is located. Second, it contains nothing, being constituted by absence and emptiness. Third, the margin communicates the notion of borderline, limit or edge, insofar as a margin demarcates the edge of a written or typed page. People at the margin or the "marginalized" are often viewed as existing at the border between order and chaos.[2]

Referring to a person or people as marginalized is a practice of rather recent custom. To which person or group the designation applies is not always as clear as it may first seem. People at the margins may not always represent the minority of a population. The majority of the Latin American population is comprised of the poor, yet they are marginalized by the systems of power and influence that shape their lives. Women are marginalized in the Roman Catholic Church, barred from official deliberation and decision-making which affect their lives, yet they by no means constitute the minority of the ecclesiastical population. Lay persons—the great mass of the people of God—live at the margins of a hierarchical system that includes only celibate, male clerics.

Marginalized people may be said to be those who live at the margins or edges of a social body. The people at the "center" may be viewed as the "mainstream." The reasons for marginalization vary. Marginalization often results from poverty which relegates people to a lower economic status or class than that of the mainstream. For some in this category it may have a somatic base. The reason mentally and physically handicapped persons are often viewed as marginalized is because of their difference from "normal people," those with healthy and robust minds and bodies. Gender or sexual identity may also place people at the margins of a social body: women in a "man's world," and homosexuals in a world where heterosexual relationships are the norm, same-sex relationships being viewed as unnatural or abnormal. People and groups also may be marginalized because of race or language.[3]

In the Roman Catholic Church, besides the forms of marginalization noted above, those at the margins include, but are by no means limited to, single persons in parishes where marriage and family life are viewed as the norm in preaching and teaching, the divorced and remarried, resigned priests, and couples in interchurch marriages.

Common to all these persons and groups is the element of being different from what is identified as the acceptable, regular, normal, or status quo. Such differences more often than not place persons and groups in positions of powerlessness in the face of economic systems, political structures, or religious institutions and their predominant ideologies. The marginalized are those who have little or no access to the power of the dominant ideology, or at least their access to it is more restricted than that of those at the center. As a result, those at the margins have little or no determination over the systems of meaning and value, the predominant modes of perceiving and being, which, nonetheless, affect them as much as those at the center. From this perspective, they may be said to be voiceless.

Related to the notion of the marginalized are the terms "the alienated" and "the oppressed." The alienated are those who are marginalized primarily for political reasons. The term "alienation" also includes emotional connotations, e.g., when women or youth are described as alienated from the church. Oppressed peoples are marginated because of victimization arising from more active forms of violence.

Another related term, "scapegoat," signifies the worst form of marginalization. With origins in the Mosaic ritual of the Day of Atonement (Leviticus 16), the scapegoat was one of two goats chosen to be sent out alive into the wilderness to die, the sins of the people having been symbolically laid upon it, while the other was appointed to be sacrificed. The scapegoat is the person or group blamed for the failure or wrongdoing of others and cast out, expelled, or at least ostracized from the social body. Such a person or group is often already distinct from the main body by reason of national identity, social status, or religious practice. In many Christian countries Jews have been used as scapegoats at various times in history, often with religious sanctioning, which added to the ideological justification for their marginalization.

It might also be useful to note that the image of Christ as scapegoat has functioned throughout Christian history, sometimes bearing positive significance, particularly for marginalized peoples. A contemporary understanding of Christ as scapegoat in light of the experience of marginalization deserves fuller attention but lies beyond the scope of this study.

INTERLUDE: SELF-SCRUTINY

As a white, middle-class, well-educated male, it may appear that I fit easily at the center of the social-symbolic order and its dominant ideology. I am part of the center, the "majority" which pushes persons and groups to the margins of church and society. But as I live at the center, I am unable to dismiss the voices from the periphery: the cries and shouts of Christian feminist, liberation, political and Third World theologians addressing me from the margins of the center to which I have had easy access by virtue of race, gender, and class. But if I would hear the voices of those who speak from the margins, I must place myself outside the center of the order and move from the middle to the edges, the margins of society *and* church.

Deciding to hear and freely stand with those at the margins results in what Rebecca Chopp calls a "center/margin viewpoint."[4] It entails a willingness to see "from beneath," from the viewpoint of the useless, the suspect, the abused, the oppressed, the despised, the powerless. In short, it "sees" from the vantage of suffering.[5] From this viewpoint, I begin to understand that the dominant social-symbolic order works for no one. It thwarts even the staunchest defenders of the center in their quest for authentic meaning and purpose, in their desire for the fullness of human flourishing.

Without prejudice to the complexity of the issue, from this vantage Christ and the presence of the Spirit are never found at the center, but always at the edge, calling into question what is considered central to the centrist point of view. I conclude that my own discourse about God, Christ, church and Christian life must change. I must first listen to the suffering of those at the margins and "name" the psychic destructiveness of the center for what it is.[6]

Here it should be noted that there are two kinds of people at the margins: (1) those who are there because they have to be— there is no choice, and (2) those who freely stand with the marginalized. The two should not be confused. The experience of marginalization and the experience of those who freely choose to stand in solidarity with them is never the same. Caution must be exercised in the face of the temptation to facilely appropriate the experience of those who have no choice but to live at the margins.[7] For example, I have learned from my short time in a l'Arche community in France that the experience of being mentally handicapped and, as a result, being cast to the margins of the mainstream, is of a radically different sort than that of "normal" persons who live in intentional communities with mentally handicapped persons.[8]

From the point of view of those at the margins and the marginalized, Christian life and practice are aimed, in part, at emancipatory transformation, not of those at the margins, but of those at the center. Emancipatory transformation is *not* a matter of assimilating the last and the least, the wounded and the weak, into systems that themselves have caused such an awesome threat to human life and the world as we know it. The "normal" modes of perceiving and being are challenged through the powers of the weak.

SPIRITUALITY: THE SPIRIT AT WORK IN PERSONS

What exactly is spirituality? More specifically: what is Christian spirituality? The terms are often used with a great measure of imprecision.

Spirituality refers to both a lived experience and an academic discipline. In both instances "the referent of the term 'spirituality' is Christian religious experience as such."[9] That is to say, the term refers to experience precisely as religious and as Christian. Because it is Christian, theological insights and accuracy are crucial to it. Because it is religious, it is affective as well as cognitional, communal as well as personal, focused at once on God and others. And because it is experience, it pertains to everything that constitutes the living of Christian life.[10] James Wiseman suggests that, rather than focusing on "what" the Christian believes (credenda) or "what to do" as a consequence of belief (agenda), the focus of spirituality is on the agendum of the whole of Christian life in relation to God.[11]

Writers like Jean Leclercq and Walter Principe view Christian spirituality in a similar light. Principe defines spirituality in terms of all the dimensions of a person's faith commitment "that concern his or her striving to attain the highest ideal or goal," namely, "an ever more intense union with the Father through Jesus Christ by living in the Spirit."[12]

What these perspectives have in common is the understanding that spirituality is concerned with the dynamic and concrete character of people's relationship with God in actual life situations. Moreover, this relationship is one of development, of growth in the life of faith. Thus it covers the whole of life. Spirituality concerns religious experience as such, not just concepts or obligations.

The life situation that concerns us here is that of people at the margins and fissures of the center. In looking to them, our purpose is to uncover an understanding of power that arises from the work of the Spirit in the experience of marginalization.

UNDERSTANDINGS OF POWER

One way to speak of power is in terms of the ability to act. Power affects change; it brings about change in persons, relationships, and structures. Most understandings of power represent functional and/or practical considerations: some have it, whereas others do not. Those who have power can use it for good or for ill. Powerful people can abuse others through exercises of power that dominate, control, manipulate, and violate. The powerless often submit to such exercises of power, by choice or circumstance, and thus are controlled, manipulated, and violated. Often such exercises of power are said to be for a greater or higher good, such as God's will or the divine plan. From childhood on, abuses of power of the most subtle sort are visited upon children "for their own good" by their parents.[13]

This "some have it, some don't" understanding of power rests on an asymmetrical dualism rooted in a restricted and restrictive view of an all-powerful God.[14] In this view God is all-powerful, external to the world as the power that controls it. Human beings are ultimately powerless, subject to domination by the divine sovereign, or to divine benevolence. Such a view of God as the divine sovereign who is "in charge," and who exercises power vis-à-vis human beings "for their own good," can serve to justify exercises of power that dominate, control, and manipulate those without power, and can be counterproductive.

Feminist studies and the "linguistic turn" as it has affected much of religious and theological studies bring new perspectives to bear on prevalent notions of power.[15] From these perspectives, power is understood in terms of "naming," giving voice, speaking. Power speaks. It "names" our experience as our own, giving voice to our silent suffering and the suffering of a people at the hands of those "in charge." To have power is to have a say. For Rebecca Chopp, "power is the ability to take one's place in whatever discourse is essential to action, and the right to have one's part matter."[16] Power is "talking back," a form of resistance to the practices and principles of control, domination, and oppression.

Whether it is viewed as the ability to speak, to act and/or to change, self-determination is at issue when we speak of power. To have power, to speak or act, is to be the subject of our own history. If this is the case, then views of power that accentuate separating divine and human power must give way to other views that recognize the unity and interdependence of divine and human power.[17] This entails a fuller appreciation of the nature of God's relationship with the world in and through the work of the Spirit which is the very life, presence, and power of God in, through, and to the world. Such an appreciation allows for understanding power as a unified and interdependent reality, thus making possible the recognition and exercise of power through processes of relationality built on mutuality, reciprocity, and collaboration.

This relational view of power stands directly opposed to the view of power that rests on the kind of dualism that assumes "some have it, some don't." The latter view treats power as something given in a unilateral way by those who have it to those who do not. Viewed relationally, power is unified and interdependent because it originates in the unity and interdependence of divine and human power. This necessitates recognizing that power rests at the heart of all creation, even and especially in the most vulnerable of creation, and allowing it to stand forth.

The keynote of the unilateral approach to power is *order*. To preserve order, especially when it is judged to be divinely ordained, control, manipulation, domination, and forms of violence both subtle and overt, continue to be justified and tolerated, even in God's name. In contrast, the hallmarks of the relational view of power are fidelity, nurture, attraction, self-sacrifice, passion, responsibility, care, affection, respect, and mutuality.[18]

Here it must be noted that in fact most exercises of power do operate in the manner of "some have it, some don't." That is to say that some do hold power in such a way that others are, or become, powerless. Structures do control and dominate. So, is the effort to describe different modes or views of power more in keeping with a relational perspective anything more than an exercise in futility?

For any real change to take place, a linguistic and epistemological reorientation is required. This demands not only a description of what actually is and must be. It also requires a description that suggests what may or might be. Consequently, to serve this task, the intention of this chapter is not to offer a specific program for proper exercises of power and empowerment. It is to suggest views of what may or might be, what is possible for each and for all in our common desire for human flourishing.

A HERMENEUTICS OF MARGINALITY[19]

In light of our concern to spell out the contours of a spirituality of empowerment, it is useful to ask at this point: is the unilateral or relational approach to power more in keeping with the lordship of Christ, properly understood, and the power of the Holy Spirit? The answer depends upon how we view Christ's lordship, or how we remember the word and the work of Jesus as expressing God's intention for the world both now and to come.

In every age Christians have attempted to find appropriate ways of giving prayerful praise and thanks to God, in view of the changing circumstances and different exigencies with which they live. The prayer of individuals and communities depends in no small measure on the way they remember Christ. Persons and groups make decisions about which elements in the life of Jesus, God's Word, are central to the task of being and becoming Christian in a particular time, place, culture, and tradition. This has been done in every age. Put more simply still, hearers of the word hear the word in certain ways.

The term "hermeneutics of marginality" describes a way of looking, understanding, judging, deciding, and acting from the margins, in solidarity with those who live and speak from the periphery: from the fissures, the cracks, the edges of the center. Adopting such a hermeneutical stance, deciding that one will perceive and be in the world from the margins, is to risk being at odds with what is judged to be "normal," "established," "reliable," and "traditional." Looking to Jesus and hearing his words from a hermeneutics of marginality implies a twofold acknowledgement. First, it sees Jesus' ministry as focused on the margins and on the radical reordering of present reality. Second, it recognizes and "names" the experience of God at the margins. More succinctly: to view the word and the work, the meaning and message of Jesus in this way is to attend to the presence and action of God manifest in the margins as well as in the lives of those who manifest God's Spirit there.

What is the view of Jesus that emerges when one looks and hears from the margins? One might say that it is the *kenosis*, the self-emptying, of Jesus Christ described by Paul. The Kenotic Christ, whose lordship and dominion are disclosed precisely in his self-emptying (Philippians 2:6-11), refused to lay claim to exercises of authority and power grounded in the dualism that gives rise to a unilateral approach to power—the power of "the world." Refusing this type of power and embracing powerlessness, disclosed the power and lordship of Jesus. Jesus' refusal of external, "worldly" power and his acceptance of the human condition enabled him to enter the life of others at their most vulnerable point. But this power differs greatly from the power of "the world." It is the power of a displaced and unknown infant at Bethlehem and a crucified minister and teacher of mercy on Golgotha. The power of this *kenosis* differs completely from what brings about change by control, domination, or manipulation; it manifests itself in care, compassion, self-sacrifice, reciprocity, and mutuality.

A hermeneutics of marginality considers the Kenotic Christ precisely within the context of a proclamation of good news for those at the edges who inhabit the fissures of the social and religious bodies. Since this Kenotic Christ is the Word and is known in the proclamation of the word, a fuller appreciation of the Kenotic Christ thus requires attention to the power of the word.

THE PARABOLIC POWER OF THE WORD

Listening to the word at the margins requires attention to the proclamation and manifestation of God's action and presence in Christ Jesus in a distinctive manner. Just as everyone's point of view is *a* view of a point, so the place where we stand determines what we hear. When standing at the margins, we hear the word in ways that orient us to a new sense of time through remembrance of what God has done, is now doing, and will do in and through the Kenotic Christ made flesh in the least of the brothers and sisters (Matthew 25:31-46).

A fuller appreciation of Jesus as God's Word from a hermeneutics of marginality demands an understanding of the way the word works. Paul Ricoeur has written extensively on the nature and function of religious language. His insights on parable are particularly instructive for the purposes of this chapter. Ricoeur suggests that parables work in a pattern of orientation, disorientation, and reorientation.[20] The parable begins in the ordinary world with its familiar and unquestioned assumptions and modes of perception. But in the course of the story a radically different view is introduced which shocks and disorients the hearer(s). Through the interplay of the two contrasting perspectives (orientation and disorientation), a tension is created which gives rise to a redescription of the world and a reorientation of the hearer(s) to a new mode of perceiving and being in the world.

This insight can be extended in such a way that we may speak of the parabolic power of the word. The way in which the *parable* works is also the way the *word*, more generally speaking, works.

Walter Brueggemann suggests that the parabolic power of the word is both a radical critique of conventional standards and a source of energy for the building of a new world more in keeping with God's promise.[21]

The parabolic power of the word, whose rhythms fill the ears and the hearts of those gathered at the edges to be invigorated by its ebb and flow, wages a radical critique on society's orientation which is to accept as normative the marginality around it. This critique begins to disorient conventional standards and the unquestioned, yet tightly held, assumptions about God, self, and others. At the same time it energizes the hearer(s) of the word to live and to work for a radically new future. This future's contours can be broadly discerned in the proclamation of the Crucified and Risen One who through his *kenosis* lived and died in solidarity with people at the edges.

In the proclamation and hearing, the word shocks and disorients the hearer(s). The present situation, the now in which voices are lifted to God in praise and thanksgiving, is called into question and radically critiqued by a word that tells of the mighty being cast from their thrones, the poor holding pride of place (as in the *Magnificat*, Luke 1: 46-55), and of the child who shall be the prophet of the Most High (as in the *Benedictus*, Luke 1: 67-79). Hearing this word summons to a redescription of reality: the poor are at the top of the ladder; the rich and proud of heart no longer command the center of attention; children reveal God's reign and have something to say.

By disorienting society's "normal" orientation, the word demands a reorientation in the direction of the future, the time of God's promise, the hour when the power of love will cast out all fear, when love will prevail over all evil. Listening to the word at the margins entails that we give the parabolic quality of the word in its entirety a chance to sink into our hearts that they might be changed. This implies that all the specific words (as manifestations of *the* Word) that are proclaimed and heard from the margins become understood in terms of the parabolic pattern: orientation, disorientation, reorientation.

For example, the parable of the prodigal son begins with an orientation that appeals to ordinary, commonplace sensibilities. Then disorientation enters when it shocks and shatters those sensibilities, calling into question all standards of fairness and justice. Finally a reorientation invites the hearer(s) to live from the perspective of unrestricted forgiveness and mercy. The effect of this and other parables of Jesus is to "destabilize" tightly held views and expectations of the God-world relation, so that human beings can live by a new vision that is glimpsed in the word and work of Jesus.[22]

This new vision can also be seen in the meal stories of the New Testament. Jesus eats with "the saved" (orientation) as well as with "the sinners" (disorientation). This shatters expectations and perceptions of righteousness and holiness. It also challenges perceptions of the "unworthy." Those on the "outside" are on the "inside" through Jesus' eating at table with them. Thus those who would live by the meaning and message of Jesus are invited to a reorientation of their ways of relating along the lines of "inclusivity," with particular attention to those at the margins of society and religious institutions—"the last and the least." "Not the holiness of the elect, but the wholeness *of all* is the central vision of Jesus."[23]

The parabolic power of the word as orientation, disorientation, reorientation is nowhere more pronounced than in the life, dying, and rising of Christ. The destabilizing effect of the life of Jesus himself who identified with the last and the least is consummated in the cross. The cross is the necessary path in bringing about the new mode of perceiving and being expressed not only in the parables and the table stories, but in the whole parabolic word-made-parable. Discipleship demands a way of radical identification with all others, and entails a commitment to solidarity with the suffering and with victims of all ages. It also requires non-hierarchical, non-dualistic modes of relationship with all others, particularly the wounded and the weak, the voiceless, those at the margins, the last and the least. His *pasch*— the point of reference in all Christian life and spirituality—is itself an expression of the pattern of orientation, disorientation, reorientation.

The parabolic power of the word destabilizes, shocks, and shatters our standard ways of thinking about reality. It invites us to live by a vision in which the proud-hearted are scattered in their conceit and the poor are exalted. In light of this redescription of reality and of life within it, Christian life becomes rooted in the *kenosis*. Union with God requires a commitment to downward mobility in order to live in mutual love with the wounded and the weak, in imitation of Christ's self-emptying, rather than the upward mobility, the "upscale" vision of, let us say, the "yuppies," the social and economic ascendancy of the 1980s whose commitment to conspicuous consumption is legendary.[24]

The word of God is a bold proclamation of the discontinuity and contrast between present, conventional standards and ways of being, and the future to which God calls and commands. On the one hand, the word wages a strident critique, reminding the hearer(s) that the power of evil and sin still has sway in the world. On the other, it offers the hope and consolation that this power will come to an end. Response to this word invites repentance as well as celebration, sorrow as well as joy, lamentation as well as praise and thanksgiving. From the vantage of the margins, we see that authentic Christian living in our day entails recognizing suffering and naming the negative factors in ecclesial and social life together with the positive ones for which we rightly give thanks to God. This implies that we strive to respond to the power of the word always; particularly, though not exclusively, in prayer in all its expressions: "private" and public; individual and liturgical.[25]

The parabolic power of the word as it is proclaimed and heard at the margins reorients the hearer(s) to the realization that the way of the cross is necessary in bringing about the new world envisioned by Jesus. This is a way of radical identification with all others, particularly the last and the least. The cross symbolizes the willingness to relinquish controlling and triumphalist tactics in favor of solidarity with victims, the wounded and the weak, the last and the least. Thus a model of Christian life in the Spirit transformed by this hearing of the word in and for our time would recognize that authentic Christian praxis lies in the acceptance of the invitation to be in union with the Crucified Christ in and through the practice of solidarity with his suffering, marginated members.

POWER AND EMPOWERMENT FROM THE MARGINS

In light of this way of viewing Jesus focused on the singular importance of his *kenosis*, and this way of proclaiming and hearing the word as a work of the Spirit, what can be learned about power and empowerment in Christian life?

Whether it be viewed in terms of the ability to speak or to act and change, the power of the Spirit mediated in the word is unified and interdependent. Divine and human power are not in competition. Although they are distinct, they are not separate realities. A Christian exercise of power thus becomes a matter of relinquishing approaches to power rooted in dualism, which result in competition, control, domination, and manipulation for the preservation of what is judged to be proper order. This "normal," "accepted," "approved," "traditional" way of perceiving and being in the world, from the perspective of the margins, does not work. And from the "center/margin" perspective that I have adopted throughout this chapter, an uncritical acceptance of the social-symbolic order and its ideology contributes to the psychic destructiveness of the center. Thus the parabolic power of the word confronts the power that preserves and protects the center. From the center, refusing to lay claim to power is to be in a position of powerlessness; from the periphery it is to share in the power of the Spirit of Christ who in his teaching and very presence wages the ultimate criticism of the dominant ideology, the prevalent order. Brueggemann writes:

> He [Jesus] has, in fact, dismantled the dominant culture and nullified its claims. The way of his ultimate criticism is his solidarity with marginal people and the accompanying vulnerability required by that solidarity. The only solidarity worth affirming is solidarity characterized by the same helplessness they know and experience.[26]

From the perspective at the margins, power possesses a whole new purpose. The end, the objective, in any proper exercise of power from a hermeneutics of marginality, provides for the possibility of others not to be the subjects of the powerful, rich, and robust (orientation), but to become ever more fully the subjects of their own history (disorientation). It is to speak with our own voice, and to tell our own story, not to speak in the voice of another, or adopt the modes of discourse in which our own voice is, at best, only a faint echo (reorientation). This kind of power exists for emancipatory transformation, the process by which persons come to do the truth in love freely, not for the preservation of tradition and order. Such power enables persons to become their own subjects, to speak their own voice. In this lies authentic empowerment and reorientation of life.

From this perspective, power is expressed in manifold ways. It is enriched rather than diminished by difference. Those "in charge" are not viewed as the sole custodians of power, but rather as servants of its manifold presence. A hierarchical view of power merely tolerates difference in light of an exacting need for control. But a relational view of power rooted in a hermeneutics of marginality does not merely tolerate difference. It demands, enables, and encourages difference. Persons and communities are enriched, not diminished, by differences. Because it is in the confrontation with those who are different from themselves that those at the center can discover their own powerlessness, their own "marginalization" and alienation from their deepest selves. Authentic solidarity with those who suffer, with others who are articulating their voice at the margins, is possible only to the measure that those at the center accept their own powerlessness and marginalization which is disclosed as they are confronted by the powers of the weak.

Within the context of this relational view of power exercised for the purpose of emancipatory transformation, the question that needs to be addressed is: how does empowerment take place? How does it happen if power is not simply handed on unilaterally by those who have it to those who do not?

Walter Brueggemann's treatment of the nature of prophecy as radical critique of the priestly, royal, dominant consciousness from the perspective of marginated people is pertinent here. It suggests clues for understanding how empowerment works from a hermeneutics of marginality.[27]

First, it involves the task of uncovering symbols that convey the experience of life at the edges. This is not a matter of inventing symbols. It is rather a question of digging deeply into the consciousness of those at the margins to find therein particular stories that have provided the basis for contradicting the dominant ideology or prevalent order that has made them invisible, voiceless, powerless. Such symbols, retrieved in memory and in hope, offer possibilities for life and future to those who have been pushed and shoved to the margins. The retrieval of symbols and stories of life at the margins is a way of pushing and shoving back.

For example, there is the symbol of the weak and frail Abel, victim of the violence of his strong and robust brother Cain. It is from the blood of the weaker, slain brother that salvation comes. Similarly, it is from Jacob, the younger brother, again much more frail and fair (but far more clever and inventive) than the sinewy Esau, that salvation's promise continues. There is God's promissory address to the darkness of chaos, to barren Sarah, to oppressed slaves of the Egyptians. "The promise of God is first about an alternative future," and it is offered to those who have no future or possibility in the reigning order of the center.[28]

Second, after releasing these hidden symbols one must bring to public expression the horrors and the hopes of those at the margins. This may be the hardest task of all. If those at the margins are powerless and voiceless, how is speech possible? To this question there is no easy answer. But we see one example of this in those survivors of the Holocaust who are willing to bring to public expression the horrors they and millions of the voiceless dead suffered at the hands of the Nazis.[29]

Just as the recovery of the symbols of the marginalized entails digging deeply into the consciousness of those at the margins to find therein symbols of contradiction, so too speaking of the horror and the hope at the margins requires a recognition that there are and have always been modes of discourse within which those at the margins have "talked back" to the center from which they have been excluded. Learning to bring the horrors of the margins to public expression requires speaking about that of which many are not conscious, cannot believe, or flatly deny. The hope expressed from the margins is often an absurdity too embarrassing to speak about, because it opposes what those at the center proclaim as facts. Christian hope at the margins is "the refusal to accept the reading of reality which is the majority opinion; and one does that only at great political and existential risk."[30]

Third, empowerment requires listening to the language of grief and lamentation so that we can learn to speak it to others. From the perspective of the margins, the old order is passing away; those at the center must grieve its loss. Exercises of power grounded in dualism and a hierarchical ordering of human life, history, world, and church have resulted in violence and in the suffering of innocent millions. But the voices of these millions, both living and dead, speak about hope and newness that redefine the present situation. Indeed, the whole history of Israel begins in God's attentiveness to the cries of the marginal ones. Christian faith rests in the Crucified and Risen One who lived and died in solidarity with those at the margins. And his Spirit is nowhere more vibrant than in the voices of those who cry out in pain and possibility from the edges to the center. It is the voice of rejected Joseph assuring his brothers that things do work out for good, as well as the voice of Mary of Nazareth proclaiming the greatness of the God who fills the hungry with good things, casts down the proud and mighty, lifts up the poor and lowly and reserves for them pride of place.

A SPIRITUALITY OF EMPOWERMENT

To speak of spirituality is to speak of the Spirit at work in persons. This Spirit is the life and empowerment of God in, through, and to the world. A Christian spirituality emerges as a result of the Spirit manifest and mediated in the word and work, meaning and message of Jesus. Different Christian spiritualities, different ways of living in and by the Spirit, arise as a result of the way the Spirit works within various cultures and traditions, specific ways of remembering Christ, and so on.[31] In other words, the place where we stand will determine the way this word will be heard and this message will be received and lived.

This chapter has attempted to develop a spirituality of empowerment from the vantage of a hermeneutics of marginality. What are the contours of this spirituality of empowerment?

First, this spirituality is rooted in a view of power which is unified and interdependent, grounded not in dualism and a hierarchical ordering of human life, history, world, and church derived from a faulty notion of the separation of divine and human power. Rather, such a spirituality is grounded in a relational view of power which is exercised authentically only to the degree that it aims at emancipatory transformation which enables human persons, especially the last and the least, the wounded and the weak, to become subjects of their own history in order to do the truth in love freely.

Second, since the *kenosis* of Christ is central to this spirituality, within the context of this way of remembering Christ through the work of the Spirit, prevalent exercises of power rooted in competition, domination, manipulation, and control must be critiqued and relinquished in order to cultivate expressions of power built on reciprocity, mutuality, and care.

Third, this spirituality develops by the power of the Spirit in the parabolic pattern of the word that orients, disorients, and reorients to ways of perceiving and being more in keeping with the lordship of the Kenotic Christ. As a result:

(a) Christian life destabilizes conventional expectations and standards of the center, and upsets "normal" divisions and dualisms. Those at the edges, on the outside, invisible at the margins, are those who receive God's self-disclosure.

(b) Christian life is inclusive, requiring the recognition of the strengths already existing in the wounded and the weak, the alienated and the outsider.[32]

(c) Christian life requires anti-hierarchical and anti-triumphalist ways of human relatedness, expressed in the self-emptying of Christ, the king who became a servant, and who suffers alongside the last and the least.[33]

Fourth, this spirituality is based in the confidence that the life, breath, and power of God in and through the Spirit reside at the heart of all creation, even and especially in the most vulnerable. Its most pressing mandate is to let life continue, rather than to harness, control, and master it. Its most compelling exercise is in letting life be, instead of forcing itself in the name of good order.

Finally, those who live by this spirituality recognize that the challenge of empowerment does not lie in handing over power from those who have it to those who do not. Empowerment involves the disempowerment of those at the center. It entails seeking forgotten symbols that convey the life of the Spirit at the margins, learning to hear with open ears and speak with full voice about the horrors and hopes of those at the margins and, finally, offering a new description of ways of perceiving and being in the world more in keeping with God's intention for the world both now and to come.

* * * * * *

Perhaps the greatest risk in discourse about power and empowerment is the failure to get beyond understandings of power grounded in the "some have it, some don't" approach. Such understandings lead to strategies, often quite well-intentioned and benign (though more often than not patronizing), for turning over, giving up, or passing on to others this slippery reality we call power.

The view of power and empowerment from a hermeneutics of marginality is of a very different kind. Most importantly, authentic exercises of this power are aimed at the emancipatory transformation of persons, and the radical critique and transformation of power as it is exercised at the center. Thus, it is not a matter of giving those at the margins a share in the power of those at the center of church and society. It is a matter of recognizing new ways of perceiving and being more in keeping with the word and the work of the Crucified and Risen One whose power was disclosed in his refusal to lay claim to the power of lords, kings, priests, and patriarchs.

To share in this power is to listen to those who speak in a different voice. It is to turn our ears and eyes from the center to the edge of church and society. It is to live from and for fidelity, nurture, attraction, self-sacrifice, passion, responsibility, care, affection, respect, and mutuality.

It is to accept the mandate: let life continue, but not as it has been with the center defining life and the quality of human life. It is to set aside the inordinate desire for order, and to recognize, enable, and encourage otherness, specificity, particularity, solidarity, and transformation.[34]

The spirituality of empowerment is one of surrender to the Spirit, the breath of God anointing to speech and bringing to voice, blessing difference, specificity, solidarity, transformation, and anticipation.

Notes

1. Sallie McFague, *Models of God: Theology for an Ecological, Nuclear Age* (Philadelphia: Fortress, 1987); see esp. 45ff.

2. Rebecca Chopp, *The Power to Speak: Feminism, Language, God* (New York: Crossroad, 1989) 15.

3. As an example of the importance of race and language in shaping perspectives different from those of the dominant ideology, see Michael Galvan, Marina Herrera, and Jamie Phelps on the issue of providence and responsibility from Native American, Hispanic, and African American perspectives respectively in "Providence and History: Some American Views," *Proceedings of the Catholic Theological Society of America*

44 (1989) 4-18.

4. Chopp, *The Power* 16.

5. Gustavo Gutiérrez, *The Power of the Poor in History* (Maryknoll, NY: Orbis, 1983) 231ff.

6. Chopp, *The Power* 16.

7. Madonna Kolbenschlag, "Spirituality: Finding Our True Home," in *Women in the Church*, ed. Madonna Kolbenschlag (Washington, D.C.: The Pastoral Press, 1987) 197-213.

8. For a treatment of life in intentional community with mentally handicapped persons, see Michael Downey, *A Blessed Weakness: The Spirit of Jean Vanier and l'Arche* (San Francisco: Harper & Row, 1986).

9. Sandra M. Schneiders, "Theology and Spirituality: Strangers, Rivals, or Partners," *Horizons* 13:2 (1986) 267.

10. Ibid.

11. James A. Wiseman, "Teaching Spiritual Theology: Methodological Reflections," *Spirituality Today* 41:2 (1989) 145-146.

12. Walter Principe, "Toward Defining Spirituality," *Studies in Religion/Sciences religieuses* 12:2 (Printemps/Spring 1983) 139; see also Jean Leclercq's introduction to *The Spirituality of Western Christendom*, ed. E. Rozanne Elder (Kalamazoo, MI: Cistercian Publications, 1976) xi-xxxv.

13. For an analysis of the roots of the abuses of authority and power from a psychoanalytic perspective, see Alice Miller, *For Your Own Good: Hidden Cruelty and the Roots of Violence* (New York: Farrar, Straus, Giroux, 1983).

14. McFague, *Models of God* 17.

15. For a treatment of the linguistic turn in theology, see Michael Scanlon, "Language and Praxis: Recent Theological Trends," in *Proceedings of the Catholic Theological Society of America*, vol. 43 (1988) 80-89.

16. Chopp, *The Power* 2.

17. McFague, *Models of God* 17.

18. Ibid. 21.

19. A "feminist hermeneutics of marginality" is ably described by Rebecca Chopp, *The Power to Speak* 43-46. One of the purposes of the present essay is to extend some of her insights beyond the concerns of feminism.

20. Paul Ricoeur, "Biblical Hermeneutics," *Semeia* 4 (1975) 126.

21. Walter Brueggemann, *The Prophetic Imagination* (Philadelphia: Fortress, 1978); see esp. chapters 3 and 4.

22. For a fuller treatment of the destabilizing effect of the parables, see Sallie McFague, *Models of God* (Philadelphia: Fortress, 1987) esp. 45ff.

23. Elisabeth Schüssler Fiorenza, *In Memory of Her* (New York: Crossroad, 1983) 121.

24. An analysis of the "yuppie strategy" is found in Barbara Ehrenreich, *Fear of Falling: The Inner Life of the Middle Class* (New York: Pantheon, 1989).

25. For a fuller appreciation of lamentation as a way of naming the negative, see Brueggemann, *The Prophetic Imagination*, chapter 3; see also Michael Downey, "Worship Between the Holocausts," *Theology Today* 43:1 (1988) 75-87, chapter 15 in this volume.

26. Brueggemann, *The Prophetic Imagination* 81.

27. Here I am indebted to the work of Walter Brueggemann, especially chapters 3 and 4 of *The Prophetic Imagination*.

28. Ibid. 66.

29. See, for example, Elie Wiesel, *Night* (New York: Avon Books, 1960); see also Wiesel, *The Trial of God* (New York: Random House, 1979).

30. Brueggemann, *The Prophetic Imagination* 67.

31. See "Understanding Christian Spirituality," chapter 3 and "Liturgy's Form: Work of the Spirit," chapter 14 in this volume.

32. For a fine example of a view of power which recognizes the strengths of the poor and of those who suffer, see the work of Gustavo Gutiérrez, especially *We Drink From Our Own Wells: The Spiritual Journey of a People* (Maryknoll, NY: Orbis, 1984).

33. McFague, *Models of God* 48.

34. Chopp, *The Power* 84.

6

Participation in Communion of Persons

THE TRINITY IS SUPPOSEDLY AT THE CENTER OF CHRISTIAN FAITH. IT IS often viewed as the loftiest of Christian mysteries; indeed so lofty that it has been given relatively little attention in the pastoral life of the church. We are unaccustomed to think of the Trinity as a practical doctrine. Karl Rahner remarked that if one were to dismiss the doctrine of the Trinity as false, the major portion of religious literature might well remain virtually unchanged.[1]

In *God for Us: The Trinity and Christian Life* Catherine Mowry LaCugna has provided a vigorous theological analysis and presentation of the Trinitarian doctrine.[2] Her central thesis is that the doctrine of the Trinity is a practical doctrine with radical consequences for Christian life. Her work has been received and evaluated primarily by theologians whose expertise lies in the discipline of systematic theology. In this chapter I shall spell out some of the insights of *God for Us* for those who study and teach Christian spirituality, with attention to some of the concerns of those interested in taking seriously the connection between systematic theology and spirituality.[3] These insights arise from LaCugna's reconception of the doctrine of God in light of the mystery of salvation, to be sure. But far more importantly, her understanding of person rooted in an ontology of relation provides the basis for a vigorous Trinitarian spirituality that, if truly

89

grasped, would altogether change our understanding of living the Christian life, i.e., Christian spirituality.

THE PRIORITY OF *OIKONOMIA*

LaCugna's work is divided into two roughly equal parts. In Part One, "The Emergence and Defeat of the Doctrine of the Trinity," she attends to the historical development of the specifically Christian way of speaking about God. Her thorough survey is a veritable *tour de force* of the emergence of this central Christian doctrine. Her presentation includes the contributions of the significant voices in Christian history who have most influenced the development of the doctrine of the Trinity in both east and west. In her presentation of the Cappadocian theology of divine relations she indicates some of her own theological convictions regarding the foundational mystery disclosed in the economy of salvation: God, who is Love, is a mystery of persons in communion. Her presentation of Augustine and Thomas Aquinas is fair and evenhanded, but she is in no way reluctant to point out the ways that their emphasis on the essence of the intradivine life unwittingly assisted in banishing the Trinity to the realms of abstraction.

The first part of the work analyzes the reasons why the Trinity as the heart and soul of Christian faith was defeated, i.e., dislodged or debunked, from its high ground as the foundation and summary of Christian faith in practice. In short, LaCugna's argument might be stated as follows: original reflection on the triune life of God focused on the economy of salvation, i.e., on God's saving plan for humanity disclosed in Jesus Christ through the power of the Holy Spirit. Because of certain questions raised by Arius and others, particularly about the suffering of Jesus Christ, and about whether God is capable or incapable of being in real relationship with creation, and by implication with human beings, it became necessary within Christian theology to settle the question of the equality of the divine persons (Son with Father) on a metaphysical, intradivine basis. This shifted focus from the diversity and uniqueness of the divine persons within the economy of salvation, to the equality of the persons within God's eternal triune life. This had the effect of diminishing the central role of the economy and what can be known of

God in and through it. Reflection on the Trinity became fixed upon the intradivine structure of God's being, rendered altogether inaccessible once untethered from the economy. Trinitarian theology thus became speculative and abstract, far removed from the practice of Christian faith. The defeat and banishment of the Trinity has had deleterious consequences up to and including our own era.

It is in Part Two, "Re-Conceiving the Doctrine of the Trinity in Light of the Mystery of Salvation," that LaCugna makes her constructive move. It is here that her central methodological principle yields the greatest fruit. LaCugna's method requires that all speculation about the triune nature of God be rooted in the economy of salvation (*oikonomia*), in the self-communication of God in the person of Christ and the activity of the Holy Spirit. The guiding principle that shapes the historical analysis in Part One and the constructive argument in Part Two is that the mystery of God (*theologia*) can only be thought of in terms of the mystery of grace and redemption (*oikonomia*). Reflection on who God is that begins by looking to the economy of salvation results in the recognition that the *God who is* is *God for us*. Beginning with the economy of salvation as point of departure for reflection on a specifically Christian understanding shows up the difficulties of approaches grounded in a strict identification of the "economic Trinity" and the "immanent Trinity," of God *ad extra* and *ad intra*. For LaCugna there is one Trinity, and this is the mystery of who God is precisely as the God for us in the economy of salvation.

The author's nuanced reading of the Rahnerian affirmation that the economic Trinity *is* the immanent Trinity, her critique of the strict equation of economic Trinity and immanent Trinity, God *ad extra* and *ad intra*, has led some to question whether she has succeeded in providing a specifically Trinitarian theology if she does not give greater attention to the nature of the intradivine life. Others conclude that she jettisons the Christian affirmation that God has an inner life,[4] or that she has collapsed the totality of God into the economy of salvation[5] because she is unwilling to speculate about just what such an inner life in God is like. This is to miss LaCugna's point entirely. Because she sees speculation about the precise nature of the intradivine life as pointless does not amount to abandoning the claim that there is an inner life in God. It is rather that she is loath to focus her theological reflection on the structure of God's "intradivine life," that is, the relationships of Father, Son, and Holy Spirit to one another. And she is unwilling to allow the view that the Trinitarian God in all eternity is transposed in the history of salvation. There are not two trinities, one eternal, the other in history. What can be known of God is known in who God is for us. Who God is, is known precisely in the economy of salvation. The structure of the intradivine life is not, then, the only way of speaking of God's eternal triune life.

Indeed there may be warrant for probing theological mysteries on the basis of analogy, indeed even as a basis for reflection on the inner life of God. But speculation about the intradivine life, and the strict equation between the economic Trinity and the immanent Trinity end up claiming too much. Perhaps more modest claims about God, anchored in the economy of salvation, need suffice. God is Love (1 John 4:8). This mystery is known in the economy of salvation through Jesus Christ in the power of the Holy Spirit. When attention is fixed on the economy, and not on arguments about intradivine life which at best remain purely speculative when untethered from the economy, the radical implications of the doctrine stand a far better chance of coming to the fore and summoning Christians to a way of life that is altogether Trinitarian.

A RELATIONAL ONTOLOGY

The doctrine of the Trinity is the articulation of the central Christian understanding that God is a mystery of persons in communion. LaCugna's presentation of the doctrine provides a cogent description of the three divine persons. More importantly, the work opens up fresh horizons and future possibilities for understanding human personhood, since the doctrine of the Trinity is normative for what Christians think a person is. What is this view of human persons that derives from a proper understanding of the divine persons?

LaCugna maintains the western Christian theological traditions took a wrong turn in the focus on substance, *ousia*, or essence in developing the doctrine of the Trinity. Theologians in the Christian east, especially the Cappadocians, offer more helpful perspectives on the Trinity, particularly because of their sustained attention to the divine *hypostases*, the divine persons. In this latter view person, not substance, is the foundational and ultimate ontological category. To say that person rather than substance is primary, i.e., person is the cause, origin, and end of all that exists, even and especially God, means that the ultimate source of reality is not a "by-itself" or an "in-itself," but a person, a toward-another. The importance of this claim simply cannot be overestimated.

LaCugna here is setting forth a view of human personhood, altogether grounded in the doctrine of the Trinity, that is incompatible with notions of person as individuated consciousness, a subsistent self, or as a nature unto itself. What she is describing is a view of human personhood thoroughly rooted in the personal mystery of God disclosed in Jesus Christ through the power of the Holy Spirit. Just as God is personal, i.e., God exists in relation and would not exist at all if not in relation (Father, Son, Spirit), so human beings are personal, i.e., human beings exist only in and through relation to another, others, and God. It needs to be made plain here that in this view the human person does not exist as an individuated nature, or a subsistent self that is antecedent or prior to self-expression. Just as in the Trinity to be is to be in relation (not only the divine persons in relation to one another but also the divine persons to us), so also to be as a human person ineluctably entails being toward-another. To exist is to be in relation, i.e., out of oneself and toward another. The God disclosed in the economy of salvation is the personal God for us. The understanding of human personhood rooted in a Trinitarian ontology of personal relation is one that enables us to see that we are what we are only insofar as we are from others and for others.

This ontology of relation, i.e., the view that the primary and ultimate category of existence is person, not substance, provides a helpful corrective to many of the tendencies toward depersonalization and dehumanization that seem to have gained the upper hand in our age. Autonomy (the self as the measure of the self) and heteronomy (the self measured primarily in terms of the other) are two negative effects of the Enlightenment's emphasis upon the individual's capacity for reason, quite narrowly understood. As a corrective, LaCugna's ontology of relation maintains that the human person is *theonomous*. That is to say that the measure of the human person is not the self or the other, but the personal God. And since God is personal and *ipso facto* relational, the human person cannot be measured in terms of the self, or exclusively in terms of the other, but only in terms of participation in personal communion with the other, others, and God. To say that the human person is theonomous is to recognize that he or she is a being who participates in the very life of the personal God who is for us. Consequently, human life is relational life, i.e., the person exists only and always from others and toward another, others, and God.

This understanding of the doctrine of the Trinity suggests that persons, relationality, and communion, are at the heart of what it means to be human and Christian. If person is taken as the primary ontological category, rather than nature, and if the Trinity is looked upon as the mystery in which the divine persons exist in loving communion, then rightly-ordered relationships in accord with the God disclosed in Jesus Christ through the power of the Holy Spirit become normative and "natural." That is to say, rather than looking to some abstract conception of human nature (judged to reflect the eternal, unchanging God *in esse*) to which human persons are expected to conform, the ontological priority of person suggests that understandings, judgments, decisions, and activities that do not enhance human flourishing in accord with the reign of God are unnatural. Subordination of woman to man is not natural. It is unnatural, out of step with human nature. Subordination, or its counterpart "complementarity," does not express some pre-ordained plan for all time. It is unnatural because it thwarts the kind of human flourishing central to the reign of God preached by Jesus Christ. Racism, clericalism, and elitism of all sorts in the church, no matter how much they are claimed to be justified by some pre-ordained plan expressive of true human nature (e.g., it is proper to the human nature of women to be domestic, caring, compassionate, whereas it is more natural for men to exercise qualities proper to the public, social order), are altogether unnatural once human beings are understood to be theonomous—persons who become what they truly are through full participation in personal communion with another, others, and God. Such personal communion is perichoretic, i.e., fully reciprocal and mutual.

Precisely because persons are theonomous, they are equal in a dignity that is based in the mystery of the *perichoresis* of the Trinity by which the three divine persons participate in the divine life without subordination.

THE PERSONHOOD OF NON-PERSONS?

Two issues are raised by this ontology of relation, this view of all existence as personal, namely, that person, not substance, is the primary and ultimate ontological category. Put briefly, if all existence is personal, then what is to be said of various life forms other than the human, i.e., non-human life such as grasshoppers, palm trees, and llamas? And, second, what of those human life forms, the most vulnerable, the developmentally disabled, the mentally handicapped, those who have lost their faculties of reason, or those who exhibit no ability to think, weigh, decide, and act? If all existence is personal, then in what sense are non-human life forms and those human beings whom many would be unwilling to call persons, "personal"?

Because the origin of all that exists is personal, i.e., the personal God disclosed in Jesus Christ through the Spirit, all that is participates in personal existence through the creative activity of God. This is to say that everything that exists is relational insofar as it comes from God and is for God's praise and glory. Human and non-human life does not exist except in and through God, who is altogether personal, i.e., relational. This is to follow somewhat Thomas Aquinas' notion that all reality participates, to greater or lesser degree, in God's being. If that being is then understood as loving personal communion, then all that is exists in varying degrees in personal communion with the God whose providential plan is not just for the salvation of the human race, but of the whole world.

From the perspective of the relational ontology set forth in LaCugna's work, the mentally handicapped who are incapable of the normal exercise of intellect, deliberation, choice, and action because of damage to the brain or nervous system incurred during the pre- peri- or post-natal period, might serve to remind the clever and the robust that human personhood is not rooted in the ability to think, weigh, decide, or carry through with a specific course of action. Personhood in this view does not lie in intellect, will, or in any combination thereof. Indeed what constitutes the person as person is antecedent to intellect and will, and to their proper exercise.

Similarly, in an age such as ours that prizes achievement and productivity, the mentally handicapped are not successful when viewed in terms of the norms of efficiency and productivity. They seem to have very little to contribute. But the mentally handicapped serve as catalyst in the recognition that our personhood is not grounded in what we do or achieve. Likewise, the mentally handicapped person who is often unattractive physically and sexually, serves to remind that physical comeliness and sexual lure do not constitute the person as person. The person is a being with a heart, one who has the capacity to be open to attraction by another, to be in communication and communion with another, others, and God. This is what is deepest and most fundamental, but so often and so easily lost beneath the veneer of physical beauty or in the dynamics of sexual interchange.

On another score, the handicapped illustrate the distinction LaCugna draws between person and nature, assigning priority to the former. Perhaps the reason why the mentally handicapped are viewed as less than true persons is that they do not measure up to some rather abstract, *a priori* notion of what constitutes human nature. If a particular view of human nature is the measure of what constitutes personhood, then the mentally handicapped individual's spontaneous shouts of glee or outbursts of rage and anger will appear as unnatural (or at least not socially correct). If, on the other hand, person is taken as the prior and ultimate ontological category, then the uniqueness, diversity, and complexity of personality, rather than some prior notion of human nature, will be the optic through which we understand the human. If person becomes nature, then what is unnatural is all that does not enhance human, personal flourishing. This is quite a different position than one that evaluates persons in view of their success or failure to achieve some *a priori* notion of what it means to be human. If person, not nature, substance, or essence is prior and ultimate, then a much wider range of possibilities of human and personal becoming may be allowed in response to the call to ever deepening participation in the communion of persons in Christ through the power of the Spirit.

Though vastly unequal to the healthy and robust in terms of their capacities for intellectual growth and self-sufficiency, the mentally handicapped do have dignity equal to the clever and the strong. But this is possible because equality is grounded in personhood, which derives from the communion of divine persons. All are equal if measured by the standard of the theonomous character of life. I suggest that the theonomy described by Catherine LaCugna is perhaps nowhere more luminous than in the lives of those who have very little to say in worlds dominated by ideas and controlled by ideologies, little to decide in a world driven by a deep-seated need to manipulate and control, and very little to achieve in a world driven by lust for success, efficiency, and productivity. Indeed, we learn what it is to be human persons, precisely in and through those who, more often than not, are judged to be less than human persons. Here is one more instance of the paradoxical character of the Gospel. If we are willing to set aside preconceptions of what constitutes proper human nature, perhaps we can be open to the theonomous character of the human person disclosed in those who have little to gain by social convention, virtually nothing to contribute to a world driven to succeed, whose capacities for self-determination are severely limited.

The disclosure of the theonomous character of the person, as a being from and for others and God, is perhaps nowhere more obvious than in the very apparent relational needs of the mentally handicapped. The clever and the robust can "stand on their own two feet" (quite literally); the healthy and the strong are supposed to fend for themselves. But if the human person is a being toward the other, others, and God, perhaps this dimension of "being-toward" is most conspicuous in the very obvious physical needs of the handicapped because of which they are "thrown" into a relationship with others. The necessity of being in relationship to others is often denied by the clever and the robust. It is an illusion, no doubt, to think that one is not "being-toward" the other. But "normal" people find countless ways to perpetuate the fantasy that there is a self-subsistent self (which of course is thought to mirror God's essence envisaged as three self-subsistent selves) that is prior to and more "real" than person as necessarily being-toward-other. To exist as person is to be in relation.

If person is the primary and ultimate ontological category, then the handicapped may provide some measure of what this implies. The one who is judged to be "normal" may in fact be the composite of layers of falsehood and illusions of self-sufficiency and the self-subsistent self. Such illusions are inaccessible to the mentally handicapped because their need for another, others, and God at every level of existence is so altogether conspicuous. There is no possibility the mentally handicapped might develop a "false self." The handicapped are persons whose being is altogether toward the other. This is precisely because of the enormity of their need, the vastness of their vulnerability, their anguish, their existential pain. But it is precisely because of this that they have such a heightened capacity and propensity for authentic communion. In the lives of the mentally handicapped there is very little hope or chance of achieving some predetermined ideal human nature. If nature is prior to person, the ultimate ontological category which is thought to be the measure of personal becoming, then it is quite understandable how the handicapped never quite measure up. Their personhood is always somewhat in doubt. By extension, the same is true of the seriously ill, the comatose, the seriously injured, the aged, the dying.

A caution is in order at this juncture. The mentally handicapped do not disclose what it means to be person by living some sustained cherubic, cuddly existence, but by witnessing to the full range of human emotions, the deepest cries and joys of the human heart, without the defenses of false self, social correctness, or neighborly politesse.[6] To be sure, authentic personhood is not synonymous with giving expression to every and all feelings, desires, and emotions. These are to be integrated within the task of personal becoming if true communion of persons is to be brought to fruition. But what constitutes the handicapped person as different from the "normal" is the immediacy of these experiences as well as their expression, negative as well as positive.[7] The gift of the handicapped is their constitutional inability to be other than what they are in all its immediacy: persons whose theonomous character cannot be obfuscated beneath layers of political, religious, and social correctness.

The handicapped person thus provides an altogether different view of what it means to be a person once person, not substance, is taken as prior and ultimate. Setting aside tightly-knit ideas of human nature against which individuals are to be measured, we may look to the handicapped as teachers of what it means to be person. Through this optic we see what might be entailed in an authentic communion of persons. Such personal communion is not built on an abstract, *a priori* view of human nature, some superior ideal self. Rather, it is based in the equality of persons who are equal because they are theonomous, from God, in God, for God. This is a relational God, a God who is God for us. Grounded in this primacy of the personal God, then, relationships flourish in reciprocity, mutuality, and interdependence. Those who most clearly disclose the theonomous character of human persons remind us that whatever we may think, decide, or act, our being is from God and for God. As this God is God for us, so the human person exists by being ever more fully for others in ever deeper and fuller participation in communion of persons. The *telos* of human personhood is luminously embodied in the mentally handicapped person who invites to a fuller realization of what it means to be a human person in communion with another, others, and God.

A TRINITARIAN SPIRITUALITY

An ontology of relation grounded in the Trinitarian doctrine has implications not only for our understanding of human personhood but also for an understanding of Christian spirituality. I understand Christian spirituality as nothing more or less than the living of the Christian life, in all its dimensions. LaCugna asserts throughout her work that a proper understanding of the doctrine of the Trinity will have enormous consequences for every area of the theological enterprise. She demonstrates this persuasively in her own area of systematic theology. I should like to indicate here some of the implications of her understanding of the Trinity for the discipline of Christian spirituality.

First, our understanding of God is in and through the way God is for us, God's providential plan for the world, in and through the Trinity known in the economy of salvation. Thus the notion that there is a God as a self-subsistent community of selves constituting an intradivine Trinity for all eternity, which is then transposed in history, is no longer persuasive. A God removed from human life and history, unaffected by it and by human suffering, who lives in eternal simplicity and tranquility, withdrawn from history, has given rise to quite peculiar understandings of holiness that have prevailed throughout Christian history. The holy person has often been understood as the one who is set apart. He or she is set apart geographically or enclosed behind a cloister wall, distanced from the everyday concerns of life in the world, and from the ordinary pursuits of domestic and civil life. This notion of holiness as pertaining to those set apart may be properly understood to be rooted in the God who is apart, withdrawn in the solitary simplicity of the intradivine life, dwelling in light inaccessible, unmoved by the contingencies of human history and, because thought to be unchangeable, unaffected by human life, suffering, and history. The understanding of a God of intradivine life unmoved by the tragedies and triumphs of human history, gives rise to a vision of holiness in which persons flee the city, turn their backs on the world, in order to live for God alone whose essence is understood to be removed from and "above" the contingencies of human life. Even though the monastic (from *monos*, alone) tradition gives particular attention to the common life, monastic life is properly understood as the solitary life pursued together with others.

Second, the pursuit of the "spiritual life" has often been understood in terms of the metaphor of journey. And this journey has been understood primarily as an inner or interior journey. Such an approach is due to a number of factors and cannot be reduced to just one. But it may be useful to consider one of the more significant of these.

In Augustine's Trinitarian theology particular attention is paid to the structure of the intradivine life, i.e., the relationships among Father, Son, and Holy Spirit. He saw the human capacities of intellect, will, and memory as together constituting a mirror image of the Trinity. The more we develop in self-knowledge, the deeper our knowledge of God. Even though Augustine may not have intended to do so, his understanding of prayer and growth in the spiritual life through deeper and deeper self-knowledge tended to overshadow the communitarian and social dimensions of life in Christ. In contrast, the eastern tradition was loath to consider God "in Godself," apart from the

economy of salvation, that is, apart from God's concrete existence as Father, Son, and Spirit with us.

As a consequence, Christian spirituality in the west has often
taken the form of the individual, solitary, inward gaze. Indeed
for many in the west "the interior life" or "the solitary life" are
synonymous with the spiritual life. This should be no great
surprise. For if "God's essence," "God's being" is understood to
exist on a separate plane outside and above the way God is for
us in the economy of salvation, and if this is understood to be
who God really is (*esse*) in contradistinction to the way God is for
us in loving communion known in the economy, then the holiness of God will be understood to be best mirrored in the
Christian who is solitary and apart, unaffected by the actual
historical circumstances which ineluctably involve the great
masses of human beings. Indeed, the very notion of holiness as
being set apart (and above) is indebted to an understanding of a
God who is apart from human history, who exists for all eternity
in intradivine communion, separate and aloof from human life
and the world.

On the other hand if God is a God for us, then the holiness of
God consists in something else altogether. Consequently the
holiness of Christians will be understood differently. In this
alternative view, holiness rests in setting aside, setting apart the
self, moving beyond self-preoccupation, self-indulgence, self-
fixation, and becoming persons conformed to the image of God
in us: being toward the other. God's very nature is ecstatic and
fecund. God goes apart, away from, outside any sort of self-
subsistent self in and through self-donation and self-communication by which God's being is for and toward the other; the
divine life is of its very nature to stand apart from itself in
ecstatic and fecund love.

In this view, holiness does not reside primarily with those
who are thought to be "called apart," "set apart" to pursue
nobler and loftier truths unmoved by daily concerns and the
vicissitudes of life in the world. Rather, authentic Christian
holiness is realized by living in Christ through the Spirit who
enables us to stand apart from, set aside, or above, our own
selves. Our self-preoccupation, self-indulgence, self-fixation, are
the real grist for the mill of Christian *ascesis*. We find the deepest
gift of personal becoming not in standing apart from (i.e., above)

the affairs of human life and its concerns, but rather by entering into personal communion with the God who is for us, precisely in the economy of salvation history, and in communion with all those with whom he lived and for whom he died.

Third, this Trinitarian perspective casts light on understandings of prayer as well as on the nature of the relationship between contemplation and action. Prayer describes the movement of the human heart toward ever fuller participation in the life of God. It is the response of our whole person to the divine initiative as this is apprehended and appropriated in the economy of salvation. The heart describes the deepest, most fundamental center of the person. Heart "names" the human capacity to be toward the other. It describes the human being's openness to relate to the real, i.e., to the other as distinct from the self. And, as such, it is inherently social and communal. Its fullest expression is found in interpersonal communion—with another, others, and God.

Prayer as the response of the whole person to the divine initiative disclosed in the economy of salvation cannot be set in opposition to action. Prayer is an expression of the desire of the human heart to be in relation. The heart's openness to relation is itself an absence, a desire to be more fully in and through others.

Because human personhood is both given and achieved, prayer of the heart is expressed in simple loving attention to the gift of God's presence and action in human life, history, church, and world, as well as in human self-expression through those activities by which we seek to participate more fully in establishing an authentic communion of persons. Loving attentiveness (contemplation) and establishing rightly-ordered relations in human life, history, world, and church (action) are equally necessary in the realization of the heart's deepest desire.

From this Trinitarian perspective, prayer is not an exercise of the mind's undisturbed gaze upon eternal, unchanging truth. Nor is it methodical, organized discursive meditation designed to gain a glimpse of God's hidden purpose. Prayer does not spring from and/or nourish "spiritual life," as if such a life existed in a separate compartment of ourselves, mirroring in some vague way the true nature, *ousia*, essence of a God above human grasp, dwelling in light inaccessible. Rather, in this view, prayer is the movement of the attentive human heart to participate in the very life of God, responding to the myriad ways in which God comes in Christ through the power of the Spirit. Such a view of prayer opens one to see that the distinctions and fast separations between spiritual life and secular life, sacred and profane, church and world, rest on an unfounded and ungrounded separation between immanent and economic Trinity. Just as there are not two trinities, immanent and economic, God *ad intra* and God *ad extra*, but one God who is precisely God *for us*, so the human person is a unity. And there is in each of us a single heart called to respond to the one triune communion of divine persons made manifest in the presence and action of Christ and the Spirit in human life, history, world, and church.

A Trinitarian-based spirituality thus serves to correct skewed notions of the relationship between action and contemplation. Informed by this doctrine of the Trinity, action and contemplation do not pertain to separate spheres: the sacred and the secular, church and world, the spiritual life and the domain of the secular and profane. There is one God who in the economy of salvation is not only a God for us but for the whole world. LaCugna writes: "God is so thoroughly involved in every last detail of creation that if we could truly grasp this it would altogether change how we approach each moment of our lives. For everything that exists—insect, agate, galaxy—manifests the mystery of the living God."[8]

Notes

1. Karl Rahner, *The Trinity* (New York: Herder & Herder, 1970) 11.
2. Catherine Mowry LaCugna, *God for Us: The Trinity and Christian Life* (San Francisco: Harper Collins, 1991).
3. For a helpful view of the relationship between systematic theology and spirituality, in which the two are partners in reciprocal relationship rather than the latter remaining under the tutelage of systematic theology or moral theology, see Sandra Schneiders, "Spirituality in the Academy," *Theological Studies* 50:4 (1989) 676-697.
4. At the 1992 meeting of the Catholic Theological Society of America, the Constructive Theologies Seminar was devoted to a presentation and analysis of *God For Us*. At least one participant questioned whether LaCugna's project amounts to abandoning the inner life of God.
5. If I have read him correctly, this is Joseph Bracken's major criticism of LaCugna's work; see *Theological Studies* 53:3 (1992) 558-560.

6. The handicapped are often thought to be sweet, adorable, lovable. I recall that while living in l'Arche near Paris in 1981, visitors would sometimes come with gifts for the handicapped men with whom I lived in our foyer, "La Nacelle." The treasures included toy trucks, coloring books, crayons, and clay. But the men of our community were adults, with the full range of emotions and feelings found in other adult men. And they would have preferred a packet of cigarettes and a can of beer, to say nothing of a stiff shot of scotch whiskey, to toy trucks and coloring books.

7. The witness of the mentally handicapped is a reminder of the theonomus character of personal existence, and is an example of the ways in which person is prior to and constitutive of human nature. That is to say, and this may sound most shocking, we learn what it means to become persons from the handicapped, and by looking to them we may learn what it means to act naturally, i.e., according to our true nature rather than according to social custom. Is it too far fetched to suggest that the mentally handicapped person may act more naturally, more human, than the "normal?" I submit that it is far less natural, far less human, to exterminate millions of defenseless people than it is to shriek with joy, or to play the clown in public with friends. Yet it was the "normal," healthy, and robust, whose mental and volitional capacities were intact, who conducted the "Final Solution" during the Nazi regime. And, as survivors of the Holocaust and others are quick to point out, the methods of the "Final Solution" were implemented as if it were a quite "normal" thing to do in service of a "nobler" aim. This nobler aim, of course, had a great deal to do with getting rid of those whose personhood was in doubt because of race, ethnicity, religion, physical impairment, sexual orientation.

8. LaCugna, *God for Us* 304.

WEAKNESS
DISCOVERED

7

Hurdles to the Holy

"PRAY ALWAYS" (1 THESSALONIANS 5:17). NO EASY MATTER. IT HAS ever been thus. People in every era are faced with the challenge of praying without ceasing. And the challenge is shaped in large part by factors that seem to prevent rather than promote authentic prayer. My purpose here is to draw attention to several factors in our own culture that present themselves as obstacles to prayer. To this end it is first necessary to provide a definition of prayer. Then, I shall attempt to describe what is meant by that ever-so-slippery term "culture." Attention will also be drawn to the great diversity of cultures, a diversity often eclipsed in considering that rather unwieldy phenomenon referred to as "American culture." This great variety of cultures notwithstanding, I will spell out specific obstacles to prayer that seem increasingly more hazardous as we navigate our way through the last decade of this century. These obstacles are not insurmountable, and so I have chosen the metaphor of "hurdles," which conveys the sense that they can be overcome. In delineating these twelve hurdles, I will assert and affirm, rather than analyze. And I will not propose any solution for overcoming them. Such a task yet awaits us in our common work of fulfilling Paul's mandate.

Prayer

Prayer is the movement of the human heart toward an ever more complete awareness of God's presence. It describes the

107

lifelong process of listening long and lovingly to the beating of the heart of God. Christian prayer entails the ongoing participation in the mystery of Christ who surrendered himself without reserve and with boundless confidence to God, even and especially in his darkest night: "Into your hands I commend my spirit" (Luke 23:46).

In speaking of prayer as a movement of the human heart, I am not referring to the region of "private," "individual" feelings or emotions in opposition to other dimensions of the person. The term "heart" describes the deepest, most fundamental center of the self. Properly understood, the heart is the name for the affective dimension of the person, the very openness of the human being to be touched by another, others, and God. To have a heart is to possess the capacity to be in relation.[1] With this understanding in mind, the heart may be said to be inclusive of communal and social dimensions of human life. Indeed, it is in and through the heart, this affective region, that the person discerns his or her relationship with nonhuman life, as well. As a profoundly personal reality, prayer may be expressed privately, or individually, such as in meditation, contemplative prayer, or private devotion. But ultimately it finds its fullest expression in the communal prayer of the Christian people, the liturgy, the corporate act of worship in which the Christian community receives and expresses its identity as the Body of Christ. Even "private" prayer is not an isolated activity. It is brought to fullness through interpersonal communication and communion with another, others, and God. Describing prayer as a deeply personal movement of the heart is not meant to imply that it is a purely private matter over against the corporate worship of the church.

Culture

People express themselves in and through a variety of forms that together constitute what is referred to as "culture." We know what culture—like time—is until we are called upon to describe it. Hopefully, without risk of overlooking its complexity, culture may be described as that constellation of means by which human beings express what is deepest and most important to them, notably the family, community, society, art, literature, and ritual. Because human beings perceive and pursue the task of self-expression in various ways, cultures differ, sometimes so much so that they appear to be irreconcilable.

To put this another way, human beings create, or participate in creating, worlds of meaning, value, and purpose in and through culture.

"Culture" refers to what human beings do to the material, natural, created world in which they live, the form or shape they give to it. Culture may be described as second nature to human beings who are always and everywhere creating and recreating what is given in nature, the "stuff" of the world at its most basic level. A few brief examples may serve to clarify. An apple is in the domain of "nature," while an apple pie is part of culture. Wild daffodils belong to nature, but a brilliant bouquet of them is an expression of culture. Precious metals are mined from nature. The exchange and wearing of gold rings as an expression of love and fidelity is a cultural phenomenon. Solid marble is hewn from nature's side. When slabs of it are carefully designed or skillfully chiseled, the result may be a contribution to culture. There is the alphabet and the dictionary. But a poem or novella is something else again. Then there are musical notes. But the ordering and arrangement of them in a distinctive musical composition is of a completely different order. All these are examples of cultural phenomena as extensions and transformations of the given "stuff" of the world in order to express meaning, value, and purpose.

To develop one example further, flowers may be arranged in a bouquet and set in a place of worship as an expression of reverence and offering. They may be sent from a lover to the beloved as an expression of affection and fidelity. Or flowers may be sent to one who is ill in the hope that they will cheer and strengthen the spirit. And they are given in times of sorrow and loss as an expression of sympathy. All these uses extend and transform nature for particularly human purposes. They are part of our culture.

Again, culture is second nature to human beings. It is the way human beings transform nature, the "givenness" of things, for specifically human meanings and purposes. But culture is much more than apple pie, nosegays, wedding rings, and skillfully-crafted marble edifices. As second nature, culture includes everything involved in the task of being and becoming more fully human. Thus culture includes the *ethos* of a people, the vision, inspiration, and principles by which they live. It encompasses laws and political systems that enshrine their sense of right and wrong. Also included are the many ways in which human beings strive to express their perceptions of beauty, e.g., music, dance, architecture, the fine arts. It involves the way they conduct themselves in matters pertaining to sexuality, partnership, and progeny. The values of religious and social bodies are inextricably linked to that web of meaning and purpose named culture, which is also the matrix within which human beings construct and reconstruct economic systems in their attempt to meet basic human needs and aspirations.

The term "culture," then, involves the entire social-symbolic order in which human beings live, and through which they both receive and shape meaning and identity. It is humanity's second nature, i.e., the extension and transformation of the natural world for human purposes. A parent's attempt to instruct a child about the distinct functions of knife, fork and spoon indicates that there are specifically human ways of dealing with food. And these exclude grabbing mashed potatoes from a common plate and eating them from one's fist. Gentle reminders to "mind your manners" at table indicate that the sensibilities of other human beings must be considered even while fulfilling basic human needs.

Here it must be recognized that the extension and transformation of nature for human purposes has a checkered history. Not all cultural expression advances truly human purposes. All human purposes are not worthy as such, i.e., simply because they are human, and not every value that human beings perceive as such is in fact so. From a Christian perspective, it is in prayerful attention to the Spirit moving the human heart toward God that opens up, orients, and sometimes reorients culture to its ultimate purposes.

Cultures

In treating cultural obstacles to prayer, it must be recognized that there exists a great variety of cultures. There is a distinctively North American culture, in contrast to the culture of western Europe. But there are also quite diverse cultures under the umbrella of the quite ambiguous term western European culture. The same is true for whatever is meant by "North American culture." Under the heading of North American culture, we would first have to recognize that there is a specifically Canadian culture different from that of the United States of America. Within the framework of Canadian culture, we would have to speak of the specific culture of the Québecois and the Inuit people alongside a whole host of others. The same is true for "American culture," i.e., that of the United States. There is the culture of the African Americans, the Hispanic Americans, the various Asian American peoples, as well as those whose forebears came to "America" from eastern and western Europe. These peoples bring distinctive cultural patterns that do not become assimilated into the cultural mainstream without leaving their mark on it. The "American culture" which was given shape through the insights and orientations of the "founding fathers" looks quite different today than it did at the time of the birth of the nation.

It would be misleading to suggest that cultural pluralism is a uniquely American or western phenomenon. There is abundant evidence of this pluralism in every major metropolitan area throughout the world. And cultural pluralism cannot be said to be a uniquely contemporary phenomenon without historical precedent. Even in the High Middle Ages, a period characterized by remarkable unity and cohesion, a great variety of cultural expressions existed. Thomas Aquinas' remarkable philosophical and theological vision, synthesized in his *Summa Theologica*, is partially the result of his effort to allow the insights of cultures different from his own, ideas that seemed contradictory to those dominant in his "world," to bear upon the fundamental questions and doctrines of Christianity.[2] And Aquinas' synthesis is one among many, if indeed the finest, that resulted from the same period. Often championed as the model to which contemporary Catholics should look in recovering unity and harmony in Christian life and practice, for creating a distinctively "Catholic culture," the period of the High Middle Ages, which looms like a mythic golden age in the minds of many, was considerably more diversified in cultural expression than those who lament its demise would like to think.

The same is true of the period of Christian origins. This era is often hailed as the "Golden Age" of Christianity, a time when the pristine purity of Christian faith offered a unified, coherent, unambiguous vision of Christian life and practice, a Christian culture. But such unity and cohesion of faith and cultural expression is difficult to verify.[3] Recognizing that the issue is far more complex than may appear from such an assertion, we can say nonetheless that cultural pluralism is a constant in human life and history. Persons and groups are always creating and recreating worlds of meaning, value, and purpose in quite diverse ways. But the issue of cultural diversity and pluralism is even more complex in light of the fact that these worlds are not only diverse but at times divergent and often contradictory.

Attentive to the Spirit in Culture

For those who attempt to live by the Spirit of Christ, the work of discerning the presence of the Spirit in culture is not necessarily the same as promoting all that passes for cultural progress or social development. Those who live by Christ's Spirit must be critical of the tendency to legitimize any and all cultural developments and expressions as authentic extensions and transformations of nature, "the world," for human purposes. At the same time, we must recognize that the Spirit is at work in persons who are, precisely as human, beings whose "second nature" is to give shape to a culture. Consequently human development and the progress of peoples in and through the culture in which we live cannot be dismissed as always and in every instance incompatible with the truth, purity, and integrity of Christian faith and practice. God's Spirit present and active in human lives brings about not only specifically human purposes, but also purposes, ideals, and values that are perceived as ultimate (e.g., in the Christian schema these include self-sacrificial love in imitation of Christ, compassion, mercy, and unrestricted forgiveness in the quest for union with God). The attainment of these ideals and values cannot be accomplished either by canonizing all "social progress" and cultural developments or by turning one's back on contemporary culture, all the while deploring and deprecating the unchristian or antichristian world as depraved, debauched, and decadent. Those who live by Christ's Spirit are ineluctably part of the culture in which they live, even if they herald the fashioning of a new creation more in keeping with the lordship of Christ and the power of the Spirit.

The activity of the Spirit enables persons to constantly interpret and reinterpret, to work and rework the ultimate meanings,
values, and purposes revealed in the person of Jesus Christ so
that they are indeed meaningful and valuable for people in
different eras and cultures. Christian prayer, in this view, involves attentiveness to the working of the Spirit in culture, and
an ongoing process of reassessment, reinterpretation, and re-
working of it in order to discern and promote God's intention
for the world now and to come.

Cultural Obstacles to Prayer

Although Christian prayer involves, among other things, the
task of discerning the working of the Spirit in culture, the culture itself often presents obstacles in the path of the heart's
movement to God. At times it seems that culture, a matrix of the
Spirit's presence and action, thwarts the human desire to listen
long and lovingly to the beating of the heart of God. Rather than
support authentic human and divine purpose, culture can crush
the human spirit, resulting in depersonalization, suffering, and
disintegration. What are the obstacles to prayer that we find in
"American culture" at the brink of the third millennium?

Collision Speed. The first obstacle is the pace of life most of
us keep. Whatever our walk of life, we move through our days
at breakneck speed. There are often long commutes to and from
work. For most there are long hours at the workplace. There are
children to be dropped off and picked up from daycare, or ballet
practice, or softball, or soccer. After work and microwave din-
ner-on-the-run or from a fast food drive-thru window, there are
meetings of committees, support groups, boards of all sorts.
Many of us are on the brink of exhaustion much of the time.
Even vacation time is one more thing we "do." If we really listen
to one another, many, indeed most, are saying that they are too
busy, and there are just not enough hours in a day. So who has
time to pray? We live in an unrelenting atmosphere of busyness.
It is as if we are living in a pressure cooker most days. Consequently we are frenzied and frantic. Travelling at collision speed
is one sure way of assuring that we will not arrive safely at our
destination. In view of this hazard, how do we begin to be still
long enough to attend to the presence of the God who is the

Source and Ground of all that is, from which springs love and freedom? If this obstacle is to be overcome, greater attention is to be given to the human need for rest and leisure.[4] At leisure, at rest, we think less and look more. We don't try to please others as much, get recognition for our achievements, or gain the love of others through things that we do. While at leisure we are able to do less, and love more and better. Prayer is not just one more activity, one more thing to do. It is a habit of affection and behavior, an instinct which, when cultivated and disciplined, brings about deeper and fuller recognition of the presence of God "deep down things" (Gerard Manley Hopkins).

The Bottom Line. Our culture prizes efficiency and productivity. We want to know the hard facts and figures, "the bottom line." We are "doers." We strive and strain for achievement and success. Competition is woven into the cultural fabric. Many of us are driven, propelled by forces beyond our control, often having lost sight of why we are doing what we are doing. This presents real obstacles to prayer which is never a matter of success and achievement. In authentic prayer there is a sense in which nothing is going on; a feeling that there is nothing to do. There is nothing to prove, nothing that can be won by our efforts. We cannot produce results. Praying is something of an art. Consequently it is not a matter of how much or how often one prays as it is a matter of how well one prays. Efficiency in prayer involves abandonment, relaxing, and letting God be God on God's own terms, as well as a willingness to accept life on its terms rather than ours.

Cacophony and Clutter. Our lives are noisy and cluttered. Traffic, television, loud music which is not only harsh and offensive but dehumanizing, is pumped into restaurants, supermarkets, and even book stores. Shopping malls have replaced the town square or the city park as the place where people congregate. The mall and television have become hallmarks of the culture. There are just too many sounds and so much stuff, things, in our lives. We are filled to the brim with products, noises, things. Even and especially in a time of economic hardship or in a condition of poverty we can become driven to acquire more. I do not intend here to underestimate the importance of satisfying basic human needs. But in a materialist and consumerist culture like our own, needs and wants are confused. We believe that having more will finally satisfy us. The spiritual stranglehold in which many of us feel gripped is due in no small measure to the glut of noise and things with which we have come to believe we simply can't do without. Is a microwave oven really as necessary as some claim it to be? A color television in the living room, in the den, on the kitchen counter, and in the bedroom(s)? The effect of materialism and consumerism is to render us very poor candidates for authentic prayer. For prayer is a movement of the heart, a desire that does not desire this or that object, thing, or sound. Praying entails the cultivation of a desire that desires only its own increase. The meaning and purpose of prayer lies in the waiting. In prayer nothing is to be gotten, no thing is to be gained, indeed no sound is to be heard.

Congestive Creativity. Projects and plans give us something to work for, something to look forward to and, once achieved, a sense of satisfaction and fulfillment. But the appointment book in our briefcase, on the desk, or on the kitchen wall can rule our lives. The appointment book has become a symbol of life in the eighties and nineties. We race from one thing to the next, finish one job, scratch it off the list, and begin another. This often leaves little space in which the imagination and creativity can bloom. In praying, imagination and creativity are given room. Setting priorities and accomplishing goals are not of the utmost importance when we pray. When we give ourselves to prayer, there is nowhere to go, no task to be achieved, no mission to be accomplished. Part of the difficulty we face in prayer is a sense of our own expendability, our uselessness. We often find ourselves asking: what's the point? What am I *doing* here? But prayer is not a project, something to be done, finished, like all the other projects in our lives. Nor does it unfold according to plan or set objectives. It is a sustained process of attention to the Source of freedom and love into whose heart we surrender day by day until we breathe our last and, with Christ, commend our spirit.

Isolation. Perhaps the major problem people in our culture face is a profound experience of disconnectedness or unconnectedness. The effects of what has been referred to as the "breakdown of the family," increased mobility, massive urbanization, and high-tech communication have all contributed to a seemingly chronic state of inability to be committed to a shared way of life or community. There seems to be a large-scale failure to appropriate the values of a family, group, or community, resulting in an inability to identify and a strong inclination to stand apart. Whereas prayer is something that springs from deep within the individual human heart, it is a dimension of human and Christian life that, for most of us, cannot thrive without the support of a community. Those who experience this isolation, disconnectedness, or unconnectedness very deeply due to alcoholism, drug abuse, child abuse, sexual abuse, or violence often recognize the need for a community of support and self- and mutual help. Alcoholics Anonymous, various Twelve Step programs, and other support groups like them are based on the recognition that we cannot go it alone. For increasing numbers of people, the parish church, rather than offering an antidote to this sense of unconnectedness, drives the wedge more deeply. How well or poorly does the parish understand itself as a community of persons who are committed to shared life, shared hope, and shared practice, particularly the practice of prayer, both individual and communal?

Quick and Easy Communication. Prayer is often understood in terms of dialogue. It is a form of interpersonal communication and communion. Effective communication requires the ability to listen, to wait, in an effort to really hear the other. Ours is an age of instant communications. We are able to sit in our living rooms and watch as Iraqi SCUD missiles hit their targets on Israeli soil. Telephones make communication with parties around the world possible in a matter of seconds. Soon many homes will have telephones with small video screens, enabling the caller to view the party on the other end of the line. More and more people converse by telephone while driving (to say nothing of the ability to speak on the telephone while being driven). By means of FAX machines we can send and receive written communication across the country and around the globe in minutes. Helpful though all this may be, these modes of quick communication may be misleading and indeed detrimental if we expect prayer to be anything like this. In prayer there is no instant contact. We do not get quick information. The answers to our questions and meager conundrums are not met with ready reply, if indeed a reply is forthcoming at all. Prayer is dialogue in which one needs to be willing to wait long and lovingly, to look and to listen patiently, to let ourselves be "put on hold" for much longer than we'd like, allowing the longing and the listening to become the love.

Narcissism. Our culture highly values youth, the beauty of the human body, strength, and health. We are encouraged to find ways to stay young, not only in mind and spirit but in body as well. Men and women well into their years go to great lengths to appear younger than they are. Aging, imperfection, fragility, which are manifestations of our condition as creatures, are judged undesirable and are to be avoided at all costs. But the very basis for beginning to pray is the recognition of ourselves as creatures who are contingent, dependent upon God as the very source and ground of our being. As creatures, we are imperfect and extremely fragile. And because we are human beings, beings with a heart, we are vulnerable and wounded. We are finite and so must gradually but certainly move through stages of diminishment, frailty, dying, and death. This is what is to be faced in prayer. How are we to travel this path in serenity and poised confidence when we are glutted with information on billboards and television which, while seducing us into the cult of youth and beauty, subtly signals the denial of our contingency, woundedness, vulnerability, and frailty?

Disincarnation. The impact of urbanization on American culture has been enormous, as has that of "high tech" and the communications media. As a result of these "developments" we seem to be less and less aware of our relationship to our bodies, to other human beings, as well as to nonhuman life. We have become dull to life's natural rhythm, to the change of seasons, to the location of the sun and the stars. When we eat, we are aware, perhaps, that what is before us has come from the earth, or from "a farm." What farm? Whose farm? A farm where? Or in which part of the country? Worked and harvested by whom? Few of us would have a clue. This is just one example of the way in which we are out of touch with the earth, with our bodies, with our relationship to and dependency upon nature and other human beings. It also dulls our awareness of the injustice and suffering faced by farm workers, the damage done to human and nonhuman life by pesticides as well as the severity of the ecological crisis.

Historical Amnesia. We have lost touch with history. We tend to live with some vague awareness of what significant events are taking place in the world in which we live. But our focus on the present can tend toward a sort of historical myopia, with little attention to the consequences of our lives for future generations. Perhaps more importantly, people in our age suffer from a type of historical amnesia. We have lost sight of the bigger picture, the great story or narrative of the God-world relation throughout the ages. Being out of touch with this story, unfamiliar with the various religious traditions in which people have struggled to pray in different ways and in shifting cultural circumstances, puts us at a great disadvantage in recognizing God's presence now in ways that are consistent with God's presence in the past, while at the same time opening up fresh promises and future possibilities.

Despair and Inertia. Particularly at the present time our culture seems to be marked by a profound listlessness, signalling a loss of hope. The rise in drug abuse, addictions of all sorts, increasing violence and crime are all manifestations of the languishing of the human spirit, contributing further to its demise. What with massive unemployment, the ever-present threat of nuclear annihilation (even on this better side of the Cold War), and the suffering of innocent millions by senseless violence, what reasons can be given to our young to inculcate a hope that will sustain them? In the great tradition of monasticism the term *acedia* describes a lack of commitment to spiritual values, a loss of concern, a prolonged state of carelessness, listlessness. In contemporary parlance it is a condition of low-grade depression which, if left untreated, results in the abysmal darkness of severe depression and chronic melancholia. The only way out is to find resources of hope, seemingly against all odds, beyond self-preoccupation and self-absorption. In view of such massive hopelessness and despair, a sort of cultural melancholia (What's the point? Why go on? You take your life in your hands when you walk out the door! Why bring children into the world?), how does one find hope, "the thing with feathers/That perches in the soul" (Emily Dickenson)? For without it one cannot really pray. Prayer requires an enduring disposition of anticipation, of waiting, of longing, expecting and hoping in the God who comes.

A Loss of Savoir-Faire. Yet another obstacle to prayer is ignorance. In previous generations, believers were nurtured in cultural contexts ripe with opportunity to be steeped in religious practice. They were taught how to pray from childhood. Just how well or poorly is no doubt arguable. But many today simply do not have a clue about how to pray and, consequently, are diffident about instructing their children to do so. This is not to assign malice. It is simply to say that we are often at a loss when it comes to even the most rudimentary forms of praying. This is in part due to the attempts following the Second Vatican Council to invite believers to deeper dimensions of prayer. Such prayer involves more than rattling off memorized prayers by rote, or speeding through decades of the rosary, or paging through one's holy cards and devotional prayerbook during Mass. But what seems to have occurred is that for many of our young, the memorization and recitation of the simplest of prayers such as the Hail Mary, Our Father, have been set aside. And nothing has been offered in their place. This is to say nothing of the lack of rudimentary familiarity with the biblical story and with the Sacred Scripture. Many are simply at a loss, not just for words, but for a single clue regarding how to cultivate the intuition for God's abiding presence. To overcome this obstacle, we need to be willing to learn how to pray, and committed to finding teachers who are schooled, not just in pastoral ministry, theology, or spiritual direction, but in prayer itself. But this is not nearly as easy is it may seem at first.

Without a Compass. There is in the contemporary culture a loss of confidence in leadership and authority. This is true not only regarding civil leaders, but religious leaders as well. One might suggest that in the United States this began with the Watergate scandal. But its roots lie much deeper. For some, the credibility of leadership and authority in the Roman Catholic Church is diminished each time a priest is convicted of pedophilia, and shattered altogether when it is disclosed that the bishop or religious superior had turned a deaf ear to the plea for help from the victim's family. It seems clear that the burden of proof would fall to those who would argue that there is not a loss of confidence in leadership, civil and religious, and that there are not good reasons for this being the case. Be that as it may, if we are to overcome the obstacles to prayer that our cultural context imposes, we must seek and find those who have experience in the ways of prayer, who are recognized as trustworthy and wise guides, whose authority we can trust in leading us in the art of prayer. Such persons are in short supply. Whereas there has been a recognizable increase in the number of lay and ordained ministers trained in pastoral counseling, spiritual direction, and related fields, it is harder to determine just who and how many have real skill in praying themselves so as to lead others on the way. To whom do we turn with confidence? Who, by virtue of being schooled in the life of prayer, can authoritatively teach others? To whom do we go when there springs from within our heart the plea "Teach us to pray" (Luke 11: 1). Only the one who has listened long and lovingly to the beating of the heart of God.

* * * * * *

The Spirit of God is present and active within the culture of a people, no matter how depraved, debauched, decadent or indifferent it may be judged. Working within a culture, the Spirit enlightens, enlivens, guides, and heals in such a way as to transform the culture so that it more effectively brings about authentic human flourishing. The human heart which longs for an ever deeper awareness of the divine presence does so in the face of cultural elements which can thwart rather than facilitate its desire. Such obstacles vary given a particular cultural matrix. No culture makes the heart's movement to God in prayer a free and easy ride. In our own day there are particular cultural obstacles that must be hurdled. To recognize and delineate these is not to make the mandate to "pray always" (1 Thessalonians 5:17) seem an even more impossible task. It is rather to gain a clearer view of the terrain in which we find ourselves as the human heart longs for God in this time and place.

Notes

1. I have offered a much fuller description of "heart" in *A Blessed Weakness: The Spirit of Jean Vanier and l'Arche* (San Francisco: Harper and Row, 1986), especially chapter 5, "The Heart Knows."

2. See Marie-Dominique Chenu, *Toward Understanding Saint Thomas* (Chicago: H. Regnery Co., 1964); see also James A. Weisheipl, *Friar Thomas d'Aquino: His Life, Thought and Work* (Garden City, NY: Doubleday, 1974).

3. See Robert L. Wilken, *The Myth of Christian Beginnings* (Garden City, NY: Doubleday, 1971).

4. See Leonard Doohan, *Leisure: A Spiritual Need* (Notre Dame: Ave Maria, 1990).

8

Illegal Compassion

THE TALE IS GRIM. IN IT LIE THE BEGINNINGS OF THE SANCTUARY MOVE-ment, an expression of the Gospel of peace and justice with vast implications for the churches in North America and abroad.

The scene is the Sonoran desert. In the dead of winter the heat scorches at midday. The temperatures plummet below freezing point at night. The Sonoran is dry and lifeless. Unfriendly, to say the least, to those who come prepared; it can be deadly to those who are not prepared.

In 1980 a tragedy took place on those sands—an incident that has marked the memory of men and women of conscience throughout North America and beyond. A "coyote" paid to smuggle human lives over the border from Mexico to the United States abandoned his precious cargo. The "coyote" took the meager savings of twenty-six Salvadorans, thanked them, then led them across the border near Nogales, Arizona in the dark of night, guided them into the depths of the desert to a point at which they would not find their way back from where they had come, or to their point of destination. There he abandoned them. Women, men, and children—half of them died a horrible death within days. The others, surviving by drinking their own urine, crept toward the north, *el norte*, the land of hoped-for freedom. A rancher found the survivors near Tucson and came to their assistance.

The survivors were brought to a hospital in Tucson. They were assisted by local church people, most notably John Fife, pastor of Southside Presbyterian Church in Tucson, whose involvement was prompted by the news of the horror that had taken place in the Sonoran. As Fife and other local church people were soon to learn, the horror of the desert paled when compared to the stories of the atrocities and violations of human rights that had driven the Salvadoran survivors and hundreds (now thousands) of others from their homes in Central America. Fife's interest in the plight of these refugees was anticipated by that of Jim Corbett, a Quaker and a rancher from the Tucson area. Corbett had long been providing havens of hospitality for Central American refugees within that same Quaker tradition which, in the previous century, launched the "underground railroad" to bring black slaves from the southern United States to the northern United States—the land of freedom. Corbett and Fife united, as did various religious groups in Tucson—Protestant and Roman Catholics.

In their efforts to assist the Salvadoran survivors and other undocumented refugees from El Salvador and Guatemala, they learned that though these people wanted to come to *el norte*, the north, the so-called land of freedom, the U.S. government did not want them. Because of their status as "illegal aliens," a status given them by the U.S. Immigration and Naturalization Service (INS), the refugees could be returned to their own countries, often to face harassment, torture, and death. Fife and other church people offered their churches as sanctuaries—places of protection for the refugees. In January 1982 Jim Corbett appealed to the National Council of Churches to act on behalf of the refugees, recounting story after story about the atrocities facing those who are returned by the INS to their "home" countries. Two months later, on 24 March 1982, the second anniversary of the assassination of Salvadoran Archbishop Oscar Romero, the Southside Presbyterian Church in Tucson and five churches in the San Francisco (California) Bay Area publicly declared themselves as sanctuaries, places of protection for the undocumented refugees.

In January 1985 sixty refugees were arrested in Phoenix, Tucson, Seattle, and Philadelphia. In that same month Fife, Corbett, and fourteen other key Sanctuary Movement workers, mostly from Arizona, were arraigned in federal court. For two days in January 1985, the first Inter-American Symposium on Sanctuary was held in Tucson. The conference involved people from all walks of life and challenged the conscience of a nation. From that day to this, churches, universities, and individual persons of conscience have established sanctuary, thereby providing protection and hospitality for the refugees from Central America. Yet the practice of "smuggling, transporting and harboring an illegal alien" is an illegal act. The U.S. Government insists that these undocumented refugees are "illegal aliens."

SANCTUARY: ROOTS AND PRECEDENTS

As the term is used in common discourse, "sanctuary" refers to a public welcoming of undocumented Central American refugees into the protection and care of the church. As of April 1986, approximately three hundred churches and synagogues in the U.S. have offered their places of worship as sanctuaries. The notion of sanctuary, however, has roots much deeper than in that horror of the Sonoran desert in 1980. Moreover, it finds precedents in the not too distant past.

In the Old and New Testaments sanctuary is a place of mystery, a place of holiness. The sanctuary is where the mystery of God dwells. Things, persons, and events in or near God's dwelling were sanctified; they were claimed for God and God's design. In or near the sanctuary God's sovereign authority and human obedience to that authority are declared. The sanctuary is the *focus* for recognizing a command above that of the nation or state, or of any human agency.

In the long history of Jews and Christians sanctuary has a twofold meaning. It is the location of gathering for worship, which is sanctified by the nearness of God's presence as well as by the presence of those who gather to invoke God's name. Further, the sanctuary is a place of hospitality and protection. In the current use of the term, sanctuary has taken on a third level of meaning which refers to an act, a movement, or a series of related acts. Hence, one hears tell of persons in different places who are "doing sanctuary."

The dual meaning of sanctuary in the tradition of Jews and Christians signifies the location of worship and praise as a

haven of hospitality and protection, thus bespeaking the insepa-
rability of the twofold commandment: love of God requires—
and not simply desires—love of neighbor. The sanctuary functions, then, as a symbol of God's mercy and righteousness above
and beyond all else, and the necessity for refuge in the face of
practices that violate human dignity; a dignity grounded in
God's own justice. Sanctuary thus has deeply religious and
political significance. It is the declaration and bold proclamation
of the ethical limitations of civil law and human order together
with an affirmation of the absolute priority of God's command
and the requirements it makes of human beings.

The "underground railroad" provided refuge and protection
for fugitive slaves, whose plight was severely hardened as a
result of the Fugitive Slave Law passed by Congress in 1850.
Those even suspected of being fugitive slaves could be arrested,
on sight, without warrant. All that was needed was the word of
a white man or woman that the black man, woman, or child was
his or her possession. The white person's word was all that was
needed to bring about the black person's arrest. A network of
people of conscience, most notably the Quakers, devised an
"underground railroad," a chain of committed persons from
south to north who would provide havens of hospitality while
the black woman/man made the treacherous journey from the
"land of cotton" to the land of freedom—the northern States.
The "underground railroad" was, of course, illegal. Yet people
of conscience broke the law, motivated by values and beliefs that
transcend or go beyond the laws of nation or state.

Another recent precedent for the Sanctuary Movement is found
in the efforts of small groups of Christians who provided shelter
for the Jews during Hitler's attempted annihilation of their race
during World War II. Small in number, these Christians risked,
and at times lost, their own lives because of values and beliefs
that led them to break the law. A small voice in the midst of
Hitler's roar, Christians gathered at Barman to confess their
belief in Jesus Christ and their resistance to the Nazi program.
Christian "confessing churches" resisted by confessing their
faith in Jesus Christ and their opposition to Hitler's program. In
the Sanctuary Movement Christians confess with resistance—
resistance to a practice they view as illegal as well as immoral.

THE CRUX: FAITH (RELIGION) AND POLITICS

Roman law, medieval canon law, and English common law made provision for sanctuary. There has been, then, the recognition that law can and should establish principles to protect persons in positions of vulnerability. Yet in the current situation the Sanctuary Movement has been judged as violation of the law, and a mixing of politics and religion.

To speak of the immorality of certain government policies is something that church people are in the habit of doing, though even this is looked upon by many as mixing faith or religion and politics. More problematical is the business of church people raising voices against government practices that are deemed illegal as well as immoral. This is to call the nation or the state at its own game and, for most, it is to bring the voice of faith into an arena where it does not belong.

In the dynamics of the Sanctuary Movement it is most evident that the pastoral has mixed with the political. Those involved have entered into the dangerous conflict between the laws of God and the dictates of Caesar. Conservatives raise the question: has the church gone against its own basic call and mission by becoming an instrument of partisan political agents? Those on the other end question whether the church can live in fidelity to the Gospel if it does not engage its energies in particular issues in the political milieu.

Since the Second Vatican Council the church has grown in the awareness of its basic mission in the world. The radical separation between church and world, which characterized so much of an earlier church consciousness, has been undercut during these years since the council. The U.S. Bishops' Pastoral Letter on War and Peace, together with their Pastoral Letter on the Economy are representative of this shift in consciousness. Perhaps, as never before, church people are aware that to separate the religious from the political is to create a false dichotomy, and in fact such a separation may implicitly represent another political position. All social religious activity is inevitably political. The logic which suggests that sending machines to a war-torn country is a "humanitarian" act, whereas the efforts to stop the flow of weapons or the building of nuclear weapons is a "political" act, is subject to suspicion at least. Increasing numbers of Christians are raising objections to this line of reasoning.

People of conscience, Christians and others, object that the present practice of the U.S. is both immoral and illegal. In the Refugee Act of 1980 the Congress adopted as law the principles of the United Nations Convention on Refugees.[1] In line with these principles, the U.S. should grant refuge or asylum status to those who cannot return to their "home" countries as a result of persecution or fear of being persecuted because of religious beliefs, race, nationality, or affiliation with a social body or political position. As verified by Amnesty International and other human rights organizations, these principles, adopted by the Congress as law, clearly apply to refugees from Guatemala and El Salvador. Murder, torture, and disappearance have reached horrific proportions in these countries.[2] Though persons fleeing from these countries meet the requirement of the U.S. Code, Refugee Act of 1980, and are viewed as refugees by the United Nations High Commissioner for Refugees, the Immigration and Naturalization Service is unwilling to grant them their proper status. They are still classified as "illegal aliens."

The voices of the Sanctuary Movement have cried out because of the refusal of the INS to grant either political asylum or "extended voluntary departure" status to those who flee El Salvador and Guatemala, although "extended voluntary departure," which allows for an indefinite stay in our country, was granted in high numbers to those who left Poland for political or religious reasons.

Misuse of military weapons provided by the U.S. to El Salvador and other Central American countries is a major cause of civilians leaving their countries of origin. Refusing to admit such misuse of arms by U.S.-backed troops, the Administration has maintained that refugees from Central America have been motivated primarily, if not exclusively, by economic considerations, and therefore deserve the designation "illegal aliens." To suggest that women, men, and children fleeing death squads are money-hungry entrepreneurs is preposterous, to say the least.

The Administration's endorsement of religious conscience is quite spotty. The Administration endorsed the Polish workers' resistance to a government that it found offensive. But people of conscience have come to see that they will pay dearly if the claims of their conscience lead them to positions that the government finds politically agitating.

CRISIS AND *KAIROS*

In this dangerous conflict between the laws of God and the dictates of Caesar, Christians of conscience find themselves faced with a crisis which at the same time is a *kairos*—a moment of critical opportunity. It is a moment within which the church can reexamine and rediscover its identity as one, holy, catholic, and apostolic.[3] These notes of the church, which bespeak its fundamental identity and its basic mission, take on new meaning and depth as the church struggles to respond to God's action in history, as well as to those who thwart the coming of God's reign. The Sanctuary Movement stands as a symbol of the limits of the authority of the nation or state, and the absolute priority of God's reign. It bespeaks an order that transcends the sovereignty of the states and serves as a reminder that ultimate allegiance is due to God alone.

In the Sanctuary Movement, North American church people have heard a call to conversion to their own fundamental mission to be one (in solidarity with victims), holy (in faith and love seeking justice), catholic (transcending boundaries of nation or state), and apostolic (faithful to the proclamation that the Crucified lives).

The Church as One

The Sanctuary Movement calls the church to be one. It brings the voice of the voiceless victims of Latin America into the forum of the North American churches. The challenge is to listen. North American Christians have been much better at speaking and proclaiming than listening. Old habits are hard to break. In light of the cultural and ecclesiastical domination exercised by North American churches, these churches are challenged to recognize that they, together with the churches of western Europe, are no longer the center of the Christian world. There is much to learn. Further, it is at once humbling and liberating to recognize that while North American churches may give protection and refuge to those of Central America, they are called upon to be recipients of the refugees' witness of faith—a compelling witness that unites and brings those of North and Central America into solidarity.

The summons to be one which the Sanctuary Movement offers to the churches is also evidenced in the widely ecumenical nature of the movement. From the movement's beginning, Presbyterians, Quakers, Roman Catholics, and others have crossed denominational boundaries; they have been motivated by values and beliefs that do not know confessional limits. Not only is it a movement that has summoned ecumenical energy; it is interreligious as well—Christians and Jews struggle to uphold the value of the dignity of human life irrespective of other differences.

The Church as Holy

The Jewish and Christian traditions affirm God's special predilection for the poor and powerless. The prophets look to the activity that stops oppression, and to efforts that advance the cause of justice for the weak and downtrodden, as the very activity of holiness. Further, the prophetic tradition views such activity as "holier" than ritual observance or worship. Indeed, such activity is a kind of religious observance, a form of worship. The Sanctuary Movement calls the churches to look again at their degree of commitment to the weak, the vulnerable, and powerless. It summons the church to be holy, not only through ritual observance and worship, but also through fidelity to its mission of reconciliation, advocacy of the weak and powerless, and solidarity through which the church grants pride of place to the little and those who have no voice. Social justice and worship are both holy acts, holy acts brought together in sanctuary.

The Church as Catholic

Sanctuary represents a realm and an order that transcend the limits of individual nations and states. It therefore represents the church's identity as catholic or universal, both in the all-encompassing nature of its claims beyond particular laws or dictates of nation or state, as well as in the ultimacy and absoluteness required by allegiance to God.

The Church as Apostolic

Finally, the Sanctuary Movement calls the churches to be faithful to the message of the women who visited the tomb on Easter morning—that proclamation which forms the core of the apostolic tradition: "The Crucified One lives!" In the faces, hands, and hearts of these refugees, Christians have come to see the body of Christ crucified. In these people, the body has been lanced through violation of rights, through torture and murder. Through the Sanctuary Movement Christians have been faced with the realization that their governmental policy has resulted in practices that hammer the nails into the hands and feet of the Savior (which in Spanish translates El Salvador). The central Christian proclamation, the message of the cross, is that the victim, Jesus, has become the healer. The message of the Sanctuary Movement is that the victims of violence, torture, and murder that take place every day in Central America, can touch, heal, and indeed save the Christians of North America. It is, thus, to see that today the voices of the refugees from Central America bear the proclamation and the promise: "The Crucified One lives!"

* * * * * *

Sanctuary is fundamentally an act of compassion. It is an expression of the basic Christian concern to love our neighbor. But it is not simply an act of relief and hospitality. It is a bold proclamation of protest. The practice of "smuggling, transporting, and harboring an illegal alien" is considered a crime. But the truth of the matter is that it is not people of conscience, Christians and others, who have broken the law. Rather, it is the INS which continues to violate international principles as set forth in the Convention on Refugees of the United Nations, and U.S. law as set forth in the Refuge Act of 1980. The United Nations' High Commissioner for Refugees has determined that Salvadorans fleeing from their country of origin are, as a body, *bona fide* political refugees, not illegal aliens. Hence the Sanctuary Movement is resistance to injustice. One of the movement's basic goals is to put public pressure on the government to change its policy toward these refugees and toward their countries of origin. The means: the activity of illegal compassion which is the heart and soul of the Sanctuary Movement.[4]

It is not a question, as many maintain, of confusing or mixing politics and religion. It is, rather, a question of fidelity to the mission of the one, holy, catholic, and apostolic church in history. The task is one of putting into practice the liberating message that lies at the foundation of church doctrine and practice: "The Crucified One lives!" How is the church to bear witness, in doctrine and practice, to the promise of liberation in the present time? The Sanctuary Movement makes the here and now holy by declaring in word and deed the promise and the possibility of God's justice and compassion in a world ridden with nations and states which would claim the Christian's absolute allegiance.

Notes

1. Gary MacEoin, "A Brief History of the Sanctuary Movement," in *Sanctuary*, ed. Gary MacEoin (San Francisco: Harper and Row, 1985) 14.

2. For accounts of the tragedies that have occurred in Central American countries, see the work edited by Gary MacEoin cited above, as well as Renny Golden and Michael McConnell, *Sanctuary: The New Underground Railroad* (New York: Orbis; Dublin: Gill and Macmillan, 1986). Both works include several accounts by the Central American refugees themselves.

3. This notion is developed at length by Eric Jorstad, "Politics, Social Ministry or Basic Mission? A Theological Reflection on Sanctuary," *Christianity and Crisis*, 31 October 1983.

4. Since this essay was first written, significant changes have taken place as a result of the Sanctuary Movement. Following the murder of the Jesuits, their housekeeper and her daughter, in El Salvador in November 1989, the U.S. Congress passed in 1990 the Temporary Protected Status Act. In summer of 1990 the U.S. Department of Justice, Immigration and Naturalization Services, settled the case involving the American Baptist Church et. al., which reopened the cases of some 150,000 Salvadorans and Guatemalans previously denied asylum. By the standards of the Department of Justice, these people are still illegal aliens. But granting temporary protected status, and reconsidering hundreds of thousands of these cases, indicates that the activity of the Sanctuary Movement has resulted in a change in U.S. policy.

9

A Balm for All Wounds

"ALAS, THERE DOESN'T SEEM TO BE MUCH YOU YOURSELF CAN DO ABOUT our circumstances, about our lives. Neither do I hold you responsible. You cannot help us but we must help You and defend Your dwelling place inside us to the last."[1]

These words closely written in a small, hard-to-decipher hand express the fullness of the spirit of Etty Hillesum. In a review of Hillesum's diaries, Elizabeth O'Connor claims that this work is "the most spiritually significant document of our age."[2] A bold but accurate assessment. It is quite curious, then, that the writings of this sober mystic have found their way into the hands of so few interested in spirituality. This may be due to the fact that her writings are unconventional, as is her nature. One ordinarily accustomed to reading "spiritual writers" would not be immediately inclined to relish the journals of one who makes frequent references to her lovers and to a possible abortion.[3] My intention in alluding to these sexual issues at the outset is not to shock. It is simply to nod in the direction of an explanation for the lack of attention given to Hillesum's writings by those interested in spirituality.[4]

Etty Hillesum's diaries and her more recently published letters[5] provide an account of human transformation, the maturation in spirit of a Jewish woman. Her writings recount one person's reception of the message of the divine indwelling during one of history's darkest hours: the extermination of six million Jews and millions of others at the hands of the Nazis.

Care needs to be taken in the face of inclinations to liken her to Edith Stein or to view her as an adult Anna Frank. And caution should be exercised against the tendency toward Christian appropriationism.[6] No matter how open she may have been to truth wherever it might be found, Etty Hillesum lived and died a Jew. But religious convention was alien to her, and Hillesum's religiosity, if it can be called that, was decidedly unconventional. There are no hints of conventional forms of worship or methods of prayer. She was a Jew who chose her own way.

Overall, Etty Hillesum's spiritual legacy can be viewed in terms of a search for integration. But a word of caution is in order. Hillesum was a woman of her age. This poses problems as well as possibilities. It is problematic, for instance, to know whether she took up the task of spiritual integration in an explicit or conscious way. We do not discern in her writings the longing to negotiate what appear to be opposing poles within *herself*: body and soul, intimacy and solitude, acceptance and resistance. She struggles, rather, with justice and mercy, transcendence and immanence, hatred and forgiveness, the claims of solitude and care for her people. The core of Etty Hillesum's spirituality lies in the attempt to negotiate these apparently contradictory and competing poles. The greatness of her soul lies in her struggle to live with the resulting ambiguity and even contradiction, moving toward a personal integration wherein duality is integral to unity and the integrity of this duality is accepted and affirmed.

THE GIRL WHO COULD NOT KNEEL

"What a strange story it really is, my story: the girl who could not kneel. Or its variation: the girl who learned to pray" (Diaries 194). Our knowledge of "the girl who could not kneel"[7] is based primarily upon eight exercise books in which she kept her diaries between 9 March 1941 and 13 October 1942. The first entry focuses upon her accomplishments in bed (Diaries 1). The last contains the bold affirmation "We should be willing to act as balm for all wounds" (Diaries 196). In addition to her diaries, we now have access to several letters written from her sickbed in

Amsterdam while she was on leave from Westerbork, a transit camp from which the bulk of the published letters were written. The letters describe daily life in a camp which was the last stop for Dutch Jews en route to Auschwitz and other Nazi concentration camps.

The Hillesum corpus is as yet incomplete. Selected entries from the 400 page diary have been published. We can only hope that the remainder will soon be released. Publisher Jan G. Gaarlandt notes in the introduction to the *Letters from Westerbork* the possibility that still more letters will come to light. He estimates that Hillesum wrote over a hundred during the last months of her interrupted life. But there will be no more diaries. Etty Hillesum took her last notebook with her on the train to Auschwitz.

There is one additional source of written information however. On 7 September 1943 Etty Hillesum, her father, mother, and brother, Mischa, were placed on "transport" from Westerbork to Auschwitz. Out of that train she threw a postcard, which was found and sent by farmers. On it she wrote: "We left the camp singing" (Letters 146). A Red Cross report states that Etty Hillesum died in Auschwitz on 30 November 1943. Her parents and Mischa died there too. And with them, we can assume burnt or buried, went the last of Etty Hillesum's diaries.

In the pages of her diaries and letters we find a Jewess in her late twenties living in Amsterdam. Her room overlooked Amsterdam's Museum Square. At the desk she described as the most beloved place on earth, she recorded everything frankly, clearly, and passionately. In April of 1942 Dutch Jews were forced to wear the Star of David. Deportations began that spring. But the restrictions and interruptions of Jewish life had begun much earlier, and it is in the face of these that Hillesum wrote. The personal scenario is one of liberation, whereas the public scenario being played out all over Europe was one of diminishment and extermination.

Her diary chronicles the journey through her inner world. But this inner journey rests upon crystal-clear honesty and attention to the facts of history. In the face of the disintegration and destruction of her race, Hillesum's attitude toward life is one of radical altruism. Her diaries spell out her response to racism, injustice, and innocent suffering. Her descriptions of persons, personal encounters, and historical events illustrate her astonishing familiarity with divinity. But it is not possible to envision Hillesum as one who "turned inward" at the expense of "turning outward." Rather, historical events and persons disclosed a God she understood primarily as the divinity dwelling within.

CHILDHOOD AND YOUTH

Esther Hillesum was born on 15 January 1914 in Middleburg, the Netherlands, where her father, Dr. Louis Hillesum, taught classical languages. Her mother, née Rebecca Hillesum, was a Russian Jewess. Theirs was a tempestuous marriage. Dr. Hillesum was an excellent, disciplined scholar; his wife was passionate and chaotic.

In 1924 the family moved to Deventer, where Dr. Hillesum assumed the post of headmaster of the Municipal Gymnasium. Esther, or Etty, was the middle child. Mischa, the eldest, was a brilliant musician. Jaap, the youngest, became a doctor. He survived the camps, but died on the way back to Holland. About her siblings, little more is known. What is certain is that Etty and her brothers were very intelligent and gifted.

Etty left her father's school in 1932. She took her first degree in law from the University of Amsterdam and then enrolled in the faculty of Slavonic languages. By the time she embarked on the study of psychology, World War II had begun.

While in Amsterdam, Etty lived in the home of Han Wegerif, a sixty-two year-old widower with whom she developed an intimate relationship. She earned her keep as a quasi-housekeeper and as a language tutor. Also living in the Wegerif home were the owner's twenty-one year-old son, Hans, who was studying economics, and Käthe, the German cook. Bernard,[8] described by Etty as a reasonable social democrat, and Maria Tuinzing, a nurse and close personal friend of Etty's, rented rooms in the Wegerif house. The diaries recount the various reactions of this diverse group to the restriction and extermination being played out in their midst, as well as Etty's conflicting feelings about her relationship to the sixty-two year-old Wegerif, to whom she refers as Father Han. It is to this group that the letter dated 6-7 September was written containing the news that Etty had been put on transport from Westerbork to Auschwitz where she would meet her death.

MATURING

Far more important is the group that gathered around Julius Spier, the "S." of the diaries: Adri Holm, Henry Tideman (referred to in the diaries as Tide), Dicky de Jonge, and Liesel Levie, Etty's best friend who emigrated to Israel sometime after the War. Spier studied under Jung and is credited with being the founder of psychochirology—the study and classification of palm prints. He was the father of two, divorced from his Gentile wife. Spier possessed a magical personality. He read palms and interpreted the results with extraordinary clarity. Etty's diary tells of the occasions when members of the Spier circle would gather around him. He read their palms and became a therapist to each. Etty became his assistant, intellectual partner, and lover.

Hillesum began the relationship with Spier in January or February of 1941. Through this encounter she undertook a lasting quest for the essential, the fully human, in marked contrast to the dehumanization and disintegration around her. Her "affair" with "S.," alongside her intimate relationship with Han Wegerif, helped her develop an enormous religious sensibility which gives her writings an all-pervasive spiritual, indeed mystical, character. The term "God" appears in some of the early diaries, but in much the same way as the colloquial "O my God!" or "God knows!" used in contemporary parlance. It was "S." who taught her to speak the name of God without embarrassment, and it was he who invited her to the depths of human intimacy and solitude within which the presence of God is awakened. Gradually Etty moved toward an ever more consistent and intense conversation with the divine. She wrote from the transit camp at Westerbork on 18 August 1943: "My life has become an uninterrupted dialogue with You, Oh God, one great dialogue" (Letters 116).

Even so, Etty's history was filled with interruptions which should not be given short shrift. The regulations and restrictions on the Jews were viewed as minor interruptions in the lives of the Spier circle. Separated from him by three streets, a canal, and a little bridge, Etty continued to make the journey to Spier's quarters. There the circle would gather around their mentor, savoring the luscious aroma of freshly perked coffee, which was in ever-diminishing supply, at least for the Jews.

When the others were gone, Spier's room became the forum for Hillesum's therapy, their admittedly bizarre wrestling matches, and eventually their amorous exchanges. Some of the most breathtaking of her insights and meditations occurred as she journeyed back to the Wegerif home, night after night on her bicycle, the sweet smell of jasmine still filling her senses.

Everything was interrupted, however, when Etty assumed a post as typist for the Jewish Council, a group of twenty important Jews with a staff of several hundred. The job of the Jewish Council was to mediate between the Nazis and the Jews. Established by the Nazis, the Council was under the illusion that by negotiation it could spare some Jews from the worst of their fate. The organization soon became a weapon in the hands of the Nazis.

WESTERBORK

Etty walked to and from her job at the Council headquarters, describing it as "hell." Her work there exempted her from internment at Westerbork, a transit camp near Assen in northeastern Netherlands. After just fourteen days at the Council, however, Etty voluntarily decided to go to the camp as a social worker: an interruption in her life that she herself chose. Her diaries indicate that she was convinced that she could be true to herself only if she did not abandon those in danger, and if she used her energy to bring life into the lives of others; to be balm for their wounds. She would not be exempt from the fate of her people.

She arrived just as the relentless deportations to Auschwitz were beginning. For more than one hundred thousand Dutch Jews, Westerbork was the last stop before Auschwitz. Between August 1942 and September 1943 Etty Hillesum spent her time keeping her diary, writing letters, and nursing the sick in the hospital barracks. During this period she traveled by permit to Amsterdam approximately a dozen times, carrying letters, securing medicines, and bringing messages. Most of her time there was spent in bed, ill and suffering. The last part of her diary was written in Amsterdam after her first month in Westerbork, and tells of the sudden illness and death of "S." She went back to Westerbork but returned to Amsterdam again to be hospitalized. Finally, early in June 1943 she left Amsterdam for Westerbork for the last time. Her lover had died, and she parted with her dear friends, one of whom was Han Wegerif, whose relationship with Etty seems to have reached no formal resolution. It was to these friends that most of her letters from Westerbork were written.

Whether she writes from Amsterdam or from the camp, Westerbork is the consuming subject of Etty's letters. In her diaries we see the inner journey of a Jewess in love with someone who allows her to stand on her own two feet, and to speak God's name without embarrassment. That speaking developed into an uninterrupted dialogue which grew more passionate and enveloping in the life of Etty Hillesum, who became the "thinking heart of these barracks . . . the thinking heart of a whole concentration camp" (Diaries 191). In Westerbork "a plaything that had slipped from God's preoccupied hand" (Diaries 180), Etty Hillesum's soul found its deepest expression. She gave herself without reserve to the service of her people. "I have broken my body like bread and shared it . . . And why not, they were hungry and had gone without for so long" (Diaries 195).

It is the nobility of her soul in the face of the final interruption of her life that leaves us awe-struck. She faced her deportation from Westerbork and from those she served there, as well as her anticipated extermination at the hands of the Nazis, with honesty and acceptance. On 30 November 1943 the balm that was the life of Etty Hillesum was poured out in the ovens of Auschwitz in solidarity with her own people, and with millions of others. And it was given willingly for all wounds, even those of her persecutors.

ROOM ENOUGH FOR EVERYTHING

Etty wrote that the soul has a different age from that recorded in the register of births and deaths. "One can . . . be born with a thousand-year-old soul" (Diaries 194). She possessed such a soul herself, and in it lies wisdom "forged out of fire and rock crystal" (Diaries 195). Hers is a wisdom arising from honesty and the capacity to see the truth in all its nakedness, to bear it, and find consolation in it. This thousand year-old soul is like a vast inner space where there is room for everything. By looking to the gradual transformation of her soul and her astonishing realization of the divine indwelling, we are not turning our backs on the facts of history that were forced upon her and to which she responded. The "inner world/outer world" dichotomy seems foreign to this woman: "Yes, we carry everything within us, God and Heaven and Hell and Earth and Life and Death and *all of history*" [emphasis mine] (Diaries 131).

THE OTHER

Curiously, attention given to Hillesum's life has focused on the hope she inspired in others and upon her service to them with little or no regard for the singular importance of the relationship that, at least in the diaries, was her abiding passion. The "other" of Etty Hillesum's life was the person who served as catalyst for her radical spiritual liberation in the midst of excruciating restrictions and confinement. Etty's affective depth was tapped by the relationship with "S." He was her lover and mystagogue. Through him she came to see that suffering, when accepted, does not diminish but enhances life. Theirs was a love both erotic and contemplative. Spier set her on the search for the essential with an urgency brought on by their awareness of the fate that awaited the Jews. It was he who taught her to speak of God without shame, and to speak to God without interruption.

Spier urged her toward integration, and impressed upon her the necessity of getting head and heart in balance. According to her, he knew how to put everything together properly. At first she found him "charming," but later grew to see how naturally they understood one another and complemented one another. Their union grew more passionate and consuming. She describes kissing his mouth as sipping his breath. She expresses her "desire to breathe one moment through a single mouth. So that a single breath passes through both" (Diaries 95). In this lies the fullest description of their union at once erotic and spiritual. She sees no contradiction between the two. Nor does she give evidence of undue inner conflict in the face of her strong desire for marital union with him while at the same time being quite convinced that she had to remain alone, without him by her side, standing on her own two feet (Diaries 165-166).

It was "S." who pointed to the territory where life's real battle takes place. In the face of the certainty that the Nazis wanted the total destruction of the Jews, Etty saw that the demons within were the real forces with which to contend. But she does not turn her back on the hell whose fires were ravaging the face of Europe and European Jewry.

Spier himself did not descend into the depth of that fire. He grew ill and died before he could be deported. By the time of his death Etty's mysticism had taken full form. It emerged not by denying reality, the facts of history, but by entering into reality's heights and depths, and transforming both.

She met Spier's death with acceptance. Death was for Etty life's great mystery to be anticipated, received, reverenced (Diaries 168). Her journal entry at the time of his death is like a great doxology: "I love people so terribly, because in every human being I live something of You" (Diaries 168). In loving "S." passionately, spontaneously, honestly, she was loving God, or what and who she knew to be God. It is also the case that in loving this "You," eros was not exclusive but became an inclusive love without ceasing to be particular and singular. In the aftermath of his death she wrote of Spier: "You were the mediator between God and me, and now you, the mediator, have gone and my path leads straight to God . . . And I shall be the mediator for any soul I can reach" (Diaries 169).

HUMAN NATURE

As the life of Etty Hillesum unfolds, we witness the gradual shedding of the inclination to accept solace in illusion, fantasy, ideals, or eternal truths. She gives herself over and over again to the real, to fact, to what actually is: particular persons, encounters, events. She gradually accepts her very limited situation in life, and in so doing transforms it. This gradual self-acceptance occurs to the degree that she realizes and accepts the divinity dwelling within. She looks life in the face and recognizes that one must accept things as they are (Diaries 130).

Etty Hillesum refused to countenance deception in herself and others. Her eyes look to those who will the destruction of herself and her race, and with sharp wit describes their cowardice and temerity masquerading as bravery and power. She cuts through the illusion, and sees right through the self-deception by which they have been blinded. It is the Nazis themselves who are pinned in by barbed wire—not their captives.

There is in Hillesum the complete absence of posturing and embellishment. Her view might seem like unmitigated romanticism but for the fact that it develops in the midst of the most grotesque and dehumanizing of circumstances. In light of the fact that they were planning the systematic extermination of her race, Etty maintains that if there could be found "one decent German" (Diaries 8) there would be reason enough not to hate the whole lot: "despite all the suffering and injustice I cannot hate others" (Diaries 72).

Her view of human nature can be properly described as radically altruistic. In light of the darkness and disintegration around her, she believed that there could always be found meaning and beauty: "if we are consigned to hell, let us go there as gracefully as we can" (Diaries 130). If we accept our own nature and things as they really are, we gain confidence in the reliability of life and of death on their own terms.

It was said of Etty: "You never expect anything and that's why you never go away empty-handed" (Diaries 117). As she grew in the deeper acceptance of facts, her expectations were fewer and fewer. Good things in life were unexpected gifts, accepted with gratitude. But "one must face up to everything that happens," and accept all (Diaries 136). Whatever her attempts to effect change, they were part of her acceptance of the things that could not change. It is this sober realism which forms the core of Etty Hillesum's view of human nature. In her we find the movement of a soul inclined to live in fantasy and illusion (the original sin—pretending to be what one is not: God) toward the gradual acceptance of the truth of what is:

> . . . one must keep in touch with the real world and know one's place in it; it is wrong to live only with the eternal truths, for then one is apt to end up behaving like an ostrich. To live fully, outwardly and inwardly, not to ignore external reality for the sake of the inner life, or the reverse—that's quite a task (Diaries 20).

Hillesum's view of human nature recognizes that the longest journey is the journey inward, but that we can never turn our backs on fact. Human life is a project of integrating the internal and external world without compromising either. And this enormous task is the destiny of everyone. Etty poured out her life in service and sacrifice for others and in willingness to die in solidarity with the victims, cognizant that those around her, victim as well as oppressor, did not accept the facts of their existence, denied their destiny, and betrayed life's beauty and meaning. It is not God she blamed for the disintegration and destruction of her people, but human beings. Staring this reality in the face, and knowing what awaited her and her family, she nonetheless insisted relentlessly that meaning and beauty could still be found.

Central to Hillesum's vision of the human person is suffering, which she learned to embrace in embracing "S.": "Through suffering . . . we must share out love with the whole of creation" (Diaries 125). Suffering is an art (Diaries 128). We can suffer with dignity or without. But suffering, like death, is part of life. In her own life Etty learned the art of suffering which gave rise to compassion; born of a quivering, trembling, but thinking heart in the face of the enormity of the suffering of her people.

In the light of the mud and the endless deportations from Westerbork to Auschwitz, she writes: "I am in a strange state of mournful contentment" (Letters 70). She eschewed romanticism, idealism, uninformed optimism. She affirmed that life is large and long, and the human soul wide enough and strong enough to bear everything it carries within it: God, heaven, hell, earth, life, death, and all of history: "there is room for everything in a single life. For belief in God and for a miserable end . . . It is a question of living life from minute to minute and taking suffering into the bargain" (Diaries 129).

HISTORY AND DESTINY

Hillesum saw her own soul as a battlefield on which history's great dramas were played out. "I feel like a small battlefield, in which the problems, or some of the problems, of our time are being fought out. All one can hope to do is to keep oneself humbly available, to allow oneself to be a battlefield" (Diaries 25). The great task of her life, living fully in the inner and outer worlds, would not allow her the luxury of self-indulgence. She did not turn her back on the history being enacted in her midst.

In the face of what was going on around her, Etty was often accused of indifference and resignation. Indeed many of her entries lend credence to this position: "everything is accidental" (Diaries 23). Etty's deeper insight is discerned from what she says about the nature of acceptance vis-à-vis resignation. Resignation means to give up deliberately. She insists that she is not resigned to the history of horror unfolding around her. But she does accept. Acceptance here may be understood as a positive, active response. It is the most mature and responsible action in the face of events and circumstances over which one is quite powerless. Thus, in the midst of the horror from which so many tried in vain to save themselves, Etty possessed a peace and calm born of mature acceptance of the fact of what was taking place around her.

The notion of destiny is fundamental to Etty's view of history. We do not shape our destiny. We determine our inner responses (Diaries 71). The events of our life, our own personal history, as well as the events of human history, are not of our own doing. Yet destiny is not fate or pure chance. Events are strung significantly together. Maturity resides in assuming our destiny, "to cease living an accidental life," (Diaries 112) to come to terms with life and death on their own terms.

Etty understood this primarily in light of the one thing she was compelled to do: write. She states repeatedly that writing was the thing she wanted and needed to do most. Her journal entries often give evidence of her struggle to accept her destiny as a writer: to be faithful to the daily round of taking up the pen to record the shape of history in the making in her inner and outer worlds. She was profoundly aware that circumstances were simply beyond her control, and that her only responsibility was to attempt to determine her responses. Response, often understood as a passive thing, is for Etty Hillesum a positive action. Her response was to write with unmitigated honesty, absence of posturing, and lack of embellishment.

Etty accepted her destiny only gradually. She came to know the small part she would play in human history—to shape it by writing everything down with a clarity springing from a mystical apprehension of truth and beauty in the midst of one of history's darkest hours: "I shall wield this slender fountain pen as if it were a hammer and my words will have to be so many hammer-strokes with which to beat out the story of our fate and of a piece of history as it is and never was before" (Diaries 146).

GOD AND ETTY HILLESUM

Etty's God is the God within. She addresses God as she does herself. With good reason we could ask if her God is her self-projection. She writes: "When I pray . . . I hold a silly, naive or deadly serious dialogue with what is deepest inside me, which for the sake of convenience I call God" (Diaries 155). That probably best expresses her feeling for life: she reposed in herself. And that part of herself, that deepest and richest part in which she reposed, is what she called God. It may be said that her God resides in her own capacity to see the truth, to bear it, and find consolation in it. Etty recognized a deep well inside herself, and in it the divine indwelling. God is found in the soul, in what might be envisioned as its apex or heart. And this God is discovered to the measure that she discovered her own self and her own destiny.

Hillesum suggests that there are people who pray with eyes gazing heavenward, and those who pray with heads bowed, their faces in their hands, seeking God within. She is undoubtedly one of the latter. Her desire is "to be true to that in me which seeks to fulfil its promise" (Diaries 52). Her prayer is dialogue. It is a conversation recorded in the pages of her diary. She also freely admits that there are moments when she honestly cannot pray. She does not pretend otherwise.

She reads the Bible and "worries" about its meaning (Diaries 22). The psalms were familiar to her, and so was the New Testament, particularly the Gospel of Matthew 6:34. She also read Jung, Dostoevsky, and especially Rilke. She found delight in Augustine. It is no wonder. In one who prayed for knowledge of God through knowledge of self she recognized an early echo of the awakening to God in the deep well of her own self:

> Truly, my life is one long hearkening unto my self and unto others, unto God. And if I say that I hearken, it is really God who hearkens inside me. The most essential and the deepest in me hearkening unto the most essential and deepest in the other. God to God (Diaries 173).

She tells little of who this God is. And never does she claim that this God tells her anything. This God does not speak. And she calls this God "God."[9]

Here Etty Hillesum, unconventional though she may be in the way she views her relationship with this God, understands God to be the God of her people: "I am who am!" "I will be who I will be." This provides her with a great confidence in the face of all that is going on around her. God is at the heart of all that is, active in history and present to creation. This is the One whose name is above any name, in whom all beauty and holiness dwell. Her diary reveals the progressive awakening of this God within herself until God is understood as the ground of her being and of all that is: "I am who am." She reaches out to embrace this God, she hearkens to God, only to find that it is God in her self hearkening to God. Is this an unconventional view of a conventional God? Or is God, like herself, also unconventional?

RELATING TO GOD

Two focal points help us understand Etty's relationship with God: kneeling and the content of her most intriguing prayers. She herself says that her story is about a "girl" learning to kneel, learning to pray. Far more important than her reading, e.g., Matthew's Gospel, or Augustine, or Rilke, learning to kneel—not a familiar posture for prayer in Jewish tradition—bespeaks the nature of her relationship with God. Her diary recounts many occasions of her gradual adoption of kneeling for prayer: in the bathroom on a coconut rug, among other places. She suggests that the act of kneeling is more intimate than the intimacies of her love-life (Diaries 89).

Most instructive is her growing awareness that one can pray anywhere, behind barbed wire or in a room in Amsterdam. As she grows in the awareness of her ability to pray anywhere and always, she writes of her desire to kneel inside, a kind of interior posture which she assumes regularly and with increasing frequency. She kneels before the God who is the Holy One, a strong God to be revered. It is a wordless, imageless, interior kneeling in the depths of her soul before the One who is therein discerned, thanked, and praised.

This God is not accountable to us for the events of history. We are accountable to God for the ways in which we betray the divine gift and presence within. Etty lived with an undeniable sense of God's nearness. The great and Holy One present at the heart of all creation and active in history is to be protected and cared for in the depths of the soul. Etty's most significant insight pertains to the vulnerability of the divine within the soul, and this linchpin holds together the various ambiguities and paradoxes of her interrupted life.

THE COST OF INTEGRITY

There is a gradual unfolding and progression in Etty's awareness of the divine indwelling. Likewise, her developing perception of the vulnerability of the divine life is slow and gradual. As a result, it is difficult to pinpoint exactly when and how she arrives at certain insights about the divine. It should be noted, however, that she begins to speak about helping God and defending God very shortly after writing "somewhere there is something inside me that will never desert me again" (Diaries 130). From this point, what she had described as her "schizoid tendencies" fade (Diaries 46). Apparent contradictions and conflicts, the opposing poles of her personality, seem to have reached a point of reconciliation correlative to her astonishing leap into familiarity with the divine vulnerability within.

Spiritual integration is a process of negotiating apparently opposite and conflicting realities. It requires an ability to live with ambiguity and even glaring contradiction, not to *resolve* opposition and conflict. In the life of Etty Hillesum we can discern the ongoing struggle to reconcile a wide range of factors that are often deemed immediately incompatible. She speaks of the various dimensions of heaven, hell, earth, life, God, and all history existing within one soul. She writes of her inability to be comfortable with her body, inclusive of the sexual, and with God on the same day. We witness the apparent conflict of her maintaining simultaneous, intimate relationships with two older men, all the while growing in self-reliance and independence so that she could stand on her own two feet without either of them. There are the competing claims of solitude and care for others, whose needs and urgent demands required her to be willing to be balm for their wounds. And there is a myriad of other conflicting factors she holds together in her "thousand-year-old soul."

But in Etty Hillesum's interrupted life we also see a gradual movement toward integration. I submit that she attained spiritual integration by recognizing and accepting duality as integral to unity and affirming the integrity of this duality. Maturity and wholeness come through such recognition, acceptance, and affirmation, as does simplicity. She achieved this by unrelenting attention to the awakening of the God within, and by accepting that the Holy One who is reverenced and adored is a presence both strong *and* vulnerable. That divine vulnerability is the ground in which her soul found rest.

On 21 July 1942, during the same month she voluntarily decided to go to live and work among her people at Westerbork, Etty Hillesum wrote: "I believe I have gradually managed to attain the simplicity for which I have always longed" (Diaries 158). A little over a week previously, she had written a Sunday morning prayer:

> I shall promise you one thing, God, just one very small thing: I shall never burden my today with cares about my tomorrow, although that takes some practice. Each day is sufficient unto itself. I shall try to help You, God, to stop my strength ebbing away, though I cannot vouch for it in advance. But one thing is becoming increasingly clear to me: that You cannot help us, that we must help ourselves. And that it is all we can manage these days and also all that really matters; that we safeguard that little piece of You, God, in ourselves. And perhaps in others as well. Alas, there doesn't seem to be much You Yourself can do about our circumstances, about our lives. Neither do I hold You responsible. You cannot help us but we must help You and defend Your dwelling place inside us to the last . . . You are sure to go through lean times with me now and then, when my faith weakens a little, but believe me, I shall always labor for You and remain faithful to You and I shall never drive You from my presence (Diaries 151).

In these words lies the fullness of her spirit—a noble integrity gained through the recognition of ambiguity and contradiction and through an acceptance of God, destiny, and death. Etty

Hillesum poured out her care for all creation, but first and foremost she cared for her own people at Westerbork, most of whom, like herself, were on their way to death. She became a balm for all wounds. In her the fullness of God was pleased to dwell.

Notes

1. Etty Hillesum, *An Interrupted Life: The Diaries of Etty Hillesum, 1941-43*, tr. Arnold Pomerans (New York: Pantheon, 1983) 151. This work will be referred to as Diaries. Page references are included in the text.

2. Elizabeth O'Connor, "The Thinking Heart," *Sojourners* (October 1985) 40-42.

3. Hillesum makes references to her ability as a lover in the first page of her diaries. There are allusions to an abortion on pp. 52ff, especially 58 and 60.

4. O'Connor, "The Thinking Heart," provides this as a possible explanation for the lack of attention given to Hillesum's writings in Christian circles.

5. Etty Hillesum, *Letters from Westerbork*, tr. Arnold Pomerans (New York: Pantheon, 1986). Referred to hereafter as Letters. Page references are included in the text.

6. In his otherwise perceptive review of the Diaries, Robert Imbelli lies open to such criticism by making claims such as "Hillesum's transforming journey more and more assumes the quality of a eucharistic celebration." See *National Catholic Reporter* (6 April 1984) 11-12. I have compared Etty Hillesum to the Christian spiritual writer Thomas Merton in "Penning Patterns of Transformation," *The Merton Annual*, vol. 4 (New York: AMS Press, 1991) 767-95. In so doing I have attempted to avoid this tendency.

7. From a contemporary perspective it seems odd to refer to a woman in her twenties as a girl. This, however, is how Hillesum refers to herself; see Diaries 194.

8. Bernard's surname is not provided in the diaries or letters.

9. There are a few exceptions to this. For example, she uses the term "Lord" on pp. 46 and 189 of the Diaries.

VULNERABILITY IN
CHRISTIAN LIFE
AND PRAYER

10

"Mercy within Mercy within Mercy"

BLUE-UNIFORMED SECOND GRADE BOYS IN SISTER M. ALOYSIUS GONZAGA'S class all learned that it is more important and indeed more admirable to die for Jesus than to kill for him. To die for Jesus demanded strength, virtue, and a good deal of tough skin. Weakness and a recognition of one's fragility were undesirable in one who professed to be a soldier of Jesus Christ as we did at confirmation earlier in the year. Above all else we were to be strong and powerful witnesses in the face of the evils besieging our world. We were at war, and engaging in the spiritual battle demanded the armor of faith and the power of virtue.

Sister M. Aloysius Gonzaga is dead now. She died in 1978 at the age of sixty-five. In 1960, when I was a second grader, she looked as if she were ninety. She was tough—a boy's nun. She taught her boys to be tough for Jesus and his mother, of course. There is little doubt that she has been rewarded for all her efforts to attain eternal bliss. So I trust that she will look down graciously and forgive me as I write boldly (those who misbehaved in class she referred to as "bold little articles") about another way of Christian life and of prayer. It is an approach much different from what I was taught, one that has been learned the hard way. It is not the way of a soldier.

The first and most important step in mature Christian life and in praying is to recognize and accept our limitation and vulnerability. Augustine writes about humility as the first and most important disposition of the Christian. Ignatius Loyola invites the Christian into an experience of prayer that demands, in the first place, acceptance of ourselves as creatures. Nothing is as basic and fundamental to growth in the life of the Spirit as surrender and acceptance of ourselves. Self-acceptance then enables us to accept life, others, and God on their own terms. But to surrender, to let go, is not to give up.

Each one of us is quite limited and vulnerable. There are limitations of personality, temperament, or material resources. Perhaps it is a limitation in the ability to make and keep commitments. For some there are the quite visible physical limitations. Our vulnerability comes to the fore when we enter into any relationship with another. To recognize our limitation and vulnerability is to see that we are weak and fragile. We are not as "together" and powerful as once we might have thought. We need others and God.

Often a repulsion wells up within us when we begin to recognize our limitation and vulnerability. Contemporary society values competition and efficiency. Weakness and vulnerability are the greatest evils, and are to be avoided at all costs. Duped into believing the dictates of our contemporaries, we spend our energies trying to cover up and flee from the basic human situation which indeed is one of limitation and vulnerability.

More often than not there is great hesitation in us when we begin to pray. Our inclination is to put it off until things get better, until we get our act together, until that time when we're not quite so messy and ugly inside. And then, of course, there is always the well-worn argument that there is not enough time for prayer. Perhaps our many excuses and arguments all stem from a basic inclination to blind ourselves to our limitations and our vulnerability.

Beginning to pray requires that we take ourselves in hand and start right where we are, as we are. Beginning will be no more possible tomorrow than it is today. Starting as we are means facing squarely our vulnerability and our wounds, the disorder and unmanageability of our lives resulting in strained relationships, loss of employment, workaholism, the tendency to dominate, our problems with intimacy and sexuality. Above all else, beginning to pray requires trust. Without it there is no relationship with others or with God. Without it there is no praying, just babbling. We need to trust that the seeds of the divine and the capacities of the human heart are found in weakness, not in strength. This is the mystery and the message of Jesus.

When we seek God in our own situation, recognizing our fragility and our brokenness, and when we cease waiting for the perfect moment of hoped-for silence and tranquility that never comes, we find that God has been with us all along. God's life, grace, has slipped through the cracks, the holes, the empty and dirty places. These are the very cracks that we have wanted, and still want, to fix before allowing God to visit us. But God's grace is loose in the world, and loose in our lives, having found a home in us where we would least likely suspect. God's life abides in our weakness and vulnerability.

The great mystery of the Christian life, and what we gain access to as we pray, is that God meets us and touches us at the most fragile point in our existence. This is the heart, the deepest and most basic part of human existence, the place where God resides. Often we approach prayer convinced that it is primarily a mental act or a verbal exercise. Often we hear that it is good to use the imagination in prayer, or that God communicates or reveals through our dreams. Whereas this may all be true, one of the richest insights of the Christian tradition is that God touches us at the deepest and most fundamental core of human life, the heart, the root of all personal life, the Spirit's dwelling. In most of us the heart is deeply wounded.

When we look to our fragility and vulnerability, rather than our strength, rational powers, accomplishments, and efficiency as the place where we meet God, we are met by a God who is not fearsome and forbidding, not a judge or mighty conqueror. In looking to our vulnerability and limitation for the traces of grace, what we glimpse is the God dwelling within who is love and compassion. Here again we approach the essence of the Christian mystery and message. God is love (1 John 4:8). We can go so far as to say that God is all loving, indeed God is all love and mercy. We know from our own experience that in loving we are vulnerable. If it is true, as we claim, that God is all love, then God is the most vulnerable of all.

Our limitation and vulnerability, then, are not to be avoided or bypassed in beginning to pray or in mature Christian living. The most vulnerable places within us, the deepest hurts and the ugliest wounds may be looked to as the very focus for the encounter and the relationship with God who, like us in our attempt to love, is vulnerable.

Such a vision of prayer requires that our vision of self, others, and God be gradually transformed. Rather than striving for strength and power, excellence and virtue in Christian life and prayer, we begin to see that our vulnerability and limitation allow for attraction to and communion with God and others. Weakness and vulnerability unite; strength and power divide.

Prayer thus understood enables us to see that those who bear quite visibly the scars of woundedness and limitation, be they the handicapped, the elderly, the poor and marginalized, or the threatened unborn, are all signs of God's life, love, and vulnerability in the world. They deserve our absolute reverence and respect. In the hands, faces, and hearts of the wounded and the poor, we glimpse the whole mystery of God's loving vulnerability.

Christian action that results from this vision of prayer is not primarily concerned with demonstrating God's power, majesty, and authority. Those who act in mercy and kindness, but above all in service and compassion, attentive to the weak and the wounded, become the clearest signs of God's presence in our world.

When we pray, attentive to our vulnerability and limitation, we are drawn to the mystery of God's vulnerability and weakness in Jesus in his infancy at Bethlehem and on the cross at Calvary. This focus helps us overcome the gap between the "active" and "contemplative" dimensions of our lives, or the call to prayer and the call to service. Attention to Jesus in his mysteries (prayer or contemplation), especially the mysteries of the crib and the cross, and service (action or ministry) on behalf of the weak and wounded are both rooted in the heart, the place in us where we are most fragile. The wounded heart is the meeting place with God who, precisely because God is all love, is most vulnerable.

There may have been a time when second graders needed to be taught a soldier's strategy for overcoming the trials and tribulations of the world of darkness and evil. Sister M. Aloysius Gonzaga equipped us with certain tools for fighting the good fight. Above all else, she introduced us to the message of the Gospel which is a word of compassion.

In our terrible age we witness the manifold fruits of the unbridled quest for power, the fight to be right, to win, even for religious reasons. The clearest examples of the drive to win, to be right, in our age are the Nazi Holocaust of the Jews and the threat of nuclear holocaust. Both give occasion to pause and consider our vulnerability and limitation. To pray demands trust that God is with us no matter what we have done or what has been done to us, to bring about this mess we're in, be it personal, communal, or social. God is present with us, precisely in our weakness. This is the greatest grace of all, and its acceptance the beginning of prayer without ceasing.

11

A Costly Loss

It seems I've always known the truth of the age old wisdom that the eyes are the windows of the soul. Eyes speak. And our own heart's eye must prepare to be attentive. But it's his hands I still see. They were long and graceful. Elegant. Not feminine. But delicate. "Piano fingers," Mother was fond of calling Dad's. They did not seem to fit with the rest of him. Short and stocky, he had tree trunks for arms. He was built like an Irish boxer, and showed the ire of one more than I'd care to tell. Piano lessons would have been out of reach for this "runt," last in a line of nine born of Irish immigrants. He worked hard and, as I remember, almost always. Given the sort of work he did, his hands should have been rough and stubby, like the rest of him. But they were as if soaked in grace and, in my mind, they had a way of changing everything they touched. Especially us: Mother, my sister Maureen, and myself. It was no Midas touch, mind you. It was a touch of a different type. And those hands exuded a goodness and a grace even when gripping his cigarette, or when they were thrown up in the air with impatience.

Philip Roth's *Patrimony*, a deeply resonant portrait of a father and son, reminds in conclusion: "You must not forget any-thing." It's those hands I remember. And much more. Especially the later part.

TREMORS OF LOSS

He looked forward to his retirement, those golden years. He glimpsed them, from afar, albeit ever-so-briefly. He fully expected that he would spend his retirement "just doin' nothin'."

Nothing could have prepared me for his death. And nothing has awakened me more to the reality of vulnerability than accompanying him through each fearful stage of his final ordeal. Falteringly, even now, I whisper to him. Words stretch to make room for silence as I try to learn from him about his living and his dying: both a stubborn engagement with life itself.

The aftershocks are felt nearly three years later. His death, at age fifty-seven, has been the most deeply formative event of my life. No doubt of my mother's and sister's as well. It is not a story with a happy ending, at least not yet. The chapters are still being written; the ink is not dry. The death of a beloved may bring families together. Or it may cause them to come unglued. In our case the outcome is still unclear. Vulnerable indeed. In our loss of him, we have lost one another as well. At least what we had been for one another when Dad was the glue that held us together.

I have always been reluctant to speak of the deepest experiences in my life. I tend to be a bit shy around others who so easily disclose the deepest part of themselves, and speak so unabashedly and directly to the deepest and most personal in others, even if it be in writing. It must be my purely Irish blood. We never say anything directly. Language is quite beautiful, so why say in seven words what can be said in seventeen? So we tend to talk around things rather than come out with it. Especially about the most important things. Speaking about the deep down things seems a bit like letting oneself be photographed in Calvin Klein white briefs, and then being plastered bigger-than-life in New York's Times Square. I don't mean to press the analogy, but I discern some truth to it.

What is deepest in us is most difficult to express. But then again, what is most personal is most universal. So my silence stretches to make enough room for speech.

Perhaps the value of speaking of the death of my father lies in the invitation it may extend to others to recognize something of their own experience and truth. One's experience can be for another a *jalon de route*, an indicator, a signpost along the way. I must admit at the outset that I am more familiar with the idiom of theological discourse. My own existential voice is difficult to pen. But I offer these reflections in my own existential idiom in the hope that my experience of the suffering and death of my father might help others navigate that terrain of human experience we call variously "diminishment," "separation," "sorrow," "desolation," "grief," "loss"—those slap-in-the-face-experiences that defy us to ignore our own vulnerability and that of others.

Some months after Dad's untimely death there was an air of euphoria in the nation, occasioned by the return of the military troops from the Persian Gulf. Indeed there was some cause for such ebullience, though in hindsight we can see that the victory was something of a mixed bag, from start to finish. As the photos of service men and women being reunited with their families were paraded before the American public, my mind's eye scanned to the edges in remembrance of those who did not return, those whose families mourn not one iota less because of the fact that the casualties in the Persian Gulf were comparatively few. "No amount of oil is worth one drop of my son's blood," wailed one bereaved mother. And the stark words of Winston Churchill remind of the ways in which war twists and truncates what is most precious: "In peace, sons bury their fathers. In war, fathers bury their sons."

Churchill's words echo and stir up from the depths of me what I have only imagined to be the greatest of human sorrow: the parent's loss of a child. I can think of nothing more painful to bear. July 1990 seemed a time of national peace. And it was a son burying his father. This son burying my father. That's as it should be. Yet even this realization provides no lasting consolation.

Too often we brush over the depth of our losses with pious platitudes and saccharine rationalizations. More often than not this is an exercise in self-deception or, in the language of a more contemporary idiom, "denial." I shall say flatly that from the time my father first fell ill in late October 1989 through the time of his suffering until his death in July of 1990, and even into the present day, things have not been right with the world, with my world. My most profound and lasting sense is of the loss of innocence, of the buoyancy and resiliency that had always come naturally to me. Indeed life is a gift, our grasp on it from moment to moment is so very insecure. And it is all the more precious because of its intrinsic and undeniable vulnerability. Sickness and death serve to remind. And so I have been wrestling in death's aftermath, bracing myself as I feel the tremors of loss beneath feet that walk on ground that once felt undeniably secure. I have gazed long and lovingly through the galaxy of heartfelt and half-felt condolences and consolations to the truth about my father and myself; about death and the dread of it; and about the vulnerability to which love consigns us all.

Vulnerability is often thought to refer to a weakness that places us in a position of being forced to give in indiscriminately to any and all powers and forces. It is often thought that vulnerability causes us to be adversely affected by persons, events, and circumstances beyond our own control. Properly understood, however, the term describes the fundamental openness of the human being to be affected by life, persons, and events. To be human is to be vulnerable, indeed defenseless in the face of so many of the events and persons that affect us, for good or ill. At the most fundamental level, human vulnerability is part and parcel of being a person, having a body, being embodied.

Our bodies, our selves, are really quite defenseless in the face of disease, sickness, suffering, accident, and finally death, which claims the life of each human being. No matter how strong a person or group may be, there are the never-ending reminders that human life is very fragile, a gift, and the forces that bear upon it cannot be predicted or controlled. Whatever precautionary and preventative measures human wisdom may require in order to assure human integrity and flourishing, human beings are altogether vulnerable if life is to be lived on its own terms.

Human vulnerability is often overlooked or flatly denied by individuals and by whole societies wherein cults of the young and of youth flourish, where the advertising industry exalts physical perfection and longevity, and where pain, impairment, and limitation are to be avoided at any and all costs.

From a Christian perspective, vulnerability may be understood as the human capacity to be open, to be attracted, touched or moved by the draw of God's love as this is experienced in our own life or in the lives of others. It is vulnerability that enables us to enter into relationships of interpersonal communication and communion with others who recognize their own weakness and need. Vulnerability requires the integrity and strength, indeed the power, to risk enormous pain, to bear the burdens of the darkest hour without avoidance, denial, or deception. It demands the stamina to open ourselves up in order to be touched in our fragility. Being vulnerable entails a willingness to lose ourselves in the hope of finding our true self. It demands the readiness to die to oneself so that others might live.

LOSING GROUND

In summer of 1989 I began a long-awaited sabbatical with a month-long visit with my mother and father at the New Jersey shore. They were in the best of their years, on the brink of their golden years together. They had been married nearly forty years. Dad took pride in their endurance and fidelity. "No small thing," he'd remark. Talk was easy with them. Dad had a great store of jokes, none of which, I regret, do I remember very well. But he loved the way words go, and he would often compose little rhymes and call them limericks because he thought it would make them more Irish. One I remember best:

> Love is grand, isn't it so,
> It sure is a pity for those who don't know.

Seeing them together that summer was a testament that they both knew love's grandeur. And before the cycle of seasons would come full turn, there was yet to be born a terrible beauty of their love of nearly forty years.

Conversation moved regularly to the prospect of Dad's early retirement. In the course of that summer he made important decisions about turning his life over to God, admitting his powerlessness to control his life. As part of his new way of life, that summer he went to Mass each day before work. I left the Jersey shore and went off for sabbatical. Dad continued to go to daily Mass and to work.

Autumn's crimson and gold heralded winter's visitation, and before its arrival Mother and Dad braced themselves for its icy chill by a visit to the Bahamas. Dad had not been feeling well, but in characteristic fashion, he stood by his commitment and boarded the plane for the islands. It was en route to the airport in the Bahamas to return to their home at the New Jersey shore that he fell to the ground bleeding. Thus began an ordeal that was to make Mother and Dad's foretaste of their golden years ever so brief, a nightmare that signalled for our family the beginning of ten months of seemingly endless waiting, of hopes quickly dashed, of broken hearts, and of undaunting courage against the odds.

Upon hearing the news of his illness, it was immediately clear to me that he was, and would likely remain, a very sick man. But after a brief period of stabilization in Nassau, Dad managed to travel home by air in the company of my mother. Doctor's visits Stateside confirmed that his health was very tenuous. But after a six week period of recuperation, he was permitted to return to work. I traveled from sabbatical hideaway at Thanksgiving and at Christmas, not realizing that these would be our last as a family. Doctors seemed optimistic at that time, and we breathed a sigh of relief. We imagined that we were in the clear.

As we rang in the decade of the 90s, I left Mother and Dad and embarked on stage two of my sabbatical: a six-month long study/retreat at the Abbey of Gethsemani in Trappist, Kentucky. The autumn had been riddled with interruption and disappointment, and I anticipated with great relish all those wonders one usually associates with a retreat in a Trappist monastery: solitude, rest, prayer, reflection, tranquility. My taste of these was brief indeed. Jonquils were up in late February, and I had just left the monastery's doors to walk among them on a fine Sunday afternoon. One of the monks raced to catch me with the news that Mother was on the telephone. And I knew.

Dad had fallen again, bleeding internally. Intensive care could not stop the bleeding. Surgery would be undergone only as a last resort. Chances of survival were slim. I traveled home to be by his side. Surgery followed. And he survived, much to the amazement of us all.

Once Dad came home from the hospital, I felt free to return to sabbatical's rest. But regular telephone calls home brought news that he was not gaining ground. He was weak, had lost appetite, was losing weight, and grew more and more listless. By Palm Sunday he was back in intensive care, with further complications. It became clearer than ever to me that he would never be himself again. We made it through Easter, and Dad came home again, now with a protocol of antibiotics to be administered by

Mother three times daily for a course of seven weeks. I traveled home to visit, and watched him waste away.

In the early 80s I lived for a time in the l'Arche community of Jean Vanier in Trosly-Breuil, France. While there I had the responsibility of living very close to a severely, profoundly retarded man, Jean-Luc. He was dependent upon me for meeting all his physical needs, even the most basic. At times I wondered where I would find the strength to assist him with washing, dressing, toileting, eating. My heart would turn to God as I grew faint. Life in l'Arche prepared me in some small way for Dad's diminishment. I had learned in theory and in practice that the seeds of the divine and the capacities of the human heart are found in weakness not in strength. But the truth comes home anew. It is a message altogether sharp and heart-rending when it is written in the flesh of one of your own family.

As Dad grew sicker and sicker, wasting away before us, I was able to assist him in caring for himself. As I washed his feet, trimmed his nails, put lotion on his body to soothe his flaking skin, I sensed that all my time in l'Arche was in anticipation of this. I remembered that Jesus washed feet. Prior to Dad's illness, gospel stories about footwashing, and all the sermonizing about the significance of such an act on Jesus' part, had made some modest impression on my theological mind. For many years I was particularly attentive to the footwashing as part of the Holy Thursday liturgy. My small hands touched Dad's feet, bathed them in cool water, felt them against my skin, loved the feel of them, sensed the still-living blood running through them. I thought how small a thing to give my father in exchange for all that he had me given. And I heard again the truth I had learned in l'Arche, one that lies hidden at the heart of the Gospel: ours is not to do great things, but to do little things with great love.

Father and son. How different! He loved sports. The earliest photographs of me are with book open, working at my play-desk. For as long as I can remember, I read the paper as he watched the ball game on television. He loved to be with people—all kinds and always. I tend to prefer my own company. It's not that I dislike people. It's just that being around them a lot does not seem to come naturally to me. My father talked to bus drivers, gas station attendants, mail carriers, secretaries, waiters, anyone and everyone—all the time. He was of good humor, whereas I live with a deep dose of the "Celtic twilight," that brand of Irish melancholy which tends to judge even realistic optimism as a kind of giddy frivolity. He never stopped believing in the goodness of life and in the merits of sticking it out. I'm not always so sure. But I am sure that making good on life is no easier without him.

He was good natured. And in that he was quite different from his only son. He knew that I was different. And I was more different than he knew. But he never tried to make it otherwise. In this lies his greatest gift to me. His was a life dictated by the restrictions placed upon him as the last of a large immigrant family. Mine is a life that is a testament to his gift: the freedom to pursue an education and to find work that is meaningful and pleasurable.

When I remember my father, it is his generosity that visits me like some gentle ghost. And his pride in me. How deeply he loved us, his family. His friends said that our three names, his wife's, son's, and daughter's, rolled off his lips like names of the Trinity—Peggie, Michael, and Maureen. And then there were his grandsons, Richard and Mikey, who were as much sons to him as was I. Far more like him than me. When I recall his generosity and good will, his pride in me and his care for us all, I am saddened a bit. Saddened because of my own impatience with him, of my tendency to judge, of my hardness in recognizing that he had feelings, real feelings. He was so proud of our accomplishments, yet spoke so little of his own. And, of course, we did not know until after he was gone how many and how great they were.

As Dad grew sicker and sicker I would often wonder if it is harder to lose a loved one through accident or other incident that snatches in an instant, or through the course of long and excruciating suffering. I am as yet unable to answer. Perhaps the question does not even merit being raised. But the question itself enabled me to recognize the enormity of the gift that my father's illness and suffering offered for forgiveness, tenderness, and for the speaking of words that so needed to be said. And for touch, real touch. Sitting by my father's bedside, I held his hand while looking down at those long beautifully sculpted fingers. It was as if they had been manicured by some kindly angel who accompanied the angel of death during those early nocturnal visitations. Ordinarily poised in unselfconscious dignity, they began to dangle at the end of arms on which now hung sacks of sagging flesh.

BETWEEN LIFE AND DEATH

Spring gave way to summer, physicians' answers to complex questions grew fewer and fewer. And more baffling. Dad had to be moved from one hospital to another. He spoke openly that he felt abandoned by the doctors: those he had trusted, to whose hands he had entrusted his life, were now washing their hands of him. They said they didn't know what else to do; they had no more answers. And so the focus of our life and energy shifted from the hospital by the Jersey coast to a major medical center near Philadelphia. The move itself was not easy, and was complicated all the more by the restrictions of insurance companies that more and more of us face as the medical and nursing professions give way to the canons of the "health care industry." We were fortunate to be able to arrange for Dad to be transferred to a hospital in the care of Franciscan sisters, one of whom was a friend of mine. Maureen's sister-in-law was also part of the hospital's administration. We felt relatively secure with the move, and the reputation of Dad's physician added to our sense of hope. Yet another range of tests began, seemingly from the beginning again. And Dad's body continued to waste away under the strain.

It is true that a family can be brought together by a long period of illness and suffering. But emotions and passions run high, disappointment gives way to anger, resentment easily gives way to rage. We were quickly dubbed "the family of the year" at the hospital: one of us was at Dad's side during each waking hour. At the risk of seeming like nags, we made sure that Dad was taken care of by nurses who had many other things to do.

As a steamy summer's June gave way to Philadelphia's sticky July, the results of the gamut of tests were pointing to what was now obvious: a second surgical procedure. It was what we feared most. If Dad had beat such great odds less than six months prior, would he be able to do so again—now ever so much weaker? Chances were slim.

From my sabbatical's hideaway I spoke to Dad on the phone. He knew that traveling back and forth by car was taking a toll. But when he told me of the forthcoming surgery, I asked him to tell me what he wanted of me—clearly and directly. I asked him to forget about what I wanted. I told him that it was very important for me to know what he wanted of me. He told me that he had always been so proud of me and my accomplishments. And he had always told others of my successes. Now, he said, he was beginning to tell others what a great son I was. "Just tell me what you want, Dad." "If you can," he said, "and if its 'doable,' I want you to be here when I open my eyes after the operation." "I'll be there." I left next morning from the quiet of the Kentucky knobs to the city of my birth, and of my father's.

When I arrived at the hospital room the evening before surgery, my sister was by his side. They were so alike, "pals" to one another, Dad would say. They had their secret stories, their private jokes. Maureen had never left home; she had stayed near Mother and Dad after high school. When she married, she lived near the family home. I left home at age eighteen. I had become accustomed to life without father. Following his death, Maureen repeated from time to time: "he was with me, or called me on the phone every day of my life." That evening as I arrived, they were having there last "Hi" and "Bye" as "pals" to one another.

Mother was always the last to say goodnight to him. My sister and I tried to leave a little early so that Mother and Dad could have a minute together, and a goodnight kiss. She was unwavering. Months spent by his side. His hope dimmed, but hers needed to be ebullient. From whence this strength and hope? In her own telling, she is not very religious. But she prayed to God for strength. Above all, she prayed that God would save her "Sweetheart." Even after she left the hospital, she would telephone him upon arrival home to say goodnight. He worried about her driving in the dark.

On the morning of Tuesday 17 July 1990, I awakened with a clear sense of reminiscence: we had been through this before. And so the day of the surgery was a bit like other days: rising early, everyone a bit tense, breakfast thrown into nervous stomachs on the run, the road to the hospital traveled as if on automatic pilot. We arrived to see him haltingly readying himself. Some of the Franciscan sisters who had visited him regularly had already been to see him that morning. The pastoral care worker brought him consecrated bread from the eucharistic celebration. We all partook and prayed with him in communion with the Body of Christ. Nurses were of good cheer, and assurances that all would be well were in ready supply. He was carried away from us on the gurney with his two thumbs up. We did not know until later how courageous an act this was, for only then did we learn that the doctor had told him privately that there was only a slight chance he would survive.

He was wheeled away at 9:00 A.M. We did not see him again until 1:40 the next morning. The surgery began at approximately 11:00 A.M. on Tuesday and lasted the better part of fourteen hours. And the results were not good. Complication led to complication. But where there's life, there's hope. And we did. We went by his side to console him, surrounded by blinking machines, oxygen tanks, ventilators, respirators. And I held his hand, listened to my mother console him, and watched my sister watch him.

Our visits with him throughout that night and the next day were brief. We were not sure if he could see us, but would respond with a squeeze of the hand. It was hard for us to leave his side, hard to stay there, and hardest of all to watch him clinging to something between life and death.

Through the kindness of the Franciscan sisters, we were provided rooms in the convent at the hospital so that we could be near him in his final hours. We had been advised to go to our rooms just after midnight of that long, long Wednesday. We had asked, as on so many occasions, to be notified of any change in his condition. Sometime before dawn the young resident doctor telephoned my room. As the phone rang to wake me from sleep, I felt myself moving to answer it as if in slow motion. I can still feel myself as if mummified in Mother Paracleta's old room, reaching for the phone and echoing "hello?" The resident told me that the time was very near. He asked if we wanted to wait and let my father pass before coming to the intensive care unit. I told him that we would come immediately.

I shall never forget the look on my mother's face and the sound of her voice as she spoke to him as she drew near to what we now knew was his deathbed. I went near his side and took his hand, pledging that I would cling to it until the last, come what may. It was hours, I do not know how many. But we stayed and whispered. I offered my forgiveness, and told him that I knew he forgave me—for everything. I thanked him for the freedom he gave me and for his fidelity to us. I told him that I knew he had done the best he could, and that he was free to go now. In that vast empty space of a hospital room he took my hand and, unable to speak, joined it to my mother's. Then taking my sister's hand, he joined hers to both of ours. We prayed over and over to God, to Mary, and to my father's beloved Saint Joseph, patron of husbands and fathers. Monitors blinked, numbers in flashing red dropped, nurses drew near, Franciscan sisters came from seemingly out of nowhere, and I held his hand. I cannot remember just when, but I know that I gave him to God, and God took him. The doctor came and pronounced him dead. And my mother, still and always the mother of her children, told us it was time to go now. As I went to leave his side, I let my gaze fall once more on those hands. And then, for the first time I noticed that it was his hand holding mine, not mine his.

A TERRIBLE BEAUTY

It would be untrue to say that his funeral and burial were occasions for the celebration of his life. We mourned his loss, and got through those steamy days of late July. Things have not been right with the world for me since. This is a fact I cannot gloss over.

Perhaps it is the enormity of his suffering that has left such a scar on us. He suffered so greatly and complained so little. None of us knew just how sick he was. And if I have only one thing for which to be grateful in all this, it is that I was able to be with him in his darkest hour. Whatever misunderstanding there may have been between us, whatever harsh words exchanged, it was all redeemed in the grace of standing by him at death's door.

In the hours after his death, a dear friend who is a contemplative nun listened as I told the story of those last weeks. I told her how grateful I was that after twenty years away from the family home, I was still able to be with my father in his darkest hour. "But you never left him," Clare said, "not twenty years ago, and not at the time of his death." To have given Dad the gift of simple presence at his time of need seems to me to have been the one thing for which I was created. Love itself.

Many months after his death I remain convinced that he was too young to die. Little consolation comes from odious comparisons with those who have met death even more prematurely. But some consolation does come in the realization that he lived long enough for the self that was my father to be born as if for the first time in the terrible beauty of his last year. Merton's words echo to remind: hell is alienation from the true self for all eternity. In the last full summer of my father's life he admitted he was powerless to control his life, and surrendered his life into God's hands. He stayed there growing weaker and weaker as illness took his life. We watched and waited as something new was born of his vulnerability, and of ours: those qualities of heart that are born in weakness and need, not in strength. In his vulnerability my father gained a self to give, as if for the first time. He wanted to live and to give it to us—again—fresh, renewed, changed. This is what we received of him, and cling to it we would had we half the chance. There was a new husband, father, and grandfather to receive, to take—a man born of a terrible beauty. But God took him. He was no longer ours to have and to hold.

His time with us was precious, indeed golden, and ever so brief for those who loved him. And rare indeed are the likes of him who now lives with God.

It is his generosity that I remember, and the freedom to have a self to give. His power and strength in living and in dying did not obscure the divine vulnerability born in him as he was consigned to love. Would that I have the courage and the strength of my father to give myself to God when comes my darkest hour. And where will be his hand?

12

When Commitments Crumble

"WILL YOU EVER DO SOMETHING WITH YOURSELF?" NAN FOX'S QUESTION
stings still. She ran the shop in the little village of Glen in the
County Donegal, on the north westernmost coast of Ireland.
Mother, Dad, and I were visiting family in High Glen, the place
my maternal grandmother left in the hope of making a better life
in Philadelphia. Mrs. Fox was unrelenting as I, then at the
threshold of midlife, rattled off: "No, not married. No, I'm not a
priest. Not a monk." Nan, ostensibly quite desperate: "Well,
what then?"

While growing up in a predominantly Irish Catholic neighborhood in Philadelphia, it was made absolutely clear that commitments are made in marriage, the vowed religious life, or
priesthood. The Pyramid of Sanctity, drawn on the chalkboard
in the early grades at Most Blessed Sacrament school by nuns
who had made the perfect sacrifice, the "ultimate commitment"
to God, made me aware that there were clearly differentiated
degrees of commitment and holiness: pope, cardinals, and bishops at the top; unmarried, unvowed laypersons at the bottom.

It is a great irony, then, that someone like me should dare speak
of commitment. Because I have none. At least not the kind that
matter to Nan Fox. Or to Sister M. Aloysius Gonzaga, I.H.M., my
second grade teacher. And to others for whom commitment is
made of the strong stuff that keeps you going when the flame

goes out of the desire for a spouse, or when the vision dims and the religious vows must still be observed over the long haul.

I dare to speak of commitment because I have learned something of it by little and by little since those early grades at Most Blessed Sacrament school. My understanding of commitment and commitments—making them, keeping them, breaking them, and reshaping them—has grown gradually and sometimes quite painfully. It is a knowledge gained in the going, insight born of my own struggle with commitment, and given over the years through participation in the lives of others whose commitments are made up of the strong stuff of marriage, vows, and ordained ministry.

LOVE AMIDST THE RUINS

Though I do not have occasion to attend as many as I did in earlier years, I fight back tears each time I go to a wedding. There is something staggering about it all. Two very fragile and wounded people, ever so limited and vulnerable even and especially in their strength and radiance at that moment, promise to lay down their lives for one another, to make their lives one, to be with and for one another in and through life and death. It's this radical self-giving and this promise of fidelity, so audaciously and boldly proclaimed in word and deed, that make of marriage the most conspicuous sacrament of God's abiding presence. To witness the making of such a commitment is altogether breathstopping.

Then again I've been shaken repeatedly as the commitment of spouses, boldly and heartily embraced, has been shattered by unforeseen circumstances. And my naturally melancholic Celtic disposition has been bolstered with reserves of hope in short supply as I have delighted in beholding the fashioning of those same commitments anew, as if for the first time. There has been the pain of loss when the way of life followed in a monastery is "outgrown" and must be set aside to follow something quite unknown but too deeply experienced to be denied. I think often of those devout college classmates whose piety bordered on the cocksure and who, in midlife, have been forced to raise fundamental personal questions, "abandoning" their celibacy to follow the deepest desire of their hearts. And then there are those whose commitment to a spouse seemed to give their life its sole meaning and direction. For them, life was inconceivable without the other. In short order the other was gone because of illness, accident, or old age. "Well, what then?"

Students these days are often gingerly berated about their generation's trouble in making and keeping commitments. I empathize. As a "relic of the 60s" myself, my generation is said to be at the root of the "problem with commitment." In this view the problem was seeded in the 60s when draft dodgers challenged the legitimacy of an undeclared war, thereby stirring questions about loyalty to their own country. The "sexual liberation" caused many to disregard venerated traditions of sexual conduct and mores. Those involved in the civil rights movement clashed with normative patterns of social arrangements among different racial groups. Women's liberation posed a fundamental assault on common perceptions and tightly-held convictions about male-female relations. Sisters in the Roman Catholic Church went from billowy black dresses and foot-length veils to smart suits and closely cropped hair, sometimes in a matter of months. In each of these instances it was their commitment to cherished values and institutions that was in question.

It is a rather facile reading of a complex mystery to suggest that people today have lost the ability to make and keep commitments. There remains a deep and abiding desire for commitment within the human heart. It has ever been thus. But there is at the same time an abiding uncertainty about the reliability of cherished institutions to carry, nurture, and sustain our deepest desires. It is not that people today cannot make commitments. It is rather more a matter of finding or making ways of giving expression to what makes us go on living.

Our commitments are our ways of making good on life. They are ways of expressing, of naming, what and who we live for. In and through our commitments we make a way through life. We give shape to our living. Our commitments express our sense of the highest values we perceive and pursue. And we do this in different forms of life, whether as single persons, spouses, parents, vowed religious, or ordained ministers.

At this juncture of history, making good on life is no small thing. Oftentimes we feel that we are left without a compass while on a journey. We are often unsure of the reliability of the guides in whom our forebears confided. Trusted sources of leadership and guidance in church and society have all too often proven unreliable. The trust of some has been blatantly betrayed. Cherished persons and communities have been tainted with scandal heretofore unimagined. Beacons of light along the way have been snuffed out. There are often very few recognizable signposts along the way. Landmarks have been irreparably tarnished. Many seem to have lost their way altogether. Indeed the metaphor of journey, which implies that there is a point of destination, is itself subject to scrutiny. Is the journey any longer a fitting description of the Christian way?

We stand in the midst of a ruins: cultural, socio-political, and religious. The violence inflicted upon innocent millions, the massacre of whole races of people, the aggression of powerful races against the defenseless, the generations-old conflict in Northern Ireland, the horror of the AIDS epidemic, the banality of senseless crime, the obscenity of gangsta rap music—all these events baffle and disorient. The interruption of our worlds of meaning and order brought on by the shock of events, the "terror of history," calls into question the tightly-knit belief in a divine plan and a provident God. We are overwhelmed with a sense of chaos and are pressed to wonder whether what we do has real potential to make any difference whatsoever. We doubt whether we are able to make the world a better place for the next generation. And if a provident God is not "in charge," calling for a final reckoning, then why spend all the energies of heart, mind, and soul trying to make good on life? Why make good decisions? Why be reasonable? Why act responsibly? Why be loving? Why stay faithful until the end?

The cultural, socio-political and religious ruins in which we stand has impact upon every dimension of life. Whole worlds of meaning and purpose and value are in a shambles. Much of what made the world secure and reliable has been shattered. And so commitment is indeed a more complex thing than in earlier generations. Not because of some moral weakness on the part of people in today's world. But because those very things to which people once committed themselves have come apart at the seams. Where is one's commitment to be placed? The seepage and spillage signal caution. Why stake my life's energies on something so shaky?

In earlier generations God's will for one's life was thought to be discerned through efforts to second guess the secret at the heart of the divine mystery, a plan preordained by a provident God. Today it seems the only place to look is to the interruptions and disorientations, those smack-in-the-face surprises wherein God's grace is discovered between the cracks of a world in collapse. God's will and way for us is not given once for all. We need to make a way amidst the rubble of institutions and worlds of meaning and value that once were home us, but are no longer.

An ancient Peruvian saying reminds:

> Pilgrim, pilgrim, pilgrim,
> There is no way, there is no way, there is no way.
> You make the way, you make the way, you make the way,
> By walking, walking, walking.

WALKING

Their faces shine, radiant amidst the ruins. It is in efforts such as theirs to make good on life in worlds that have come apart at the seams that the deepest mystery of commitment is beheld. It is the way that they have gone on amidst the ruins that illuminates our own halting and half-baked efforts at commitment. In them we glimpse the "costingness" of commitment in a world that offers so few guarantees, the kind of guarantees cherished by Mrs. Fox and Sister Aloysius Gonzaga.

Agnes

As a teenage girl Agnes would rise at 4:00 A.M. to pray in silence before the others awakened and they all went off to school. When the strictly cloistered Carmelite nuns established a monastery in town, she was the first to join, just after high school. And she was their hope for a future. In the first ten years, she was "formed" as a Carmelite nun, and spared no effort to assure that her whole being would be given over to God's transforming grace in this form of life. Her promises were made, her commitment was sealed. Perpetual vows.

While the others were busy with household chores or taking their rest, Agnes would read. Voraciously. In a cloister with only pious and devotional literature, she managed to read everything she could get her hands on, within and from outside the cloister walls. A visiting lecturer heard her questions in response to his presentation and was staggered by her insight. He arranged for scholarships, first to Harvard, then to Stanford. Her superior let her undertake studies with the hope of using her talents in the formation of future nuns. Her commitment to a sustained life of prayer was unwavering throughout her time away. As was her heart's desire to read and to learn. So abiding was the latter that she found it impossible to remain within the cloister upon returning. She had to remain true to her deepest call, her vocation.

She is a Carmelite nun in perpetuity, and two dimensions of her life are inseparable: the "intellectual" and the "contemplative." These are commitments made in her effort to make good on life. They are names of that for which she lives. But the institution in which she has vowed her life cannot accommodate both these desires, both commitments within its walls. She has been forced to choose between them, and cannot. To do so would be to do violence to herself, to betray what and whom she lives for. And so she stands amidst the ruins of a form of life to which she gave herself without reserve and with boundless confidence, but which now has no space within which she can live out her call. And so she goes on. She lives alone, forfeiting the profit of recognition in order to do what needs to be done. Making a way where there had been none before. Given to God by vow, perpetually.

Bernie

"I've just change my mind." This was the beginning. Or were there earlier signs? Bernie thought that they had agreed that marriage was until death. How can she just change her mind? But there was more to learn as the truth was brought to light. Gloria had fallen in love with a woman. She didn't want to be married anymore. Bernie and Gloria were the proverbial couple atop the wedding cake. A perfect match, a handsome couple. But something had gone amuck. Their lives were a shambles. She had to follow another way, make good on life in a way that has a different name than marriage. As did he. After years of suffering in the dark abyss of severe depression, he was able to find the hidden reserves of hope stirred up by someone to whom he could give his whole heart and soul, again. He was given something to live for once more. Someone. Together they live in the country of marriage, but their church will not name it so. And so they make a way in a church that will not recognize remarriage between divorced persons, and holds as sacred and indissoluble Bernie's marriage to a woman who loves women. To maintain his commitment to his beloved, Bernie is forced outside the very church that constitutes so much of the world of meaning and value in which he dwells. He cannot but be committed to that church and to his beloved. He has risen from the rubble, and stands as a beacon to countless others whose lives are shattered by love's dying. He is making good on life through his commitment to her, in a church that calls their union adulterous.

Judy

It happens often enough. A friendly conversation gives way to a heart's deepest revelation. I hadn't known Judy long. She was troubled because he does not support her in her efforts at self-enrichment through education. "He thinks I should be home all the time. Meals on the table promptly. Kids chauffeured to ballet, tennis, and soccer. He doesn't like it when I'm not home in the evenings." I waited for the other shoe to drop. "What happens in the evenings?" She shied: "Not too much." I blurted: "Does he drink?" "Yeah." "How often?" "Every night." "How much?" "A bottle." "A bottle of beer?" "No, a bottle of whiskey." I knew the other shoe would slam as it hit. "A pint?" She demonstrated by spread fingers: "No, what do you call those things, is it a liter? Or a quart? Or a fifth?" She seemed surprised that I judged that an inordinate amount, no matter how great his tolerance might be because of weight and brawn. She called him a good husband and father, a great provider, though the children don't like to see him "like that." And they don't like to be alone with him. She talked about not leaving him for the sake of the children.

Their love has grown cold. He lives to drink, quietly and at home. She lives for the children, and tries to "better" herself. They no longer live with and for one another, not really. She is trying to make good on life, and he shows signs of being defeated by it. He stands amidst a ruins of one sort. She stands in the rubble of a marriage that she hopes to rebuild by convincing him that he drinks too much. Should she break through, there will be no rebuilding. They will need to fashion new foundations, make a new way. They will have to see one another as if for the first time, shining in a shambles of their own making.

Sean

Sean lives in the woods in Oregon. He has been something of a mystery to his family. He was in the first group of university students I taught in Los Angeles a dozen years ago. Because of his native intelligence he quickly mastered the principles of accounting, and this assured him a post with one of the major firms in Los Angeles upon graduation. He did figures for a year. His parents had reason to be proud. But Sean was not happy. There was something deeper. He thought it might be a call to the priesthood. But it is deeper still than that. He now says that his vocation may be to seek his whole life long. And his commitment is to that. He lives to seek. That's what gives shape to his life. I share in his search to some degree. And in his pain. He is all too aware that he could have been quite stable and secure had he put to use his very practical accounting skills. Instead he lives in the woods, teaches English for a pittance to migrant workers, hikes on hidden trails in the wilds of the Pacific Northwest and thinks dangerous thoughts put into his head by an upstart professor of theology and spirituality in Los Angeles. He has no clear idea where he is going. But he has given his life to something. To Someone. With his whole heart.

Brendan

Paul preaches on the occasion of Brendan's profession of vows. He speaks the obvious. A word that no one in the monastery is willing to hear. The monastic life at this abbey is dying. Most of the brothers are grey-headed. Many are in the infirmary, and have been for quite a few years. The sheep have just been sold because there are not enough hands to keep and care for them. The monks are exhausted with the work once done by nearly twice as many of them. There are few recruits. They come. Most go. Some, like Brendan, stay. And on an occasion such as this he pledges his life to God in this monastery, with these brothers, until death. In former days, all present for such an occasion knew that the word "death" referred to that of the brother professing vows. But Brendan wonders whether the monastery will die before he does. How then to keep the vow to live in this house with these brothers until he dies? The echoes in the cloister corridor remind him that this house, once filled to the brim with vigorous and zealous young monks, is experiencing something of an emptying, a *kenosis*, Christ's self-emptying. His commitment is to give himself to that, fully, completely, without reserve; to empty himself, even and especially of the desire for the guarantee that he will live and die in this house amidst these brothers. He is to make his way in life through participation in the mystery of the *kenosis* of Christ. He knows that this is his call, his way to make good on life.

Mary Ann

Mary Ann has long been aware that her community is dying. It has been so for most of her life. Bit by bit cherished customs and traditions have been set aside. It seems that nothing of the old way is left. But she continues to walk with the community. "What would you do if the community ceased to exist?" was my query. As if she had been quizzed like this before, she replied without a second thought: "I'd continue to live as I have lived all these years." Her commitments have shaped her life in such a way that they are who she is. She cannot undo her commitments any more easily than she can undo herself. But none of what drew her to the community, carried her in the earlier days, sustained her in her life-long desire to be of service, remains. The community that she embraced and that enfolded her in security and stability continues to collapse. And she continues to make a way, finding on the way that she has been true all along to that which, to those whom, to the One for whom, she has given her life.

ENTRUSTING

Rising from the rubble of the cultural and religious ruins in which we live, lives such as these lives bespeak the deepest meanings of commitment. They serve to correct our rather rigid and static, indeed legalistic notions of this complex mystery. If indeed we live in a "litigious" society, its ethos has impacted our understanding of commitment in no small way. Often thought of in terms of a permanent and irrevocable *obligation* through thick and thin, commitment may more properly be understood by considering the roots of the term. This leads to an appreciation of commitment as *entrusting*. From the roots of the term, commitment connotes engagement with something or someone. Its most literal significance is to send or to put together, but even this conveys the sense of joining or undertaking at risk.

In Christian perspective, commitment implies joining oneself to, entrusting oneself to, engaging one's whole heart and mind and soul with the person of Jesus in the presence and by the power of the Spirit. This Jesus is Alpha and Omega, beginning and end, point of origin and point of arrival. But he is the Way. And it is for all who live by the Holy Spirit to make a way with him. To make a way with Jesus, to make good on life with, through, and in him, entails a way of relinquishing guarantees, the sort of which he himself had so few, not even a sure place to lay his head. It ineluctably involves creating a way of life on the road of downward mobility, walking with the wounded and weak, the last and the least, with whom Jesus lived and for whom and with whom he gave his life. Christian commitment requires risking security and stability so that his way is the only way in which we place our trust. It demands that we make him and what he lived and died for our God.

Standing in the midst of the ruins, we are staggered by the interruptions, the discontinuities, the disorientation brought on by our failed plans, the force of circumstances beyond our control, our seeming inability to make a difference for the better. But this also presents us with the opportunity to realize that the God of the Hebrew and Christian Scriptures is not first and foremost a God of order and providence. God is, rather, the One whose word is a promise of presence. But there are no guarantees as to how this presence will abide. This God has promised to be active in history and present to creation. But we want more certainty than that, the sort no doubt that prompted Moses to take his staff and slam it against that rock (Exodus 17:1-7). And the followers of Jesus to demand signs. Small consolation in the sign of Jonah for those who want sure guarantees (Matthew 12:38-40). Indeed Jesus interrupted rather than fulfilled conventional certainties about God's plan of salvation for the chosen people. The promises offered by the Christ flew in the face of tightly held expectations. Indeed his very coming and cross were interruptions, discontinuities with all that was judged to be God's way and work in the world.

Even and especially amidst the ruins we can be buoyed up by the conviction that in the discontinuities and interruptions of our lives, precisely in the midst of the movements and events of our lives that boggle and baffle, God's presence abides. This abiding presence inevitably calls to vigorous engagement. It entails movement toward something or someone. It requires entrusting ourselves to a Way, sometimes making a way where none has been made before us. It means participating in a way of life grounded in the knowledge that beyond or beneath our specific commitments in the single life, marriage, parenting, vowed religious life, or the ordained ministry, there is one thing we desire; One whose beating heart our hearts long to listen to long and lovingly.

In the collapse of worlds of meaning and value, in the insecurity and uncertainty that riddles personal and communal life, there is room to make a way. But we are to make a way through the cracks, amidst the rubble and the ruins of a life, in a world sorely disheartened by the disorientation brought on by the great disparity between events and our expectations of what might have been. Like Mary and the Beloved Disciple at the foot of the cross. We are swathed in the consoling hope that in giving ourselves in and through this mystery, God comes.

WIDENING
WORSHIP

13

Widening Contexts of
Sacramental Worship

WHEN CONSIDERING WHAT IS DISTINCTIVE ABOUT CATHOLICISM OR THE
Roman Catholic Church, people of all ages often think of the
pope, papal infallibility, the role of the Virgin Mary, teachings
about birth control and abortion, or the role of priests and nuns.
Whatever importance these may have in Catholic doctrine and
life, they must be seen in view of a much larger picture. In this
larger view, there is specific focus on the disclosure or manifestation of God's grace, the presence of God and the transformation this brings about, in and through a community of faith and
sacramental worship: the church.

For nearly a dozen years, I have worked exclusively within
Roman Catholic ecclesial and academic circles. In recent years I
have had more frequent occasion to lecture in wider academic
and ecclesial contexts. In my judgment it is fair to say that in the
traditions of Protestantism, greater attention is given to the
importance of the word in the Scriptures and to personal belief
in the salvation that comes through faith in Jesus Christ. This
priority of faith in the word both proclaimed and heard is clearly
expressed in the gatherings for prayer and worship within these
traditions. By contrast, in addition to the attention given to the
proclamation and hearing of the word, the Roman Catholic
tradition emphasizes the singular importance of sacramental life
as expressing the fidelity between God and humanity.

The line should not be drawn too sharply here. Whether the emphasis is on word or sacrament, members of different Christian traditions would agree that worship plays a crucial role in fostering the life of Christian faith and practice. And without doubt Christians of various denominations would agree that what is said and done in a community's worship must have bearing on the way believers live their lives from day to day. What is said and done in word and worship must bear fruit in the wider contexts of Christian living. Said otherwise, when worship is taken seriously there are practical implications.

There is common ground here between and among various Christian traditions.[1] Whatever differences may exist in terms of their particular "beliefs," Christians of different traditions would be hard pressed to disagree with the point that there is a necessary connection between what is said and done "in church" and in the living of everyday life. Taking it a step further, this conviction is not just shared by Christians. People of different faiths, i.e., those other than Christian, would not quibble over the point that their prayer and worship must bear fruit in the way they live the rest of their lives. But just how this is to be done is a far more complex question. My own approach is rooted in the conviction that there are always socio-political ramifications of Christian worship, indeed that worship itself is a socio-political act. No doubt some will find serious objections to this claim.

My purpose here is to explore the sacraments of Roman Catholic Church, attentive to contemporary people in parishes in North America who strive to integrate what happens in church with what happens in the home, at work, and in political life. Such integration is even concerned with the question of how the sacraments bear upon human relationships of the most intimate kind, and how human intimacy, including the sexual, is expressed sacramentally. I am persuaded that one of the more pressing questions in the hearts of the majority of people active in the life of the churches is: how do I integrate the actual experience of sacramental life in the parish setting with the demands of Christian living day by day, week by week? Ordinary laypersons constantly feel the rub between worship and practice, and the locus for the conflict is quite often the pastoral context within which they worship. They are acutely aware that there are practical implications involved in sacramental worship, and earnestly seek to put them into practice.

My aim is to chart a sacramental world that ordinary Catholics might share, in which all activity, even the most mundane, is—at least potentially—sacramental. The purpose is to assist those who are earnestly striving to integrate the sacraments with Christian living. By first looking to the sacramental life of the church we can aim at cultivating a deeper appreciation of its pastoral implications. It is my hope that in taking these implications to heart, a contribution will be made to those who take seriously the lifelong task of being and becoming Christian. Strategies for the implementation of these practical implications will need to be developed in light of different cultural contexts, and in view of shifting modes of being and perceiving at this juncture of modernity and postmodernity.

Be it noted that my aim is not to engage in moral exhortation. The intention is not to argue that faithful churchgoers should or must practice what they preach (and/or what they have preached to them) in word and worship. The assumption is that those who celebrate God's presence in word and worship do not need strident exhortation. Rather, the need is for guidance in the task of living ever more authentic Christian lives in the wider contexts within which everyday life is lived.

Before moving on to an exploration of the practical implications of sacramental worship, it is necessary to offer a description of a sacramental worldview as a context for understanding sacrament and sacramentality. Grace, sign, symbol, and sacrament will then be described. A treatment of the seven sacraments attentive to their practical implications will then be offered. In addition to the word in Scripture, the teachings of the church and its tradition, and the role of an informed and formed conscience, these practical dimensions provide perspective on how the Christian is to live his or her life in relation with another, others, and God.

SOAKED IN GRACE: A SACRAMENTAL WORLDVIEW

Faith and religion are often understood as matters of personal taste, based on individual, private religious experience, and lived out in a "one-to-one" relationship with God. By contrast, it may seem a bit strange to speak of one's relationship with God as something that includes every dimension of life. This perception is rooted in a sacramental worldview. It rests on the faith that despite the vast dissimilarity between God and the world, God's presence is communicated in and to the world. In this view, human life, words, actions, objects, and events have the capacity to disclose or manifest the very presence and activity of the invisible God. Grace, the very life of God, is present in and to the world bringing forth the transformation of human life and world. All created reality exists and is empowered by the life and breath of God.[2] Thus everything that exists is, at least potentially, sacramental. Because the presence of God is active in history and present to creation, all human life, activity, and speech, as well as events and history, are capable of disclosing the presence and action of God whose very nature is to express and communicate love in and through the world. The central Christian insight that God is Love (1 John 4:8) is known only in and through the way that God is for us in and through human life, the world, and history.[3]

More specifically, in this sacramental worldview there is a compatibility between human nature and God's grace. Human nature, marred by evil and sin, is not completely and irrevocably destroyed by them. The transformation brought about through grace perfects the goodness of what has been created by God. Such a view is consonant with Aquinas's view, put rather concisely as "grace perfects nature." Taking this a step further, all creation, nonhuman as well as human life, is the locus for the presence of God and the transformation this brings about.[4]

None of this implies that God and humans are the same. Nor does it suggest that human beings and their activities are divine, or that they become God in the process of transformation by grace. An important distinction needs to be made here between pantheism and panentheism. I am persuaded that the latter is compatible with a Catholic sacramental worldview. Indeed, in my judgment, panentheism (particularly as expressed in some mature forms of process theology) is modernity's most significant achievement in the ongoing effort to "name" the Christian understanding that God is Love.

In recognizing the points of connection in the God-world relation, it must be accepted that whatever region of likeness there may be between God and creation, there is at the same time a region of unlikeness wherein our words fail because of the recognition of the distance between ourselves and God.

SACRAMENT AND SACRAMENTALITY

Sacramental life is, on one hand, an expression of God's gracious offer. It is at the same time an expression of the human desire to be in relation to God. This desire is expressed in prayer, which may be described as the conscious striving to be in relation with God, and to surrender to God's coming, often in startling, unexpected, indeed disruptive events and persons. For Christians, the mystery that believers call God comes in the person of Jesus of Nazareth. More specifically, the cross and resurrection of Jesus disclose the mystery of the One whom Christians name Love, interrupting and unsettling tightly-knit understandings of the divine.

Appreciating the importance of sacrament entails recognizing that it is possible for human beings to express and communicate their response and relation to the invisible and eternally gracious God disclosed in the unique, particular, historical person, Jesus of Nazareth. In this view God's grace has been and remains available throughout all creation and history. But the mystery of God's love which inheres at the heart of all creation has become explicit in Jesus—God's grace made flesh. From this Christian perspective God's grace is, thus, ineluctably incarnational and sacramental.

Christian sacrament is, at the same time, a human response to the divine initiative in Christ. This response is possible, of course, only because God has first initiated a relationship with Christians in and through the person of Jesus. In this sense, then, Jesus is for Christians the first and foremost sacrament of God. It is in Jesus that the human and the divine meet. That is to say that in Christ's life, ministry, words and work, the invisible, eternal God is disclosed, revealed, or made visible and tangible. And when the followers of Jesus express and communicate their desire to be in relationship with God, they do so through, with, and in Christ. Their communication with God is made possible in and through the words, actions, objects, and events central to his life, such as the breaking, blessing, and sharing of bread and wine, the anointing with oil, the laying on of hands. And beyond the church's central actions that constitute the seven sacraments, there are the actions of washing the feet of those who are "less," forgiving and loving even enemies, giving alms and healing— all of which may indeed be understood as sacramental in the wider sense of the term.

The word and work, meaning and message of Jesus did not end at the time of his death. Those who followed him and believed that God's fullness was revealed in his life and ministry, claimed that God continued to come in the person of Jesus even beyond his death. Those who put their faith in him claimed that he appeared to them on the third day. The Christian tradition rests on this Easter proclamation. The gracious mystery disclosed in the person of Jesus continues to come and live in the midst of those who gather in faith and worship in his memory. And it is in their words, their actions, and their communal life that the presence and activity of the gracious mystery continues to come. The life and communal activities of the disciples gathered in Christ's name becomes the locus of expression and communication with God in Christ. Thus, in addition to the life of Christ, the church itself in its shared life and practice is a sacrament of God. For in its remembrance of Christ, its commitment to his word and work, its pursuit of Christ's meaning and message of self-sacrificial love in light of changed circumstances and shifting modes of perceiving and being, the followers of Jesus who constitute the church manifest the continuing coming of the gracious mystery in human life, history, and the world.

As the life of the church continued beyond the period of its origins, as its members became more and more numerous, and as those members took on the task of living the meaning and message of Jesus in diverse cultures, the relationship of the Christian people to God came to be expressed in ways less and less similar to the religious practices of earlier times. Said another way, practices that carried over to Christianity from Judaism were set aside if judged to be out of step with the meaning and message of Jesus. Determining which practices were in accord with the mind of Christ was not an easy matter. Clarity on which writings constituted the authentic Christian Scriptures, as well as what were the essential Christian practices, took a long time in coming. But over the course of Christian history, the church's sacraments have emerged as those communal ritual activities which are most central to the task of being and becoming Christian. In the sacraments of the church, then, we find another, more particular expression of sacramentality. For it is in these seven communal ritual actions of the church that the Christian community expresses and receives its identity as the Body of Christ.

Thus, within this Christian sacramental worldview there are several dimensions.[5] First, Christ is the sacrament of God. In Jesus the Christ, in his word and work, indeed in his person, the ultimate mystery that believers name God is manifested in an explicit, definitive, and irrevocable way. Second, following the death of Jesus, his disciples gathered in his memory. In their common life of faith and worship, in their commitment to service in self-sacrificial love in his memory, God continues to come. That is to say, the church is sacrament of Christ. As the Body of Christ, the church constitutes the sacramental presence of Christ in and to the world. Third, in those communal ritual activities judged to be central to the task of being and becoming Christian, the church expresses its relationship with God in Christ. In word and sacrament, preeminently in the eucharist, the church celebrates the mystery of God's self-communication in the life, death, and resurrection of Jesus. The sacraments of the church, then, express the sacramentality of Christ and church. Finally, because the presence of God is expressed in and through the world, all human life, activity, events and history, as well as nonhuman life, constitute the wider contexts wherein God's presence may be discerned. God's grace, the presence and activity of God and the transformation of life which this brings about, is loose in the world.

THE LANGUAGE OF SACRAMENT
AND SACRAMENTALITY

At this juncture it may be useful to offer a brief description of some of the key terms in discourse about sacraments: grace, sign, symbol, and sacrament.

A crucial term in the language of sacraments is "grace." For many, grace is a quantitative reality—an invisible object or thing "poured into" human beings. We get it if we go to church on

Sundays; we have some taken away if we don't. Properly understood, grace is God's own free and personal self-communication to creatures. From this perspective we can say that sacraments are not so much vehicles for transferring grace as they are unique and particular expressions of God's gift of self and the transformation of human life which occurs in response to God's self-communication.

In defining sign, symbol, and sacrament, we come to a crucial point in our exploration. Some readers may be familiar with an earlier definition of sacrament as an outward sign (of inward grace) instituted by Christ to give grace. Though there are distinct advantages to the clarity provided by this definition, contemporary studies persuasively demonstrate the advantages of understanding sacraments as symbolic realities.[6] "Symbol" here does not refer to something that is not really real, for example, when people refer to a gesture that is "merely symbolic," or to the power of a king or queen that is "only symbolic." Symbol is a rich and complex reality, deeper than sign.

A sign is an action, gesture, word, or object used to communicate precise information, or clear instruction about how to function in the world. The meanings of signs are clear and precise, or at least they are intended to be so. Stop signs mean "don't go!" There is little room for interpretation here. Street signs are meant to provide motorists and pedestrians with a sense of direction. The information they provide, i.e., that the right of way belongs to the *other* traffic, should be clear and direct so as to avoid confusion and to serve the function of helping people find their way without accident or injury.

On the other hand, symbols are words, gestures, activities, and objects that communicate meaning and value. Symbols help bring about interpersonal communication and communion. Giving a rose never means just one thing. Nor does a handshake. Shaking hands may be a gesture of reconciliation, it may be an expression of greeting or farewell, it might be the activity that seals an agreement between two parties. An invitation to dinner may be the first step in courtship, it may be the occasion to begin or settle a business deal, or it might be the activity whereby old friendships are renewed. Symbols differ from signs in that the latter have to do with the world of function and information, whereas the former have to do with the world of meaning and value. The difference is not always as clear as it may seem, but it may be useful to keep this distinction to the fore.

Symbol (Greek: *sym-ballein*, "to throw together") invites to participation in deeper realities. It beckons to mystery. Symbols are objects, gestures, and activities that

> belong within a given cultural context, bear of repetition without being rigid stereotypes, meet affective needs of meaning and belonging, express group identity, even though some are more immediately related to the group and others to the individual, and are subject to the changes that come with the evolution of time, moving perspectives and changing values.[7]

With this understanding in mind, we can speak of Christian symbols, whether it be the breaking of bread and the blessing of a cup, pouring or immersing in water, lighting and carrying candles, all as concrete objects, activities, gestures, and words that express the meaning and the truth of the Christian community as the Body of Christ, by means of which the community receives and expresses its identity as the Body of Christ.

Here it must be remembered that Christian symbols are like other symbols in that their meanings are rich and multilayered.

> Symbols, being roomy, allow many different people to put them on, so to speak, in different ways. Signs do not. Signs are unambiguous because they exist to give precise information. Symbols coax one into a swamp of meaning and require one to frolic in it. Symbol is rarely found among the inactive, the obtuse, the confused, or the dull. Signs are to symbols what infancy is to adulthood, what stem is to flower, and the flowering of maturity takes time.[8]

Symbols never have just one meaning. For example, in baptism, the pouring of water over the head or, better, the immersion of an infant or adult into a pool of water "In the name of the Father, and of the Son, and of the Holy Spirit" communicates the forgiveness of sin, but it also signifies incorporation into the Body of Christ, commitment to participation in a community's way of life, and ongoing purification and enlightenment by the word and work of Christ. But its meaning does not stop there.[9]

DEFINING SACRAMENT

In light of this understanding of grace, sign, and symbol, is it possible to provide a straightforward definition of sacrament? Given that symbols are understood as objects, activities, gestures, and words that are used to bring about interpersonal communication and communion, and given that they invite fuller participation in the ultimate meanings and highest values that human beings perceive and pursue, sacraments may be defined as symbols of God's presence in human life, history, world, and church. To say that they are instituted by Christ is to recognize that these activities, objects, gestures, and words are actions of the church rooted or grounded in the meaning and message, the word and the work of Jesus.

The sacramental life of the church has changed and grown in the course of Christian history. Like any process of growth, mistakes have been made, and wrong turns have been taken. And sometimes it is fitting to ask whether this sacramental practice or that, past or present, adequately expresses the church's attempt to express and receive its identity as Body of Christ, to live in accord with the meaning and message, word and work, of Jesus. Whatever the answer to this question, it has usually been and remains the case that Christian people understand the sacraments as manifestations of grace, central to the task of participating more fully in the Paschal Mystery of Christ in and through the church.

SACRAMENT AND WIDER CONTEXTS

From the perspective of a sacramental worldview, the seven sacraments are not isolated moments that can be restricted to certain times and places, e.g., in the church on Sunday. Both the New Testament and the documents of Vatican II, as well as the history of sacrament and worship, emphasize the strong connection between liturgy and life, sacrament and living. What believers perceive and pursue as the highest values and purposes in human life, they express in worship. Sacramental celebration is an expression of how Christians hope to live their lives. That is to say that in the sacraments of the church, Christians can discern practical implications, contours of a vision of how we are to conduct ourselves in the wider spheres of life. Clues to the ways in which Christians are to live in relation to another, others, and God are found in the Scriptures and in the traditions of the different Christian communities. Indications are found in the teachings of the church. For Roman Catholics, the magisterium plays a central role, to be sure. An informed, formed conscience is a vital dimension in the quest for living an ethical, or moral life. But for those whose tradition is marked by a strong sacramental worldview, what is said and done in sacramental worship expresses the deepest convictions of a people regarding how they are to live in relationship with others and God.[10]

INCORPORATION INTO THE BODY: BAPTISM AND CONFIRMATION

Baptism, confirmation, and eucharist are the sacraments by which a person is incorporated or initiated into a community of faith and worship. To be baptized in Christ's name is to be incorporated into a body of persons who share their lives in a community through participation in the dying and rising of Christ. This demands ongoing conversion in Christ through participation in the life and mission of the church, through sharing in its teaching, and through the ongoing struggle to live by and to promote its values. In baptism, water and word signify that this infant, child, or adult has gone down into the tomb with Christ and has been raised with him to a new way of life. The baptized are a new creation, dead to sin and alive in the light and life of Christ Jesus. Those who are baptized become members of Christ's Body, animated by the Spirit, participating in the life and mission of the church, and living in light of the word and work of Jesus. Incorporation into Christ's Body, the church, is a response in faith to Christ's death, and a commitment to the life of Christian discipleship, taking up the task of ongoing transformation of self and world by the grace of God in Christ.

In confirmation we are strengthened and sealed in the Spirit given in the water and words of baptism. The anointing with chrism, ordinarily by the bishop, is a marking or signing with the Spirit which strengthens and empowers the Christian to live a life of peace, patience, love, joy, gentleness, humility—some of the hallmarks of the Christian life (Galatians 5). In confirmation the commitment to ongoing conversion to deeper life in Christ is sealed and strengthened. And it is in the celebration of the eucharist that commitment to ongoing conversion in Christ is expressed and strengthened regularly and repeatedly. In this sense, in addition to baptism and confirmation, we may speak of the eucharist as a sacrament of initiation insofar as in its celebration we are initiated ever more fully, week by week, or day by day, into the fullness of the Paschal Mystery.

Practical Dimensions

In the sacrament of baptism we are initiated into a *covenant* through incorporation into Christ's death and resurrection. Sharing in Christ's dying and rising calls for a new way of life based on the covenant in his blood and motivated by his preaching and teaching, particularly the beatitudes. This way of living is rooted in *love* and *fidelity*, rather than law or obligation. It is shaped by a sense of *responsibility* to another, others, and God rather than a preoccupation with obligations and requirements. Living this way is characterized by a sense of responsibility that arises from membership in God's people through baptism. Such a way of life is grounded in relationship to others in community, and to Christ the Lord. In this perspective Christian life entails the ongoing task of viewing our actions, and those of others, in light of the lordship of Jesus Christ so that the ongoing conversion in Christ begun in baptism may be completed. Everything and everyone is to be seen in light of this lordship and in view of the transforming power of Christ's Spirit.

The anointing with chrism is the central act in the sacrament of confirmation. In this action and in the words that accompany it, the individual and the whole community recognize and submit to the attraction and leading of the Spirit, and invoke the Spirit's increase. Confirmation is not primarily the sacrament of choice or commitment, as is often thought. It signals *abandonment* and *submission to the power of the Spirit* and the *empowerment* that results from the Spirit's presence. One abandoned to the sway and power of the Spirit is led to live according to the Spirit, not according to the flesh. Those empowered by life in Christ Jesus and the Spirit are known by their fruits. Their lives are marked by peace, patience, kindness, long-suffering, gentleness, faithfulness, single-hearted love of God and neighbor. The absence of the Spirit is recognized in hatred, jealousy, envy, greed, lust, and despair (see Galatians 5)

SACRAMENT OF THE BODY: EUCHARIST

In the celebration of the eucharist Christ is present to the community in the memorial of his death.[11] In the breaking of the bread and the blessing of the cup, the Christian community expresses and receives its identity as the Body of Christ. At the table of the Lord the faithful gather to hear the story of Jesus' life, ministry, passion, death, and resurrection. It is to this table, to the fullness of Christ's mysteries celebrated there in word and sacrament, that baptism and confirmation lead. And it is in their relationship to the sacrament of the eucharist that the other sacraments—reconciliation, anointing of the sick and dying, marriage, and ministry—are properly understood. Consequently, the eucharistic liturgy is to be understood as the source and summit of Christian sacramental life (SC 10). The eucharist is the center of Christian sacramental life in that the other sacraments derive their meaning in relationship to it, and have their purpose in drawing Christians more fully into its celebration. It differs from the other sacraments in that it is the gathering and celebration of the Body of Christ, the celebration of Christ's presence to the community in the memorial of his death, the center where the church comes to full expression. In the eucharist the Christian community finds the focal point which brings together in common expression of faith and celebration all the symbols that belong to the Paschal Mystery of Christ in the church.

In proclaiming and hearing the word, and in breaking the bread and blessing the cup, Christ's presence is discerned. Central to an understanding of the eucharist is that in the simple gifts of bread and wine, the church celebrates a meal of thanksgiving. In this simple meal God's presence and activity in Christ are remembered and proclaimed as present and as an offering of hope for the future. This is a meal in which Christians celebrate their communion with God in Christ and with one another, especially the poor and the weak, the oppressed and the alienated, those at the margins of social and religious institutions.

These are the ones who are to be first in the kingdom of God, about which Jesus preached and for which he died.

Practical Dimensions

As the central expression of the church's call and commitment to *communion* and *justice*, the eucharist is the heart of a Christian way of life. Divisions and failure to share signal an inability to discern the Body of the Lord. Unwillingness to share in the wider regions of life as well as in the eucharist, self-preoccupation, self-absorption, and self-indulgence all constitute a failure to discern God's presence which is remembered and hoped for in the breaking of the bread and the blessing of the cup. Those who celebrate Christ's presence to the community in the memorial of his death commit themselves again and again to live in accord with the covenant through which they are members in God's people: to live according to the Spirit and not according to the flesh (Romans 8).

This willingness of Christians to share has implications for life with others beyond those gathered at the table. It pertains to all who constitute the human family, with particular attention to the poor and wounded—those whom Jesus promised will hold pride of place in the reign of God which is anticipated in the eucharistic meal. As participation in a ritual meal of communion and justice, the eucharist does not permit distinction of persons: divisions, separations, and distinctions of persons based on race, class, sex, handicap, status, and rank are decried; a willingness is expressed to work toward overcoming such divisions, factions, and distinctions so that Christ may be all in all (Galatians 3:27-28). To celebrate the eucharist implies that we live our lives motivated by a vision of communion and justice. To break bread and bless the cup is to live in the memory of Christ's passion and death, to have died with him. To have died with Christ is to live for God and for the coming of God's reign wherein the power of love prevails over all evil.

FORGIVENESS AND HEALING OF THE BODY: PENANCE AND ANOINTING

The communion celebrated in the sacrament of the Body of Christ, the eucharist, is at once God's gracious offer and human response. As such, it may be likened to a gift offered and accepted. As with any gift worthy of the name, it cannot be taken for granted and must be treated with great care. The life in Christ Jesus celebrated in the sacraments of initiation, and participated in ever more fully in the eucharist, is often diminished by neglect or abuse of the gift of grace. The lives of individuals and communities are often scarred and broken by the presence of evil, sin, and suffering. The sacrament of penance expresses God's unrestricted mercy and forgiveness. It is an offer extended to both individuals and communities in light of the need for ongoing conversion in Christ, even and especially when the presence of evil and sin bring about a severe break in our relationship with God, our own deepest selves, and the community of the church. The sacrament of penance from a contemporary view need not be understood as a repayment for offenses committed. It is, rather, a celebration in praise of God's mercy which brings about healing, conversion and reconciliation with God, conscience, and community, no matter how grave the wrong, or how many or serious our offenses.[12]

The sacrament of anointing and pastoral care of the sick and dying is an expression of Christ's continuing ministry of care, comfort, and healing necessitated by the effects of evil and sin in the world. It manifests the presence and action of Christ in the church in the face of human sickness, suffering, dying, and death. Anointing the sick and dying with blessed oil is intended to offer support to the seriously ill, the aged, or the dying, in the hope of gaining strength, consolation, and healing in mind and body. And this strength, consolation and healing are to be hoped for even and especially when serious illness leads to death. Pastoral care and anointing of the sick and dying are the sacramental expressions of the church's larger ministry of healing in and through its struggle against sickness, suffering, and depersonalization.

Practical Dimensions

In celebrating the sacrament of penance, Christians express a distinctive view of reality. They articulate their intention to live within the perspective of God's *mercy* and *forgiveness*. The lordship of Christ and the empowerment of the Holy Spirit are the criteria by which judgments and decisions are made. Here, *com-*

passion is the hallmark of Christian life. Judgments about our own lives and the lives of others are made in light of a consciousness of sin and grace in the events of human life. As a result, the lives of the rejected and the scorned, the outcast and the forgotten, those judged to be worthless and useless by the criteria of efficiency, productivity, and propriety, are to be seen from the perspective of God's mercy and forgiveness. In light of the consciousness of sin and grace, the wounded, the weak, the little, the fragile, and the poor are viewed as disclosing God's grace and mercy which touches us in the greatness of our need. Those who respond to God's love and attraction in the heart of the repentant sinner, in the little, the forgotten, and the weak become the clearest signs of God's reconciling love in our world. Life itself becomes an echo of the testament of Paul: in our weakness is God's strength (2 Corinthians 12:9-10).

Through the sacrament of anointing the Christian community lives in remembrance of Christ's *healing* ministry. As such, Christians are called upon to *care* for the sick and dying, to struggle against illness, suffering, and depersonalization. In celebrating the sacrament of anointing of the sick and dying, the community expresses a new perspective on suffering, illness, and death that enables Christians to live in the hope and with the confidence that nothing escapes the grasp of God's healing and compassion in Jesus Christ.

BEING AND BUILDING THE BODY: MARRIAGE, MINISTRIES, ORDERS

Both marriage and holy orders are sacraments that express the importance of self-sacrificial love, fidelity, and service in the church. In the sacrament of marriage two people commit themselves to live a life of self-sacrificial love and fidelity to one another until death. This commitment is to be lived out first and foremost with respect to the life of the spouse, and includes whatever children may be born of their union. But there are wider implications here. In Christian marriage the couple responds to the call to live a life of inclusive communion. And this is sacramentalized *in* the church, *before* the church and *for* the church. Christian marriage is thus a way of being and building the Body of Christ. In their pledge of lifelong fidelity, in the sexual union of their flesh, in the new life born of their intimacy and ecstasy, the couple becomes ever more fully a sacrament of the self-sacrificial love of Christ for those to whom he gave, or laid down, his life.

Ministry is service for the building up of the Body of Christ, the church. All the baptized receive gifts that are to be used for the life and growth of the Christian community. Some may have the gift of teaching—in whatever forum it is exercised, teaching should be aimed at building the Body. Some have the gift of offering wise advice. It is to be used in service so that others might have fuller life. And then there are others who have no apparent gift other than that of being able to pray, however well or poorly. Whatever gift it may be that one has been given by the Spirit in baptism, strengthened in confirmation, and regularly reaffirmed in the celebration of the eucharist, it is to be used in a way that builds the Body of Christ.

Of these many gifts given in baptism, one is the gift of leadership in the community of faith and worship. In the Catholic tradition the leader and teacher in the community is also the one who presides and preaches in the context of the community's prayer, particularly the eucharist. Through the sacrament of holy orders the priest participates in a distinctive manner in the ministry of Christ the servant and healer, especially—though not exclusively—through preaching, teaching, and celebration of the sacraments. This ministry is brought to focal expression in the activities of preaching and presiding at the eucharistic liturgy. What is particularly distinctive about the ordained ministry is that the priest assumes a public leadership role in the church. In a manner of speaking, he is a public servant of the church, and in no small measure, a representative of it. When presiding at the eucharist, the priest brings to the fore in a particular way the characteristics of the life of the church as *one, holy, catholic,* and *apostolic.* Around the table of the Lord at which the ordained minister presides, the assembly gathers as *one* people. By their baptism, and by their ongoing conversion in Christ and service of his mission, they are a *holy* people. Their eucharistic prayer is joined to the prayer of all those throughout the world in every place and of every tongue who constitute the congregation of the true church. They are thus a *catholic* (universal) people who gather at this table. And they join their voices in praise and thanks to God in memory of Jesus Christ as has been done from the time of the church of the apostles. They are thus an *apostolic* people, not only because their worship is in continuity with the faith of the apostles, but because, like the apostles, they are sent forth as servants of peace and heralds of the reign of God. The one who receives the sacrament of holy orders is empowered to serve this people in manifold ways, but particularly through preaching, teaching, administering the sacraments, and presiding at eucharist—the community's central sacramental action. His life as public servant of the people of God demands a commitment to life-long fidelity in service of this mission, so that Christ may be all in all.

Practical Dimensions

In matrimony or the sacrament of Christian marriage the entire Christian community as well as the two persons united live out of a vision of God's *personal, loving fidelity.* Christian marriage is thus the model par excellence of love and fidelity and provides a new way of living from the perspective of God's self-sacrificing love and faithfulness to the divine promise. The relationship between these two persons united in marriage, together with their relationships with others, are thus undertaken in light of the value of God's fidelity to the person and to the human community. The couple thereby becomes a sign of God's own loving fidelity through their union with one another, and in their dealings with others in the human and Christian communities. Particularly through the bearing and rearing of children, fruit of faithful union and invitation to a more inclusive fidelity, the couple gives expression to the values of self-sacrificing love and fidelity, and to the whole church's intention to live by these values.

Ministry expresses the value of *service* to the human and Christian communities modeled on Christ's own service. It is rooted in the church's *care* of the various needs of the community throughout the ages and in remembrance of Christ's own life and ministry. Whatever its disadvantages, the discipline of clerical continence and celibacy has been and remains an invitation to, and expression of, faithful service to the human and Christian community. All ministry—ordained and lay, undertaken by persons married and single—aims at concretely expressing the value of *self-sacrificial love*, a love motivated by a new vision of reality shaped by the perspective of Christ's own servanthood and faithfulness to God's promise unto death.

SACRAMENTAL LIVING

The practical implications of the church's sacramental life do not constitute specific directives or answers to complex questions that people who follow Christ must face. Sacramental worship empowers Christians to develop and grow in the life of Christian discipleship. Sacramental celebration does not result in ready-made prescriptions to alleviate the pains and burdens involved in decision-making and in discerning the most appropriate Christian response in a complex world. Rather, the sacraments express a Christian worldview with practical and pastoral implications. They give shape to an ethos that informs the Christian understanding of the God-world relation, and this offers insight regarding appropriate ways for human beings to relate with another, others, and God.

The specific and often very tough choices that Christians must make are facilitated by different strategies and processes of moral decision-making. One such strategy is to consider what is written in the Scripture so that the word might throw light on a particularly thorny issue. Another approach might be to take stock of the church's teaching on a particular issue, or to attempt to glean from the Christian tradition some insight regarding a moral dilemma in which one feels trapped. Many attempt to arrive at a good decision by considering what Jesus himself would do in this or that situation. A more mature Christian decision-making process entails paying very close attention to what the interior movement of the Spirit is prompting us to do in this or that situation. Some find that choices are clarified by considering the values that we judge to be important and that we hope to embody in all our decisions and actions. But here it is important to be certain that the values we hold dear are in fact good, worthy, and noble.

Any process of decision-making has both strengths and weakness. And all are to be undertaken with a prayerful disposition and in a spirit of willing consultation with others who may be more advanced in the life of the Spirit. Whatever strategy we adopt for the purposes of decision-making, the practical implications of sacramental worship provide a perspective by which Christians can give shape to a life in response to grace and Spirit.

There are areas of Christian life where the practical implications of sacramental worship are extraordinarily complex: human sexuality and social justice. In considering the choices faced in the area of sexuality, we might ask: how does this course of action relate to the *covenant morality* that we hope to live with the other, others, and with God? What is our *responsibility* to them and to ourselves? How does this choice express a *commitment* and *fidelity* to a life of peace, patience, gentleness, joy, chaste love, and long-suffering? Does this choice lead to an increase of these fruits, or does it lead to an increase of anger, envy, lust, despair? What is the bearing of this choice upon our promise of *fidelity, self-sacrificial love, care,* and *service*?

Social justice is the activity of cultivating and promoting rightly-ordered relations with others. In considering this or that choice pertaining to our dealings with another or others, it may be useful to consider: does this course of action or that option lead to deeper measure of *communion* and *justice* with others, or does it alienate and impoverish, especially those who are wounded and weak, the last and the least, those who were central to the preaching and teaching of Jesus? Which intention or course of action leads to an increase of *justice, mercy,* and *forgiveness* in one's own life, in the lives of others, in the life of the community, and in the world at large?

* * * * * *

Whatever differences may exist between and among Christians, to say nothing of the differences between and among Christians and those of other faith traditions, certainly there is agreement on the importance of practicing the implications of what is said and done in prayer and worship. Rather than starting with matters of doctrine, i.e., the statements of belief of different faith traditions, it is more helpful to recognize that the key to understanding faith traditions lies in their life of prayer and worship, and in their efforts to put into practice in the wider context of life what is expressed and impressed in worship.

In this chapter I have provided an exploration of sacramental worship in the Catholic tradition and attended to some of its practical implications. It is my hope that the result is not only a greater familiarity with this tradition, but also a deeper appreciation of the truth that in any and all authentic religious living, prayer and practice, worship and the way one lives within wider contexts, must go hand in hand. Living in the presence of the mystery Christians "name" Love (1 John 4:8) involves absolutely every dimension of human life. Taking seriously what is said and done in sacramental worship necessarily implies attending to its practical implications. Appropriate pastoral care will enable Christians, both as individuals and as communities, to develop means whereby the practical ramifications of sacramental worship might be discerned and implemented when facing increasingly complex issues.

Notes

1. For example, see *Baptism, Eucharist, and Ministry*, Faith and Order Commission of the World Council of Churches, Paper 111 (Geneva: World Council of Churches, 1982).

2. For a concise treatment of this worldview in contrast to other views of the God-world relation, see Sallie McFague, *Metaphorical Theology: Models of God in Religious Language* (Philadelphia: Fortress, 1982).

3. For a splendid treatment of this point, see Catherine Mowry LaCugna, *God for Us: The Trinity and Christian Life* (San Francisco: HarperCollins, 1991).

4. Sallie McFague, *Metaphorical Theology*, is quite instructive on the importance of including nonhuman as well as human life in consideration of the God-world relation. Other perspectives informed by ecological concerns can also be helpful in developing a wider view of sacramentality.

5. Here I follow Edward Schillebeeckx, *Christ the Sacrament of the Encounter with God* (New York: Sheed & Ward, 1963).

6. See David Power, *Unsearchable Riches: The Symbolic Nature of Liturgy* (New York: Pueblo Publishing Co., 1984).

7. Ibid. 64-65.

8. Aidan Kavanagh, *Elements of Rite* (New York: Pueblo Publishing Co., 1982) 5.

9. For a treatment of sign and symbol in light of the task of teaching sacramental theology to students at different stages of faith development, see Michael Downey, "Teaching Sacramental Theology," *Liturgy* 5:1 (Summer 1985) 61-67, 90-93.

10. See Michael Downey, *Clothed in Christ: The Sacraments and Christian Living* (New York: Crossroad Publishing Co., 1987).

11. See David N. Power, *The Eucharistic Mystery: Revitalizing the Tradition* (New York: Crossroad Publishing Co., 1992).

12. See Roger M. Mahony, *In Praise of God's Mercy: A Pastoral Letter on the Sacrament of Penance* (Los Angeles: Archdiocesan Office for Worship, 1990).

14

Liturgy's Form:
Work of the Spirit

AT THE OUTSET IT IS IMPORTANT TO NOTE THAT MY CONCERN HERE IS NOT
with liturgical spirituality as such or a liturgical spirituality in
particular. My intention is not to demonstrate the necessity or
essential characteristics of a liturgical spirituality which could
then be situated in a row alongside Ignatian spirituality,
Benedictine spirituality, Franciscan spirituality, a lay spirituality, and the rest. Rather, the purpose here is to describe the kind
of relationship that exists between Christian spirituality and
liturgy. In so doing, I hope that the nature and function of both
will be clarified.

Much contemporary thought and writing on liturgical matters is directed to the question of the formative role of liturgy in
Christian spiritual life. Kevin Irwin's work in this area is primarily concerned with this issue. He offers a well-developed "liturgical spirituality," the essential contours of which are presented
in detail.[1] In like manner Robert Duggan, in a rather brief article,
suggests what he considers to be the constitutive elements of
liturgical spirituality.[2] The point of both authors is quite the
same: Christian prayer and spiritual life suffer when they are
not rooted in the liturgical life of the church. Such studies are
useful in that they contribute to a deeper understanding of both
liturgy and spirituality. What is needed, however, is further
reflection upon the nature of the relationship between the two
with an eye to spirituality's formative role in the liturgy.

A well-developed Christian spirituality recognizes the formative role of the liturgy. That Christian prayer and spiritual life are to be based in the life of common worship is beyond dispute. But efforts to treat liturgy and spirituality remain incomplete if they do not see the formative influence of spirituality upon the liturgy. In attempting to understand liturgy and spirituality, the task is not one of culling out of the liturgy specific elements that are thought to have a formative influence on the spiritual life of an individual or a group. For example, one might claim that since the *anaphora* is essentially a prayer of thanksgiving, any authentic liturgical spirituality will be characterized by a spirit of thanks. Or others, in the wake of the Second Vatican Council and with the attention given to the importance of the liturgy of the word, may maintain that a liturgical spirituality must be marked in a singular way by its focus upon the Scriptures.[3] The task is more complex and requires the recognition that the relationship between liturgy and spirituality is reciprocal. Not only does liturgy shape spirituality: spirituality shapes liturgy.

TWO MODELS

To arrive at a better understanding of this relationship, a glance at two different models may be helpful.

The first model, which shall be referred to as a model of derivation, is useful in understanding the concerns of Irwin, Duggan, and those who are primarily interested in the importance of the formative role of liturgy in a person's or group's spiritual life. Looking to this model, the concern is to illustrate the elements of spirituality that flow from the liturgy. Spirituality is shaped by these. Such elements which derive from the liturgy are understood to comprise liturgical spirituality. In an effort to pin down these elements, there is an attempt to develop not only the contours of liturgical spirituality but the rather specific elements of a liturgical spirituality or *the* liturgical spirituality. The relationship here is rather one-sided. Elements from liturgy carry over so as to shape the spiritual life. If there is a conviction that the relationship between liturgy and spirituality is in any sense reciprocal, this is hard to detect, and the question of the influence of spirituality upon liturgy does not appear to be a major concern when operating from this model.

The strength of this model lies in its recognition of the import liturgy has, or should have, on the spiritual life of an individual or group. Its deficiencies lie in the assumption that elements of spirituality derive from liturgy without explicit reference to the interrelationship that exists between the two and, further, that there are very specific elements that constitute a liturgical spirituality or *the* liturgical spirituality. What's more, there seems to be an implicit assumption that *the* liturgical spirituality would be somehow more authentically liturgical, or spiritual, than others.

In an effort to introduce a more adequate understanding of the relationship between liturgy and spirituality, a second model is worth considering. This might be referred to as a model of reciprocity and critical correlation. Here the dominant concern is with mutuality of impact: liturgy and spirituality are shaped and formed by one another. The reciprocal relationship between the two gives rise to a variety of spiritualities and liturgical forms. This view of liturgy and spirituality allows for dynamic interaction, openness to change under the Spirit's lead, and multiplicity of future possibilities. If for no other reason than these, this understanding of liturgy and spirituality commands attention.

SPIRITUALITY: THE SPIRIT AT WORK IN PERSONS

When discussions of spirituality focus exclusively upon methods of prayer, forms of asceticism, or religious disciplines, or when liturgy is understood in terms of a given, rather unchanging, static, approved rite, the whole story is hardly told. Likewise, when attention is given to the rather extraordinary experiences of the ascetical and/or mystical currents within the Christian tradition, some of the more important lines of the story of Christian spirituality go unheard. A good deal has been said of late about the "underside of history" in an effort to explain the process whereby insight is gained through the telling and hearing of a story from a radically different perspective than that of the dominant, prevailing viewpoint.[4] Similarly, in an effort to gain fresh insight into the nature of Christian spirituality and its relationship to the liturgy, it is necessary to shift perspective in order to recognize that Christian spirituality is not in the first place concerned with religious exercises and/or extraordinary experiences. Rather, Christian spirituality has to do with the Spirit at work in persons. Whatever is said of religious exercises and experiences, or of liturgy, needs to be said in this light.

In speaking of the Spirit at work in persons, we must pay attention to seven focal points wherein the Spirit may be seen to be at work: (1) within a culture; (2) in relation to a tradition; (3) in memory of Jesus Christ; (4) in relation to contemporary events, hopes, sufferings, and promises; (5) in efforts to combine elements of action and contemplation; (6) with respect to charism and community; (7) as expressed and authenticated in praxis. By looking to these, it is possible to envision the broader context of a foundational Christian spirituality within which particular questions and concerns find their proper place. It is within this context that questions regarding the nature of the relationship between liturgy and spirituality are properly addressed.

LITURGY'S FORM: SHAPED BY SPIRITUALITY

The Spirit at work in these seven focal areas affects the form liturgy takes. In speaking of liturgical form, I am not referring to a fixed, static, unchangeable way of worship. I reject any notion of liturgy that maintains that it is unaffected by contemporary experience of the Spirit at work, as well as any notion that liturgy *could* remain unaffected.[5] What I have in mind in using the term "liturgical form" is much the same, and is characterized by the same flexibility, as what Joseph Gelineau describes as an operational model:

> The operational method thus emerges as a form of symbolic behavior which the celebrating group is familiar with, the participants have fully assimilated, and the main actors have adequately mastered. It allows the group to celebrate with peace of mind because the game and the rules are familiar. But it does not paralyse the action. Whatever is done is done, as it were, naturally and instinctively. The liturgy can emerge both as something remembered and as something new.

> The operational model may be said to be the concrete form that the local way of Christian worship actually takes for a specific human group in a particular area at a given moment.[6]

A variety of liturgical forms or operational models emerge precisely in response to the way in which the Spirit is at work within a particular culture, in relation to a specific tradition, in light of different ways of remembering Jesus, and so on. Such liturgical forms are assimilated to various cultural models and will vary according to the cultural model in each case.[7]

THE SPIRIT'S WORK: SEVEN FOCAL POINTS

To speak of the Spirit in persons it is necessary to see, in the first place, those persons as located within a culture and in relation to a tradition. It is in the very particular customs, rites, myths, narratives, metaphors, and ethos of a people, all of which are culturally conditioned and transmitted through a particular tradition, that the Spirit is at work. Traces of the Spirit are to be found in the various cultural patterns and currents of tradition through which persons and groups manifest God's being in the world and humanity's being in God. Thus, the particular culture and tradition of a people, with attention to all those channels which facilitate self-expression, interpersonal communion, and communication, are the very places of the Spirit's operation. We look to the whole network provided by culture and tradition wherein we find the primordial locus of God's self-manifestation celebrated in liturgy. It is within the whole gamut of human experience, which is always "situated" within a culture and tradition, that God's word is first spoken. Whatever is said of liturgy must be related to this.

The history of Christianity demonstrates that any number of different spiritualities have emerged in the lives of various people and communities all formed, shaped, or schooled by liturgy. For example, the Beghards and Beguines, the followers of Francis and Clare and Dominic, were all formed by the same liturgical life of the church. But the spirituality that each group lived was noticeably different from the other, each with its own particular characteristics. Liturgy invites participation of persons who, in memory of Jesus Christ and by the power of his Spirit, respond to the Gospel in any number of ways, given the influences of their own historical, cultural, context. Such context will determine not only the way in which things are done and said in liturgy, but also the response to what is done and said. The variety of traditions and cultures together with the historical particularities of a given person or group all shape the context within which liturgy is celebrated and its meaning communicated and received. When looking to groups like those mentioned above, we find a distinctive liturgical form in each case. What is most striking is that each form emerged from within medieval culture which was quite remarkably the same throughout western Europe. Not only is it true, then, that different cultures give rise to different liturgical forms and spiritualities, but a variety of liturgical forms and spiritualities may emerge from the same culture.

The same may be said of the present day. Recognizing that there are nuances and differences within it, one can speak of a North American culture. Yet no one is surprised that the liturgical form operative in a North American Cistercian monastery is considerably different from that of the local parish church. Some may be surprised to hear that a group of aging priests and brothers of a religious congregation celebrate the liturgy at a different time, place, and in a very different style than the younger seminarians and brothers in the same house, seeing in this an expression of irreconcilable differences. But this is not the only reading of the situation. This may be viewed as a case in point, wherein persons within the very same culture, living under the same roof, respond to and shape different liturgical forms recognizing that they are living quite different spiritualities, even in the same religious congregation.

Another area to be considered in assessing spirituality and liturgy is that of contemporary events, hopes, sufferings, and promises. It is a great temptation to think and to write about issues in spirituality with the aim of retrieving insights from a bygone era, be it that of the New Testament or another, and applying them to the contemporary situation of a person or group. Far more difficult, yet more to the point, is the task of interpreting and responding to contemporary events in remembrance of Jesus Christ by the power of his Spirit. Response to the divine initiative operative in relation to the contemporary events and hopes of a people will take a variety of forms to meet the changing and varied needs and circumstances of the age. Indeed, some responses may find no precedent in the history of Christianity. To the massive crises of our own age, there are simply no easy solutions, and too often the facile application of insights or principles derived from a cursory reading of classical religious texts only aggravates the growing senses of despair. David Power has written of the great hopelessness of our age signaled in the dual holocaust of the present century.[8] The first is that of the willed and systematic attempt by the Nazis to annihilate the Jewish people as well as other groups. The second is that of a possible nuclear holocaust still threatening the world today. The issue here pertains to the truth and integrity of Christian faith and of its meaning. In light of these two contemporary events, one a fact, the other a possibility, can we profess faith in Jesus Christ?

What does it mean to profess Christian faith between the holocausts? Further, what should be the form of Christian prayer and worship between the holocausts?[9] Should it continue in the same form after Auschwitz as before? If there is a reciprocal relationship between liturgy and spirituality, then the Spirit at work in persons in relation to the contemporary event of the dual holocaust will impact the shape the liturgy takes, as persons and communities struggle to articulate prayer and celebrate hope in the face of such tragedy. This requires more than the inclusion of a prayer of petition here and there that God protect us from the threat of nuclear disaster, or that God show compassion and give hope to those who live in despair. It is rather a question of allowing liturgy and sacrament to enter and so transform the collective human experience of helplessness and hopelessness signaled in the dual holocaust, by bringing these experiences to expression, and by relating such experience to the memory of Jesus and his abiding presence in the People of God through the Spirit.

In words said and things done in memory of Jesus Christ we find another *locus* of the Spirit's activity. Memory is the heart of liturgy. The diversity of Christian spiritualities illustrates that Christians have remembered Jesus differently in different times and places. To remember Jesus as triumphant Lord of the universe results in a view of church, ministry, and worship shaped by such remembrance. To remember Jesus as suffering servant results in a different understanding of church, ministry, and worship. Contemporary currents in theology point out the importance of remembering the forgotten, the victims, the oppressed, and those living in solidarity with them, in the memory of Jesus Christ.[10] Not only is the role of the liturgy to include in memory the words, actions, and promises of Jesus and his followers throughout the ages of Christian history, but also those who have stood at the edges of history, at the periphery of church and society. Those forgotten through a willed and systematic forgetfulness can be gathered into the memory of Jesus Christ, and with this a certain freedom can be won. Traces of the Spirit are found where persons and groups choose to remember all those who in the course of history have been victimized by systems and by the fears and hatreds inculcated therein—victims of racism, classism, sexism, sacralism, environmental pollution, and the like.

To choose to remember the victims is to stand in "anamnetic solidarity" with them, acknowledging within ourselves and our community whatever stands in need of pardon and reconciliation in Christ. The liturgical forms that result from this kind of remembrance would have no room for "high church" motifs. Rather, they would make room for lamentation as well as thanksgiving, and the memory of suffering as well as hope.

In the efforts to combine elements of action and contemplation we find another locus of the Spirit's work. The way in which these are blended has formed the core of the rich tradition of Christian spirituality. It is true that both ingredients need to be balanced in any wholesome Christian life, and yet it is also true that one or the other dimension will be accentuated, given the temperament, cultural conditions, and historical circumstances of person and/or group. The way in which these are combined gives rise to different liturgical forms in such a way that we can notice considerable differences between the liturgy of a Poor Clare monastery and that of a Catholic Worker House. Whatever similarities may exist between these two groups, the difference in liturgical form in each community results—at least in part—from the way in which their respective members attempt to combine action and contemplation.

In considering charism and community as the next focus for understanding the Spirit's work, it is useful to point out that the liturgy is the activity that fully expresses the faith of a community of believers. This is a community of grace and Spirit whose members, by baptism, have been granted charisms or gifts for the service of the Body of Christ, the church. The gifts differ. The form liturgy takes will vary according to the type and measure of gifts operative within a specific community. Given this diversity of gifts, we might ask if the present state of liturgical affairs is characterized by an openness to diverse charisms, such as prophecy and wisdom. Or is the operative assumption that such charisms are a bit unwieldy and so have no place in the church's liturgy?

Finally, liturgical forms are assessed by praxis. That is to say that there is a critical correlation between liturgy and praxis. Here the question is one of the adequacy of the liturgy to the life experience of a people. David Power puts the question well: "Do common and accepted modes of liturgical expression respond adequately to contemporary ways of perceiving and being, and do they allow for hope in the future when we are threatened with awesome destruction?"[11] Liturgical forms must constantly be assimilated, assessed, critiqued, and reworked in light of their ability to relate to and address the deepest experience of a people wherein the Spirit is at work.

CHANGING FORMS: AN EXAMPLE

Perhaps an example may serve to illustrate the point of the reciprocity and critical correlation existing between liturgy and spirituality. The growing consciousness among women of the oppression which the long tradition of patriarchy has foisted upon them has led many women and men to call for greater self-determination and participation among women in the church and society. As women gain greater freedom from the shackles of sexism, the possibilities and responsibilities of promoting the truth in love, of moving toward God's future, become clearer, though these possibilities may find no apparent precedent in the history of Christianity. Where persons grow in greater self-determination, moving forward in truth, freedom, and love toward the fullness of human personhood, the Spirit is to be found. Where the "women's movement" in all its various forms has enabled persons to do such, it must be rightfully recognized as a work of the Spirit. With this emergent consciousness has come a rather critical posture in the face of the "exclusive," "sexist" language used in church and society.

"Man," "mankind," "he," "him," used even in the generic sense all evidence a deeply embedded patriarchal bias. When used in the liturgy, this type of language has only served to deepen the sense of alienation and exclusion from a life of full participation in the mission and ministry of the church. For many this was aggravated when, during the institution narrative, the cup of salvation was offered "for you and for all men." In recent years this wording in the liturgy has been changed in some countries so that the form the liturgy now takes has been reshaped. And it has, in this case no doubt, been shaped by the work of the Spirit in women within a specific tradition, in relation to their culture, in light of the contemporary events and circumstances that have enabled them to arrive at greater participation and self-determination. When such women gathered in remembrance of Jesus Christ to celebrate God's reign they found, at least in this particular instance, that the liturgy did not address them in their possibilities, needs, or aspirations. It required critical evaluation, given its inadequacy and its tendency to exclude women from the celebration of God's presence in Jesus Christ. But the work is not yet finished. Even as regards sexist, exclusivist language in liturgy, there is much to be done.

This is to say nothing of the great variety of alternative liturgical forms that are emerging from the women's movement, some of which do not appear to be immediately reconcilable with church life, practice, and policy. There remains the need for assessing what works are works of the Spirit and which liturgical forms are authentic expressions of the Spirit.

* * * * * *

Rather than providing a blueprint containing specific guidelines for a healthy Christian spiritual life, liturgy offers canonical parameters within which particular and quite diverse spiritualities (as expressions of the Spirit at work in persons) may develop. The Spirit at work in persons has resulted in new liturgical forms and expressions to meet the exigencies of diverse and particular persons and communities throughout history. The formative influence of liturgy upon spirituality is beyond question. But the deeper issue is that of the openness of liturgy to diverse spiritualities and hence spirituality's influence upon the form that liturgy takes.

Notes

1. Kevin Irwin, *Liturgy, Prayer, and Spirituality* (New York: Paulist Press, 1984).

2. Robert Duggan, "Liturgical Spirituality and Liturgical Reform," *Spiritual Life* 27:1 (Spring 1981) 46-53.

3. Ibid. 48-49.

4. The term is used frequently in currents of what is referred to broadly as "liberation theology"; for an interpretation of liberation theology, see Rebecca Chopp, *The Praxis of Suffering* (New York: Orbis, 1986).

5. In light of the history of the liturgical and sacramental life of the churches, the burden of proof would rest with those who argue otherwise.

6. Joseph Gelineau, "Tradition-Invention-Culture," *Concilium* 162 (1983) 15-16.

7. For a fuller treatment of this point, see Anscar Chupungco, *Cultural Adaptation of the Liturgy* (New York: Paulist Press, 1982).

8. David N. Power, *Unsearchable Riches: The Symbolic Nature of the Liturgy* (New York: Pueblo Publishing Co., 1984) 1.

9. I have developed this at further length in "Worship Between the Holocausts," chapter 15 in this volume.

10. See Matthew Lamb, *Solidarity with Victims* (New York: Crossroad, 1982); see also Johannes Baptist Metz, *Faith in History and Society* (New York: Seabury, 1980).

11. Power, *Unsearchable Riches* 5.

WEAKNESS BROUGHT
TO WORSHIP

15

Worship Between the Holocausts

IN DESCRIBING THE RELIGIOUS PRACTICE OF HIS BOYHOOD, JOHANN BAPTIST Metz writes: "With our back toward Auschwitz we prayed and celebrated our liturgy. Only later I began to ask myself what kind of religion is it that can be practiced unmoved by such a catastrophe."[1] Acknowledging the singular importance of the Holocaust for contemporary Christian life and theology, Metz holds that "everything has to be measured by Auschwitz."[2] He maintains:

> There is no truth for me which I could defend with my back turned toward Auschwitz. There is no sense for me which I could save with my back turned toward Auschwitz. And for me there is no God to whom I could pray with my back turned toward Auschwitz.[3]

What we find in the writings of J.B. Metz is a recognition of the fact of the Holocaust, an acknowledgment of the Christian's complicity in this event, and a determination to engage in Christian life, prayer, and theological reflection in memory of its victims.

In light of the Holocaust, a question must be asked: can we pray at all in the wake of the Holocaust? Metz asserts that Christians can pray after Auschwitz only because there were prayers in Auschwitz.[4] I basically agree, but I would nuance this a bit. Christian prayer after the Holocaust must be *informed* and *shaped* by the prayers at Auschwitz. And it must make room for the memory of its victims. I would also say that Christian worship must take place in full view of the imminence of a second Holocaust—the threat of nuclear annihilation.

My purpose here is to reflect upon the Holocaust of the Jews and a possible nuclear Holocaust, while being attentive to their significance for Christian worship. I begin with the assumption that liturgy can, in principle, recognize and be open to alteration by contemporary events. Ruled out is any theory holding that liturgy remains unaffected by contemporary event or fact. The question I am concerned with here may be simply stated: what shape or form will liturgy take if the reality of the twofold Holocaust is taken seriously? My hope is to advance the discussion of those whose concern is liturgy after the Holocaust of the Jews by pressing the question as to whether or not Christians have taken the Holocaust seriously.[5] But I would also like to take the discussion in a different direction by raising the issue of a possible imminent nuclear Holocaust as anticipatory symbol, and by attempting to determine what impact the two Holocausts might have upon our understanding of prayer and worship.

HOLOCAUST OF THE JEWS

Yaffa Eliach's anthology offers a sampling of the way in which Jews prayed during the Holocaust. In "The First Hanukkah Light in Bergen Belsen"[6] she recounts how the victims construct a makeshift hanukkiah from a wooden clog, strings, and shoe polish to serve as oil. Not far from the heaps of bodies, the living skeletons assemble to participate in the kindling of Hanukkah lights. Aware of the heap of the dead and the assembly of living skeletons, the rabbi hesitates and then proceeds with the third blessing—in which God, addressed as Lord and King of the Universe, is blessed for keeping, preserving, and enabling the people of the covenant to reach this season. When questioned as to why (under the circumstances) he would address God in such terms, the rabbi explains that the large crowd of living Jews, their faces expressing faith, devotion, and concentration as they listen to the rite, provides the justification for this kind of prayer. According to the rabbi, if God has a nation such as this, that in times like these, when during the lighting of the Hanukkah lights they see in front of them the heaps of bodies of their beloved fathers, mothers, brothers, sisters, sons, and daughters, and death is looking from every corner, then the rabbi has grounds for reciting the third blessing in praise of God's goodness and providence.

The recognition of the "orienting event"[7] of the Holocaust in its own historical particularity brings with it an awareness of our own experience and situation, the fact of what we are living with and confronting—meaninglessness and powerlessness. In what sense can meaning, hope, and promise be found in light of such massive evil and suffering inflicted upon humanity by humanity? Being confronted by the Holocaust, the primordial symbol of evil in our age, brings with it a crisis of vision and a crisis of hope. The churches must deal with the question of how faith in Jesus Christ can be proclaimed and celebrated in worship in light of this event.

The fate of the Jews, who are the people of the covenant and the kingdom, has everything to do with the way we as a Christian people understand and speak of the kingdom. A Christian sense of meaning, hope, and promise derives from and is dependent upon this covenant people. Christians recognize this in the import accorded to the Exodus and the Messianic covenant in Christian faith, theology, and worship. But if we have allowed the originating event of Jewish faith, the Exodus, to shape our religious consciousness, have we also allowed the orienting event of the Holocaust to do so? The Jewish people's experience of abandonment by God, abandonment by the rest of the world, and the purposeful attempt by the Nazis to dehumanize and exterminate them has everything to do with our understanding of hope, promise, future, and ultimate meaning, precisely because they are the people of the covenant and it is upon them that ours depends.[8]

For the Jew the Holocaust is the paradigmatic example of evil. As symbol, the Holocaust is evocative of conversion to a God who is there on the other side of this evil, this meaninglessness, this senselessness, this powerlessness. Moreover, it is conversion to a God who stands with the chosen precisely in the midst of all this. If Christian faith takes seriously this event, the same sort of recognition of meaninglessness and powerlessness, and conversion undergone in its light, is demanded. Liturgy is to facilitate this. Yet it seems that contemporary Christian liturgy continues to be celebrated with its back to Auschwitz, much like the liturgies of the time when Metz was a boy.

The imminent nuclear Holocaust threatens the existence of everything as we know it. Whether or not it is accepted and appropriated as possibility or probability, the imminent nuclear Holocaust serves today as the anticipatory symbol of futurelessness. Even if persons and groups do not accept that the world will end in nuclear destruction, the fruits of the anticipatory symbol of the apocalyptic end play deeply upon the contemporary psyche. Examples of this may be seen in movements among the young that are built upon and thrive on images and expressions of violence and self-destruction (punk and heavy metal among others), and in the little concern among the young in many countries when faced with the prospect of long-term unemployment. This is to say nothing of the growing fascination with what has come to be called "Armageddon theology."

THE APOCALYPTIC

The two Holocausts—the one fact, the other possibility—bespeak the reality of powerlessness, meaninglessness, and futurelessness. Here memory and anticipatory symbol converge. As symbols, the two Holocausts are evocative of conversion to a God who is there in the midst of human powerlessness and meaninglessness—a God who is ahead of us, before us, on the other side of extermination or complete destruction of humanity and everything as we know it.

Whereas conversion is not liturgy's only function, liturgy is to be formative in the ongoing conversion of the Christian community. What is expressed is impressed. What form will liturgy take if memory and anticipatory symbol are taken seriously, so as to facilitate the conversion demanded by the crisis brought about by the twofold Holocaust? The introduction of prayers of petition that God grant us protection from (or for) nuclear war, or that we recognize the Jews as forebears of Christians hardly tackles the issue. Such gestures further the impression of "situation normal." The trouble with normal is that it always gets worse. Liturgy, if it is to respond adequately to contemporary modes of perceiving and being, and to contemporary fact, must allow itself to be impacted by the memory and anticipatory symbol of meaninglessness and futurelessness signaled in the twofold Holocaust.

Such impact may be made as Christian assemblies begin in earnest to work toward integrating into worship a more profound appreciation for authentic apocalyptic as well as a remembrance of the dead Christ and the descent into hell. A recovery of the remembrance of the dead Christ and the descent into hell, and of authentic apocalyptic, would address Christian communities in light of their experience of meaninglessness and hopelessness brought about by the twofold Holocaust, while summoning Christians to trust and hope in the midst of their adversity.

Apocalyptic rhetorics gain force when continuities are shattered. A distinguishing characteristic of authentic apocalyptic rhetoric is that it emerges from and speaks to a situation in which everything is at stake.[9] Common to all true apocalyptic is a situation characterized by instability, disorientation, anxiety, and isolation. The apocalyptic emerges where there is a loss of cohesion and an erosion of psychic and cultural structures. Everything is on the line. The motif of panic dominates, due to the "all-or-nothing" nature of a situation involving opposing forces of light and darkness, life and death, order and chaos. It is not merely a matter of the individual in isolation. The matter is one of the survival of the whole of existence, the viability of all life.

Much contemporary fascination with the apocalyptic, especially though not exclusively where this is joined to speculation about the nuclear Holocaust, focuses rather narrowly on its negative or catastrophic dimension. A recovery of authentic apocalyptic would draw attention to the stage of miraculous renovation and world affirmation, the stage which has passed through the phase of world negation. The hierophany central to the apocalypse entails both nay-saying and yea-saying.[10] The catastrophic imagination alone is, therefore, not genuinely apocalyptic. Apocalyptic in the true sense includes salvation as well as judgment, restoration as well as destruction, the eucatastropic as well as the catastrophic.

Ancient apocalytic, replete with revelations, dramas of cosmic warfare, symbols and motifs that strike as fantastic, spoke effectively to the consciousness and perception of many. Perhaps only its recovery can speak to our threatening sense of the catastrophic and destructive when faced with nuclear annihilation, while holding out a vision and possibility for the new age to come which evil cannot overcome.

In the rhetorics of the apocalyptic, hope and future play a central role. Since everything is in jeopardy and since all trusted securities are unreliable, the only future that is possible must be thought of in terms of the provident and the miraculous. The hierophany central to the apocalytic is characterized by enormity and paradox. The language of the apocalytic is a sort of nonlanguage, as it were. It is a language that breaks continuity with accepted patterns of speech and perception because all is forfeit to chaos. Yet, it is a speaking of meaning out of meaninglessness. The rhetorics of apocalyptic are peculiar in that they dramatize a group's vision in a situation of hopelessness, broken promises, and disappointment. Into this situation, forfeited to chaos, the apocalyptist rings out in yea-saying. The apocalyptist says that, in the midst of dire adversity, meaninglessness, powerlessness, and futurelessness, God is coming against all odds and will be victorious.

A note of caution is in order here. Since the nuclear Holocaust signals the end of everything as we have ever known it, there is no "other side" or future to imagine. In this the present crisis stands in radical discontinuity with all others before it. The future can only be on this side of the Holocaust. The providential act of God, the miraculous, lies in prevention. The preservation of life through co-creational responsibility, rather than a cosmic playground on the other side of catastrophe, is the future to which we look and to which contemporary apocalyptic rhetorics must speak.

A LITURGICAL OBJECTIVE

Gordon Lathrop offers the reminder that the agenda for liturgical work is not that of "dabbling with superficial poetry,"[11] but of allowing words, images, and symbols to stand forth, all expressing present needs and allowing us honestly to stand before God with the remembrance of the twofold Holocaust.

It is a biblical, liturgical objective to let lament into the heart of our worshiping communities. Nothing less is adequate for worship in this century. With Lathrop and David Power, I maintain that biblical images of lamentation best serve to give voice to the experience of absence as a distinct mode of God's presence. Disappointment, need, lament, all bespeak an experience of a God whose presence is no longer present, yet needed and hoped for. To lament God's absence is to name a longing for what once was and what needs to be.

Here again Christian prayer needs to be informed and shaped by the prayer of the Jews during the Holocaust.[12] In such prayer thanksgiving spills over into lamentation. The deeds of the Lord recounted are held up only to draw attention to their absence and to ask for their presence once again. The prayers of Auschwitz are profoundly full of need, of lament, of frustration, of disappointment. Further, they are shot through with imprecation and cries for vengeance. Jews continue to cry to God for vengeance in their memory of the Holocaust. Imprecation and call for vengeance have a profound meaning in their way of praying. Christians generally omit such imprecations from their prayers. Why this is so cannot be answered here, but suffice it to say that imprecation and cries for vengeance would find a more central place in Christian prayer if this prayer were to take seriously the horrors of our age. Between the Holocausts, lamentation must be given room in our assemblies as an expression of the communities' experience, if such communities honestly wrestle with fact and future.

Perhaps there is no image in the Christian tradition that is more suited to lament, more evocative of God's absence, than that of the forsaken servant of God, the dead Christ. The notion of deliverance, central to the tradition of Judaism, is here interfaced with one of non-deliverance. Can we praise and thank a God who has delivered, but is not delivering?

The image of the dead Christ must be distinguished from that of the crucified. The image of the dead Christ is not of one who is rejected, persecuted, tortured, and despised, but of one who is dead, finished, obliterated, gone, no longer there or here. To keep memory of the dead Christ is to embrace, so as to integrate, the negative. With this image to the fore, the vitality of the negative can come into play in the liturgy. Without denying anything that has happened or that could happen, the inclusion of the image of the dead Christ, evocative of God's absence and of nondeliverance, gives shape to a form of liturgy that is a lamentation.

With the reforms initiated since the time of the Second Vatican Council, much of the liturgical renewal has focused upon the pivotal notion of joyful celebration. Systematic theology, as well as liturgical theology, has rather consistently stressed the resurrection as the originating event of Christian faith and worship.[13] In a community whose song is Alleluia, the vitality of the negative is easily forgotten. Only through the efforts of feminist, liberation, and political theologians have the churches been faced with the "struggle for remembrance"[14] which uncovers the original testimony: "The Crucified One lives." Yet the testimony remains semantically empty if we forget that those who claimed him alive did so after having first known and profoundly experienced his death, his absence.

Memory is the heart of liturgy. If contemporary liturgy is to project a worldview pertinent to fact and adequate to common ways of being and perceiving, the vitality of negativity must be given room. The dead Christ is with the dead sons and daughters, mothers and fathers, brothers and sisters, past, present, and future. He shares their experience of abandonment, of nondeliverance, of death, of being forgotten—and he is God. Is it too strong to suggest that our liturgy will remain inadequate, will continue to turn its back on fact, as long as it is conducted in such a way that gestures, verbal images, vestments, and other liturgical accoutrements bespeak Christ in his glory and majesty, while, if the truth be faced, the Christian community is living right smack-dab in the middle of Holy Saturday.

RECOVERING THE IMAGE OF THE DEAD CHRIST

But in what sense is a recovery of the image of the dead Christ useful or appropriate for worship in our age? What purpose does it serve to recover the image of the dead Christ, evocative of negativity, absence, and nondeliverance? Does this image, in fact, serve the purposes of bringing to expression the hope and faith of a people in the midst of crisis and confirm them in that faith and in that hope?

In itself, it does not. Here the image of the dead Christ must be coupled with that of the descent into hell. The images of the dead Christ and the descent into hell must be understood in light of contemporary Christological insights that draw attention to Jesus as God's compassion.[15] Since Jesus entered so completely in compassion into human suffering, vulnerability, and death, and since God remained faithful to him in his abandonment, the church has an image that provides the basis for its own involvement in the human community and for Christian worship. It is not a question of seeing in the death and descent a propaedeutic for the verification of Jesus' lordship in the resurrection. Nor is it a question of viewing the death of Jesus and the descent as something undergone for us or on our behalf, Jesus being understood here as one who suffers because of and for us. Rather, it is a question of seeing in Jesus the compassion of God entering into solidarity with the suffering victims of all ages, unto death and into hell. This provides the basis for hope in our age. Because Jesus entered so completely into human suffering and death, we as Christians can look to the future in hope and trust that nothing can separate us from the love of God made manifest in Jesus Christ.

It is the memory of this trust and this hope in the midst of abandonment, negativity, and absence that compels Christians to give praise and thanksgiving, and allows them to raise up voices in lamentation.

In treating the question of the possibility for an authentic Christian response to the horrors of Auschwitz "which avoids the temptation both of Christian appropriationism and Christian complacency,"[16] Mary Knutsen alerts us to the dangers posed when well-meaning Christians and others attempt to instruct the Jews about the Holocaust. The Holocaust stands in its own historical particularity. The warning against Christian appropriationism is helpful.

Knutsen speaks of the importance of three factors: solidarity, double alterity, and expectation. The first points to the need for fundamental moral sensibility and principle before the suffering of others, especially victims. The second, double alterity, suggests that within the context of compassion for and solidarity with victims, there is the need for recognizing a twofold otherness: the otherness of the victim, whose suffering can never be appropriated or fully comprehended by another, and the otherness of suffering and death from what should be. This response, when seen in light of what is often the complacency of Christians, is one of outrage, a sense of horror and disappointment in the face of such unbelievable suffering, a passionate awareness that this should not be. At the same time, however, this response includes the third factor: recognition of a promise of the redemption of suffering and death and, along with it, an attentiveness to the apocalyptic, the radically not-yet of Christian faith.

Worship between the Holocausts, if it is to be an authentic Christian response, needs to recover and make room for a rebirth of the central image of the dead Christ and the descent into hell, as well as an authentic sense of the apocalyptic. Liturgical forms must emerge that express a deepened sense of lament, solidarity, otherness, profound hope, and expectation. To allow the twofold Holocaust to shape contemporary liturgy is to give full voice to the experience of the absence of God, yet of a God who is needed and whose coming is hoped for. To face the past and the future, Christians must voice the groan that while God did establish the covenant through deliverance of the Jews in the Exodus, God did not deliver them during the Holocaust. The fate of the Jews as people of the covenant and kingdom is ours. Their prayer must inform and shape ours. Our prayer must be their prayer. Together we await in adversity a God who is to come. Nothing else is adequate in the twentieth century, for it is only through acknowledgment of the fact of the Holocaust of the Jews and the possibility of nuclear Holocaust that we can place ourselves in honesty before God's face.

USING THE IMAGES

At this point I would like to give hints as to how the churches might use the images of the dead Christ and the descent into hell, and the apocalyptic, while recognizing the great diversity of expressions and forms of liturgical practice in the churches.

The Christian year provides occasion for the implementation of remembrance of the dead Christ and the descent into hell. But the singling out of one or a few days which would then become focal for such implementation runs the risk of losing the sense in which the mystery of Christ's death and descent into hell are at the heart of the mystery celebrated in each liturgy. It is precisely my purpose to recover the images of the dead Christ and descent which have often been forgotten as an important element of Christian worship.

That having been said, a look at the Byzantine rite for Good Friday, and the procession of the dead Christ—a popular practice in the Philippines—may be useful.

In churches of the Byzantine rite, the Good Friday liturgy includes the vespers of the descent from the cross and a service of the entombment of Christ. In the evening this is followed, in such churches as the Greek Orthodox, the Melkite-Greek Catholic, and Antiochene Orthodox, by a matins service for Holy Saturday. Particular details of practice may vary. During this service an icon of the burial of the dead Christ is taken from the church building. With the icon or Epitaphion at the head, the congregation processes around the church three times. Upon entering the church, all those in procession pass under the image of the dead, buried Christ, which is elevated in bridge-like fashion by its carriers. The significance here is that of going down with the dead Christ, passing under the yoke of the dead Christ and taking it on.[17]

A good example of how popular narratives portray the Christ may be seen in the poems of the Passion read on Good Friday in the Philippines.[18] Such poems are associated with the procession of the dead Christ. In that country the lives of the people have been scarred by suffering, tragedy, and the regular threat of death. They believe in a Christ who is close to them in their struggle, who has entered into solidarity with their misery even to the point of descending into hell. Their belief in this Christ is expressed in, among other ways, the procession of the dead Christ. Instead of trying to make people move painlessly from Good Friday to the Vigil, Christian assemblies might profit from the struggle with the issue of how the celebration of the memory of the dead Christ might become, for the disoriented, anxious, hopeless, and oppressed, a cry of hope, a memory of a death that is itself the promise of liberation.

Here we can learn from liturgical history. In the earliest liturgical forms we know, the Paschal Vigil was the arena for the reading of the Passion. Good Friday did not have its own liturgy. Though later history has given rise to a telling of the Christ story on Good Friday rather than during the Vigil, there remains the task and the possibility of integrating the images of the death and descent into Christian worship in such a way that its integrity and significance are not befuddled in the vain attempt to wean people from Good Friday to the Paschal Vigil.

The two previous examples taken from different liturgical traditions might serve to instruct others in the way that the images of the dead Christ and descent into hell might be recovered in the liturgical activities of the churches. The task, of course, is not to impose such practices upon the local churches in ways that are inappropriate to their own proper liturgical practices. It is rather a question of allowing for appropriate, yet sometimes unprecedented, liturgical forms that give better expression to a people's experience of a sense of loss and the absence or hiddenness of God.

IMPLEMENTATION

Let us turn now to the question of how this implementation might occur in the various liturgical prayers of the churches, and in the eucharistic prayer in particular. In speaking of liturgical prayers, I have in mind the patterned, predictable, and public prayers, both formal and informal, written and unwritten, spontaneous and prescribed, by which Christians meet and are met by God in the intentional, corporate coming together of the church. Liturgical prayers of petition, intercession, benediction, and thanksgiving need to take account of the churches' experience of being part of a humanity which lives in a time of disintegration and destruction, a humanity continually compelled to consider whether there are any hopes by which it is possible to face the future. Liturgical prayer must name this experience of crisis of vision and of hope, and address God who is often experienced as absent or hidden. Hence liturgical prayer takes on the character of lamentation, of a cry that God, once near, has withdrawn or disappeared. Prayer becomes a protest that those who keep the covenant are, for all that, seemingly forsaken by the God who has promised to be with them. The psalms and wisdom literature are shot through with such sentiments.[19] It is simply a question of retrieving what has often been forgotten or been deemed inappropriate in liturgical prayer, and allowing such expression to come to the center of our assemblies.

In this vein no other focus is so central to this experience in the Christian context than that of the dead Christ, the forsaken servant, and his descent. This is what provides the basis for hope in our age. No other image is more adequate to name the mystery of God's absence as well as God's self-emptying and complete identification with suffering, negativity, and death. It is in this mystery that we look to the future in hope and trust that nothing can separate us from the love of God in Jesus Christ.

In the eucharistic liturgy of the Roman Catholic Church the eucharistic prayer itself needs to be seen as the locus for this type of prayer. Themes of loss, longing, desire, and lament akin to the Jewish prayers for the dead must be integrated in the prayer of thanksgiving. At present many liturgical practitioners hesitate to deviate from approved texts. But as approved text becomes understood as paradigm, not rigid prescription, greater possibilities may emerge for the expression and impression of what is communicated in the images of the dead Christ and descent into hell, and the apocalyptic, in this central prayer of the church. Where this liberty is not found, a very practical and, I dare say, realizable goal would be to place before official liturgical and episcopal conferences some eucharistic prayers of the type I am suggesting, composed by competent liturgists and/or liturgical theologians, in the hope that one or more might be approved for general use. Such a eucharistic prayer would recount what God has not done, together with what God has done. Expression would be given to a profound sense of lament and protest in the face of the evils and suffering of our age, together with thanksgiving for what God has given. Attention to the themes of deliverance and nondeliverance would be given alongside a firm affirmation that God's victory is brought about through entry into solidarity with suffering victims of all ages, unto death and into hell.

Proclamation of the word is a response to God's presence and action. Sermons must draw attention to the central mystery of the resurrection. But this can and should be done in ways that affirm the resurrection as victory and triumph over suffering, evil, and death. It is victory through and in negativity, and triumph through death. Resurrection is not passing over or around these. Evil, suffering, and death exist. Proclamation of the resurrection must take seriously the depth of evil and suffering that persons in the churches experience in our terrible age. Not taking seriously the realities of evil, suffering, and death as negative human experience bespeaks a lack of trust that God will be victorious even in them. Proclamation and sermonizing must drawn attention to the lack of cohesion, vision, and hope characteristic of our age, and hold out a vision of God's future wherein the suffering, the weak, the forgotten, and the nameless who have been trampled underfoot will hold pride of place.

* * * * * *

What I have attempted to provide here is nothing more than a hint as to how the images of the dead Christ and the descent, and a sense of the apocalyptic, might be implemented in liturgical activity in general, liturgical and eucharistic prayers in particular, and in the sermon or homily.

Between the Holocausts, the eschatological "not-yet" is the true characteristic of Christian prayer and worship.[20] A deepened sense of the apocalyptic and a remembrance of the dead Christ and Christ's descent into hell best express and impress our experience of anomie and chaos, crisis and loss of vision brought about by the twofold Holocaust. Such images are strong images, sober and shot through with hope and profound expectation for the manifestation of God's coming. They need room in our assemblies so as to move from the edges to the center.

Central to Christian worship is gathering, reading, praying, sitting, and breaking bread in memory of Christ in the church through the Spirit. Maybe it is the bread of affliction and lament that is to be broken between the Holocausts. Maybe there is (or will be) no bread at all, as at Auschwitz. But as we have learned from the voices of its victims, and the voices of the inheritors of the ancient covenant, the ethnic descendants of the first Christians: memory is the heart of liturgy. In our terrible age, we the living stand together with the dead and those yet to come, awaiting the immortality of the flesh and the glorious coming of the Lord Jesus when the power of God's love prevails over evil.

Notes

1. Johann Baptist Metz, "Facing the Jews: Christian Theology after Auschwitz," *Concilium* 175 (1984) 28.
2. J.B. Metz, *The Emergent Church* (New York: Crossroad, 1981) 21.
3. Metz, "Facing the Jews" 28.

4. Ibid. 29.

5. See John T. Pawlikowski, "Worship after the Holocaust," *Worship* 58 (1984) 315-329; see also Lawrence A. Hoffmann, "Response: Holocaust as Holocaust, Holocaust as Symbol," *Worship* 58 (1984) 333-341.

6. Yaffa Eliach, "The First Hanukkah Light in Bergen Belsen," *Hasidic Tales of the Holocaust* (New York: Avon, 1982) 14-16.

7. John Pawlikowski, "The Holocaust and Contemporary Christology," *Concilium* 175 (1984) 43.

8. Arthur Cohen puts it succinctly in the question: "If the first People of God, the inheritors of the ancient covenant, the ethnic descendants of the first Christians—if the history of this People has no relevance for the Christian Church in its fullness then what history at all speaks to Christians?" In "In Our Terrible Age: The Tremendum of the Jews," *Concilium* 175 (1984) 13-14.

9. Amos N. Wilder, *Jesus' Parables and the War of Myths*, ed. with preface by J. Breech (Philadelphia: Fortress, 1982) 156.

10. Ibid. 167.

11. Gordon Lathrop, "A Rebirth of Images: On the Use of the Bible in Liturgy," *Worship* 58 (1984) 300.

12. See Eliach, "The First Hanukkah Light," esp. part one.

13. Notable exceptions to this are J. Moltmann's *The Crucified God* and Matthew Lamb's *Solidarity with Victims*, as well as the works of the theologians of liberation.

14. J.B. Metz, "Facing the Jews" 28.

15. Examples are Monika Hellwig, *Jesus: The Compassion of God* (Wilmington, DE: Michael Glazier, 1983); Leonardo Boff, *Jesus Christ, Liberator* (New York: Orbis, 1978); and Jon Sobrino, *Christology at the Crossroads* (New York: Orbis, 1978).

16. Mary Knutsen, "The Holocaust in Theology and Philosophy," *Concilium* 175 (1984) 72.

17. The rite for matins for Holy Saturday is found in *The Lenten Triodion*, translated from original Greek by Mother Mary and Archimandrite Kallistos Ware (London: Faber and Faber, 1977) 622-655.

18. For the insights on the role of the dead Christ in the Philippines, I am indebted to David Power, "Liturgy and Culture," *East Asian Pastoral Review* [Manila] 353.

19. See, for example, Psalms 44 and 137; see also the Book of Job.

20. Lathrop, "A Rebirth of Images" 300.

16

Rhythms of the Word:
A Spirituality of the
Liturgy of the Hours

WHAT IS THE DIFFERENCE BETWEEN RECITING OR SINGING THE LITURGY OF the hours (the divine office) and praying it? And what is the relationship of the liturgy of the hours, a public form of prayer, to "private" or "personal" prayer?[1] These questions have prompted the writing of this essay.

Such questions may vex some readers. For monks and nuns whose lives are centered on choir seven times daily, such questions may never arise. But for many laypersons like myself, the liturgy of the hours is not a familiar expression of prayer. Despite the designation of the liturgy of the hours as the Prayer of Christians, remarkably few lay Christians have much experience with this mode of prayer. And so I am grateful to have the chance to bring my perspective as a lay theologian to bear on the issue of a spirituality of the liturgy of the hours. It is my hope that other "non-monastic" persons might find something of use in what follows.

In trying to describe a spirituality of the liturgy of the hours with an eye to relating this form of prayer to private prayer, I will adhere to the following strategy: first, some remarks on the terms of this essay: rhythm, word, and liturgy of the hours. Second, it is necessary to attend to the significance of the liturgy of the hours as the prayer of the church, with relationship to Jewish liturgical prayer and its role in sanctifying time. Third, attention will be given to the power of the word. That is to say, focus will be upon how the word changes our way of perceiving and being in the world. Fourth, the life of Jesus will be viewed as the parabolic word expressing God's intention for our time. Fifth, insights on the nature and function of the word will be brought to bear on the model of prayer that emerges from the writings of Teresa of Avila. In other words, the rhythms of the word that we recognize in the liturgy of the hours will be set alongside the rhythm of personal, private prayer to which Teresa of Avila invites her listener in charting the path of the soul's journey to union with God. In bringing these two rhythms together, some clarity might be brought to the question of the relationship between the liturgy of the hours, the public prayer of the church, and what is commonly called private prayer.

KEY TERMS

It is commonplace to hear that the liturgy of the hours punctuates the day. The office provides a rhythm to the day or, better, it marks the rhythm of the day, the week, the season, the year. But just what is rhythm? Simply put, rhythm is a movement or action marked by a regular recurrence of elements. Musically, rhythm is a recurrent pattern formed by notes of differing stress and duration. To speak of the office as marking the rhythms of time, or as giving a certain rhythm to the day, week, season or year, is to recognize that such rhythm lies in the arrangement of psalms, hymns, canticles, readings, and benedictions, each of different stress and duration, which together form a recurrent pattern of prayer that is repeated regularly.

The liturgy of the hours is a form of prayer whose hallmark is attentiveness to the word. This word expressed in the Scriptures is, for Christians, definitively disclosed in Jesus, the Word Incarnate. But the word extends beyond these expressions to God's proclamation and manifestation in human life, history, the world, and the church. Attentiveness to the word entails an openness to God's activity in all history and creation, but with particular attention to this presence and action discerned in the Exodus and covenant, and in the life, ministry, suffering, passion, death, and rising of Jesus Christ.

LITURGY OF THE HOURS:
PRAYER OF THE CHURCH

The focus of this essay is on one dimension of the *agendum* of Christian life—the gathering for the liturgy of the hours as an ecclesial act—for the purpose of discerning the contours of a spirituality. The divine office, even when recited alone and in silence, is the prayer of the church. As such, it expresses the notes or characteristics of the church as one, holy, catholic, and apostolic. The liturgy of the hours is an occasion for the coming together in one place of those who have been baptized into the dying and rising of Christ. As such, this gathering gives expression to the oneness and the holiness of the church. But the one assembly of the baptized does not stand alone. Through this prayer those gathered are united with all who throughout the world join in this prayer during the course of the day, as well as with all who have voiced and heard these psalms, hymns, canticles, readings, and benedictions since the time of the church of the apostles. As such, expression is given to the church as catholic (in the etymological sense of universal) and apostolic.

But this pattern or rhythm of prayer has roots in an earlier time: the life and liturgy of the Jewish community of faith. One way of examining the ritual life of the Jewish community is through the categories of passage, space, and time. From this perspective, the purpose of Jewish ritual is sanctification: of life's passage, of space, and of time. Jewish prayer at morning, evening and in the course of the day is the activity by which the community renders time sacred or holy, by remembering the Exodus and covenant, those points in time when God made of the Jews a chosen people. And so all time is viewed from the perspective of God's activity in history and presence to creation. Time is God's time, and it is sanctified precisely by remembering this and living from this perspective.

The early church set aside Jewish practices that it judged ill-suited to the new faith and to freedom in Christ. But the practice of assembling for morning and evening prayer was carried over from Jewish practice, albeit with its own emphases and orientation. Though there are clear differences between Jewish prayer forms and the prayer forms of the early life of the church, there are similarities. The similarity and continuity between them may be understood in light of this notion of the sanctification or consecration of time.[2] The most notable difference, of course, is the Christian conviction that God's activity in history and presence to creation is manifest not just in the historical events and actions of the Exodus and the covenant, but in a person: Jesus of Nazareth, the Crucified and Risen One. The life, ministry, passion, suffering, death, descent, and rising, together with the promise of his coming again—form the locus from which time is now viewed and measured. The Paschal Mystery is the measure of time: from morning to evening in the anticipation of a new dawn; from the first day of the week to the last when Christians stand again at the threshold of Sunday, the first day; from week to week to the Great Sunday, Easter, the church's celebration of the Paschal Mystery in its fullness.

THE WAY OF THE WORD

The liturgy of the hours is most fundamentally an occasion to attend to the word, to be "washed" in the word. Such attention is possible only through the presence and working of the Spirit. This word is both proclamation and manifestation of God's action and presence in Christ Jesus. The word orients us to a new sense of time through remembrance of what God has done, is now doing, and will do in and through Christ. Thus the liturgy of the hours is a celebration of the word in memory and in hope. It is an act of remembrance, in the fullest sense of the term (from the Greek, *anamnesis*), and of trust in the divine promise yet to be realized.

A fuller appreciation of the celebration of the word and of the liturgy of the hours as the occasion for repeated, patterned "washings" in the word, demands an understanding of the way the word functions. Paul Ricoeur maintains that there is in the parable a dynamic interaction of three elements: orientation, disorientation, and reorientation.[3] The parable orients the hearer of the word by introducing what is familiar and recognizable. In the telling of the parable the listener is shocked and disoriented by the events of the story. In the contrast or clash between what is familiar and what is surprising, new possibilities open up as the hearer is reoriented to alternative ways of seeing and believing. Walter Brueggemann suggests that the dynamic of the parable inheres in the word at large.[4]

The insights of both Ricoeur and Brueggemann are instructive for those who pray the liturgy of the hours. The psalms, hymns, canticles, readings, and benedictions orient those gathered by "telling the time" of God's activity in history and presence to creation, particularly in the pasch of Christ. But in the very telling, the word shocks and disorients those whose lips speak and sing, and those whose ears hear.

The word demands a reorientation to the future, the time of God's promise, the hour when the power of love will cast out all fear, and love will prevail over all evil.

THE PARABOLIC QUALITY OF THE WORD

Christian prayer, be it public or "private," is rooted in the Paschal Mystery and is intended to bring those who pray into a fuller celebration of this mystery. In every age the Christian community has attempted to find appropriate ways of giving praise and thanks to God in prayer, in light of changing circumstances and different exigencies. The life and prayer of a person and a community depend in no small measure on the way they remember the person of Jesus Christ. Put another way, persons and groups make decisions about which elements in the life of Jesus, the Word Incarnate, are central to the task of being and becoming Christian in a particular time, place, culture, and tradition. Christian history goes to show that this has been done in every age. Put more simply, hearers of the word hear the word in certain ways.

What then is the appropriate way to hear the word *in our time*? In light of the needs and exigencies of our age, it is the parabolic quality of the word in its entirety that must be given its chance in our hearing. This implies that all the words, psalms, hymns, canticles, readings, and benedictions be given the chance to pattern our prayer on parable's pattern: orientation, disorientation, reorientation.

The conviction that the parabolic character of word needs to be given its chance in our hearing is rooted in the more fundamental conviction that the life, ministry, death, and resurrection of Jesus together form the parabolic word of God. That is to say that the pattern of Christ's Paschal Mystery, which is the point of reference for all Christian life and prayer, and so for every gathering for the liturgy of the hours, itself expresses this pattern of orientation, disorientation, reorientation. The parabolic quality of the word as orientation, disorientation, reorientation, or description, deconstruction, rediscription is nowhere more pronounced than in the living, dying and rising of Christ—the Paschal Mystery.

The parabolic character of the word, whose rhythms fill the ears and the hearts of those gathered to be "washed" in its ebb and flow, gives rise to a sharp critique of conventional standards and the unquestioned, yet tightly held, assumptions about God, self, and others. But it also energizes those whose ears hear and whose lips speak this word to live and to work for a radically new future, whose contours are discerned in the proclamation of the Crucified and Risen One.

RHYTHMS OF PRAYER:
PERSONAL AND PUBLIC

Having suggested that the rhythms of the word celebrated in the liturgy of the hours might be discerned by careful attention to the parabolic pattern of orientation, disorientation, and disorientation, we can take up the question of the relationship between this public prayer of the church and personal or private prayer.

The Christian tradition abounds with descriptions of what has come to be called personal prayer, beginning with Jesus' own instruction on how to pray, addressing God as "Abba" (Matthew 6:9-13; Luke 11:2-4), and continuing in the early tradition with the treatises on prayer in the writings of Cyprian in the west and Origen in the east. But the sharp division between personal and public prayer that came to characterize later ages, and which has made its mark in our own day, was unknown in early Christian centuries. This is exemplified in the *Our* Father as the prayer of Jesus and the pattern of all early treatises on Christian prayer (even though the term "Our" is not found in the Lukan account of the prayer of Jesus).

One of the most familiar classical formulations of the life of prayer is found in the writings of Teresa of Avila, whose influence goes well beyond the parameters of the Carmelite school and those who have come under its tutelage, directly or indirectly. The *Book of Her Life* (begun in 1562 and completed in 1565), *Way of Perfection* (1566?), *Interior Castle* (1577), and *Book of Her Foundations* (begun in 1573 and completed in 1582) provide elements that have gone together to shape a model of personal prayer.[5] In this model we can discern a recognizable rhythm, as has been described above, which in many ways embodies both earlier and later understandings of personal prayer. If for no other reason than this, it commands attention in auditioning a response to the question of the connection between personal prayer and the liturgy of the hours.

Teresa of Avila's primary concern is with the soul's union with God in and through prayer. Her writings suggest that there is a certain recognizable pattern in the life of growth toward union with God. First, the soul moves toward union with God by *ascending* stages. Second, such growth entails experiencing the *dialectic of consolation and dryness*, light and darkness, both positive and negative factors. Third, the fullness of union is likened to *marriage*, inclusive of sexual consummation.

Whatever the merits of Teresa of Avila's model, the contemporary reader of the *Interior Castle* is likely to note the absence of Scripture in her writing. What role the Scripture may have had in her own life and prayer is difficult to determine if the *Interior Castle* is read as a discrete text.

In an attempt to connect public and personal prayer, the rhythms of the word described in this study will be given their chance alongside the rhythms or patterns that Teresa describes in the soul's growth toward union with God. What happens when these two rhythms are brought together in such a way that the orienting, disorienting, reorienting word of God is allowed to interact with Teresa's rhythm?

The advantages of making this connection should be clear. First, establishing such a connection enables us to cultivate approaches to personal and public prayer that are both rooted in the transforming power of the word. Second, Teresa's model of prayer described in this chapter could be redescribed in ways more suited to the life of prayer and union with God *in our own day*. To this task we now turn.

RHYTHMS OF PRAYER REDESCRIBED

The parables of Jesus destabilize, shock, and shatter our standard ways of thinking about things. In light of the redescription of reality and of life within it proclaimed in parable, Christian prayer and union with God might be more properly understood in terms of *descent* rather than ascent. Such a view is rooted in the *kenosis* of Christ. Union with God thus requires a commitment to downward mobility in order to live in mutual love with the wounded and the weak, in imitation of Christ's self-emptying. Growth toward union with God in our day includes the awareness of negative factors as well as positive ones. "Naming the negative" is part of the life of growth in the Spirit in our day. This implies more than recognizing the interior movements of consolation and dryness in a person's deepest self. The place or space for recognizing this dialectic of sin and grace, darkness and light, and "naming the negative," is not only in the interior castle of the soul. It is in the public prayer of the church that we need to make room for "naming the negative", a space for giving voice to the individual and the corporate sense of desolation, abandonment, hopelessness. Precisely how this is to be done is the responsibility of different worshiping communities to determine in light of their specific charisms, needs, and aspirations. But such a mode of prayer that would give adequate attention to desolation as well as consolation, to the public as well as personal manifestations of the negative factors in human life, would require a deeper appreciation of the role of *lamentation* in Jewish prayer. This tradition needs to be given more room the public prayer of the church.[6]

A model of personal prayer informed by the word in and for our time would recognize that the consummation of the life of union with God is correctly understood not so much in terms of the mystical marriage between the soul and the divine bridegroom, but more in terms of the invitation to *solidarity with the Crucified Christ* in and through the practice of solidarity with those who suffer.

CONTOURS OF A SPIRITUALITY

This chapter has tentatively auditioned an explanation of the liturgy of the hours as a form of prayer expressive of the Spirit and the word at work. It has also attempted to clarify the nature of the relationship between public and personal prayer, a distinction which should not be made too sharply, lest we bring about further cleavage between them, a cleavage sometimes as troublesome as the one between action and contemplation.

In bringing the rhythms of the word to bear upon Teresa of Avila's rhythms of personal prayer, the aim has not been to set aside her contribution. Nor has it been to undercut the necessary place of personal prayer alongside public prayer. Rather, the intention has been to give the word its chance to complement a classical approach to personal prayer so that it might more effectively address the needs and exigencies of our own time. No definitive resting point has been reached, but several elements of a spirituality of the liturgy of the hours can be spelled out based upon this exposition.

First, the spirituality of the liturgy of the hours is an ecclesial spirituality. In the gathering of the baptized for the liturgy of the hours, the Prayer of Christians, the hallmarks of the church as one, holy, catholic, and apostolic, are given particular expression.

Second, this is a spirituality of the word. As such, it is a celebration in memory and in hope. Those who gather for this celebration do so in order to attend to God's presence to creation and action in history, particularly to what God has done and is doing in and through Christ Jesus.

Third, based upon of the centrality of the word, this is an eschatological spirituality. That is to say that the word's power to orient, disorient, and reorient to a new vision of God's future, summons all those who speak and hear it to a deeper anticipation of God's kingdom yet to be realized.

Fourth, following from what has been said immediately above, this spirituality is cultivated in attentiveness and anticipation.

Fifth, the spirituality of the liturgy of the hours is enriched and complemented by personal or private prayer, and vice versa. A relationship of reciprocity and critical correlation exists between the two. Through the presence and working of the Spirit in both forms of prayer, one is influenced by the other.

Sixth, following from what has been said immediately above, the liturgy of the hours is dynamic, as are personal or private modes of prayer. Neither is fixed. Both forms of prayer must constantly be reconsidered in terms of their ability to give adequate expression to the power of the word.

Seventh, in our own day, it is the parabolic quality of the word that needs to stand forth in our public and private prayer. This needs to be accompanied by a deeper appreciation of the Kenotic Christ as the central image or root metaphor in our prayer. Such an approach to Christ involves a redescription of prevalent notions of prayer and union with God, together with the praxis of compassion and solidarity with all who suffer in and through the Crucified.

Whatever our walk of life it is useful to recall that there are many roads, but one Way. Attentiveness to the parabolic pattern of the word, the way the word works, provides occasion for hearing again and again the rhythms of public and personal prayer, as if for the first time.

Notes

1. All prayer is in some sense personal. In using the terms "personal" and "private" prayer in this essay, I have in mind the various modes of prayer other than the public, liturgical prayer of the church.

2. General Instruction of the Liturgy of the Hours, no. 10.

3. Paul Ricoeur, "Biblical Hermeneutics," *Semeia* 4 (1975) 126.

4. Walter Brueggemann, *The Prophetic Imagination* (Philadelphia: Fortress, 1978); see especially chapters 3 and 4 where Bruegemann treats the word in terms of its critical function as well as its ability to energize believers in their efforts to fashion a new world order.

5. See especially Teresa of Avila, *Interior Castle*, tr. Kieran Kavanaugh and Otilio Rodriguez, introduction by Kieran Kavanaugh (New York: Paulist Press, 1979).

6. For a fuller appreciation of lamentation, see Brueggemann, *The Prophetic Imagination*, chapter 3.

17

Cry Aloud, Daughter of Zion

"WE ARE AN EASTER PEOPLE, AND ALLELUIA IS OUR SONG." AS THE liturgical reforms were being implemented in local churches in the days of Vatican II, this and other similar phrases were hallmarks of Catholic worship. Banners with words of promise and future adorned church sanctuaries. Upbeat lyrics filled song sheets and missalettes. And pious and reverent Catholics were invited to come to church in a spirit of whooping joy. Many years have passed since the opening of the council. The optimism and enthusiasm of those days have waned. "Alleluia"— the "A word" never to be uttered or proclaimed in our assemblies during Lent—is mumbled and murmured in many congregations throughout the bulk of the liturgical year.

The present state of liturgical affairs cannot simply be attributed to a loss of enthusiasm or optimism. We live in a time very different from that of the council and the years immediately following. Ours is a time of crisis, a crisis that touches on liturgy. Above all, this is a crisis of hope. We are part of a humanity that lives with a profound awareness of disintegration and destruction. This is nowhere more evident than in the twofold holocaust of our age. First, there is the holocaust of the Jews and six million others at the hands of the Nazis. Then there is the possible nuclear holocaust threatening the entire world. In light of this twofold reality, the churches are continually compelled to consider whether there is any hope with which to face the future.

In our own day we are faced with the suffering of millions and with the death of thousands and thousands by senseless violence. We are confronted with the senselessness and meaninglessness of our age signaled in the twofold holocaust. In light of this, the remembrance of Jesus Christ which is at the heart of Christian liturgy must give voice to sorrow and lamentation as well as praise and thanksgiving. In lamentation the community's suffering, pain, and sorrow is expressed and in such self-expression they can be transformed.

"Alleluia" does not resound from full throats in our assemblies because there is an ever-growing awareness that "something is quite wrong with the way things are." Christians are more and more uneasy with the naive and euphoric giggle of glee often mistaken for the sober and sane hope shaping the heart and soul of Christian faith and expressed in choruses of "Alleluia."

Lamentation "names" or articulates a community's perception of human sin and the forces of evil that prohibit the free reception and response to God's grace and word. This sense of lamentation was and remains vital to the Jewish people and to their liturgy. It must be retrieved and allowed to come to the center of Christian assemblies.

Lamentation is not endless complaining. It carries the seed of hope. Rather than ruling out praise and thanksgiving, it is the first movement in an authentic expression of both. For it is possible to accept our sin and our complicity in the sinfulness of the world only where there is a trace of hope. Whatever is remembered in lamentation, in crying out before God's face, is renewed and redeemed. To lament is to look to God's promise and to voice the desire and urgent longing for God which is yet unfulfilled. Lamentation in the Christian sense is at the same time an act of thanksgiving for the promise given in Jesus Christ which is being brought to completion by grace and Spirit.

At the level of practice, we need to make room in our assemblies for lamentation. This might be done in several ways.

First, there needs to be a concerted effort to retrieve the theme of lament so that it might be proclaimed and heard in its fullness through the liturgy of the word. There is a noticeable absence of lamentation as a motif in the public prayer of the church. The great bulk of readings from the Book of Lamentations and the psalms that are shot through with lament have been omitted, through excision or selective remembering, from the lectionary.

A second step would be to make room in worship for the apocalyptic. Authentic apocalyptic is positive discourse regarding what God has done, is doing, and what is coming to be. But apocalyptic language emerges when systems of meaning, value, and cohesion are breaking down because of evil and sin. The language of apocalyptic says "No!" to the present order of things, and "Yes!" to the new world God is bringing about. This is a world where the strong and clever have been cast down from their places of power, and where the poor and the wounded hold the place of honor.

A third area where practical efforts might be made is that of preaching. Speech about hope in these days must be sober and more realistic than it often manages to be. We live in a world in which there is little hope among the young. What grounds are there for hope in a century that has seen two world wars, tragedies of global significance, and the attempted annihilation of the world as we know it through nuclear arms? Homilies will remain "semantically empty" as long as preachers and congregations turn their backs to these facts. Whatever hope is proclaimed in word and sacrament must be a proclamation that takes such negative factors seriously.

And finally, in the church's song we must at times sing with those whose harps were hung in an alien land and whose only music was the wailing of voices nearly crushed by oppression. Our voices must be strong enough to sing of the goodness of a God whose presence we affirm precisely when we feel most abandoned. And our lips must open wide enough to weep at the ways in which we as the Body of Christ have betrayed the gifts of grace and Spirit given in baptism.

It is a strong, sane, and sober hope that is born of lament. Christian assemblies are not simply arenas for whooping joy. They are the coming together of the Body of Christ whose mystery is one of life in and through suffering, dying, and death. "Alleluia" is indeed the song of this people, a people bold enough to proclaim in word and worship: The Crucified lives!

18

Welcoming the Wounded and the Weak

My purpose here is to make some connections. Recognizing that there are real differences between the Pauline communities and the communities of l'Arche of Jean Vanier, I am convinced that there are nonetheless some striking parallels between them. I hope to advance the discussion about the function of ritual in community by arguing that ritual serves much the same purpose in the communities of l'Arche as it did in the Pauline communities. As a result of this analysis, I hope that others will give further consideration to the ways in which ritual might be more effective in light of significant social factors that shape the life of the churches.

Definition of Terms

Wayne Meeks has constructed a social history of Pauline Christianity.[1] He does not, however, use a purely sociological approach. Meeks' method is more of a dialectic between the documentary sources and the sociological analysis he employs. His sociological approach is thus part of a larger repertoire of hermeneutical tools. He ably demonstrates that within Pauline Christianity predominant figures were of a variety of social strata. Based upon this insight, he suggests that Pauline Christianity was generally made up of persons from various social strata. Meeks maintains that several of the prominent members of these churches had at least two things in common: "status inconsistency" and "social mobility."

Status inconsistency or status dissonance describes the phenomenon of moving or crossing unusually rigid social boundaries in a society within which restrictions against such crossing were quite strong. Those marked by status inconsistency in Paul's world were individual women of moderate wealth, Jews with wealth in a pagan society, and freed slaves with skill and money, but stigmatized because of origin. In contemporary parlance one might say that it was hard to know how or where these people "fit in."

The second characteristic of the prominent figures in the Pauline churches is social mobility. Precisely because of status inconsistency, the social standing of these people was relatively fluid or mobile. As a result, they had a fair measure of freedom within a society with otherwise very rigid structures. If they were unable to have the security that came from being identified with a particular social group, they were able to enjoy the freedom from the restrictions that such identification often brought.

RITUAL EFFICACY IN THE PAULINE COMMUNITIES

Meeks offers a view of ritual efficacy informed by sociological categories. My purpose here is not to argue whether a sociological approach provides sufficient explanation of ritual or sacramental efficacy. My purpose is rather to draw attention to a view of ritual efficacy that stands in marked contrast to understandings grounded in medieval philosophy or metaphysics, and which may serve as a complement or corrective to them. In the medieval understanding, emphasis is given to the formal-material constants (e.g., bread, wine, gestures, words) of a ritual. What other perspectives might be opened up by looking to the function of a ritual from a sociological view? Here the abiding question is: what does ritual do? For Meeks, given the various social strata represented in the Pauline communities, the function of ritual was to unite, integrate, bring about cohesion, and hold out a vision of hope. If ritual accomplished these purposes, it could be said to be effective, efficacious. In the language of a later school, we might say that to the degree that ritual/sacrament unites, integrates, brings about cohesion, and holds out a

vision of hope for persons of various social strata, it is efficacious, it gives grace.

As a result of the social factors of status inconsistency and
social mobility, the Pauline churches faced unique problems.
These problems were addressed and, to some degree, resolved
ritually. Their own life experience of marginalization and
ostracization resulting from status inconsistency was brought to
bear upon the rituals of baptism and eucharist, and to other
minor rituals, which provided hope, cohesion, and vision.

It is useful to note that ritual helped integrate these diverse
persons from various strata into a *communitas* in Christ. Ritual
from this perspective provides occasion for socialization. It is a
sense of belonging or solidarity which results from participation
in ritual. As such ritual is constitutive of community.

The values of this *communitas* in Christ stand in opposition to
the prevailing social stratification of "the world." The residue of
social structure and stratification seems to abide in every generation of Christians in the way they live and worship. The
influence of such structures and stratification upon liturgical
expression works at cross-purposes in a *communitas* that expresses and receives its identity in rituals projecting values of
hope, cohesion, and unity of a sort that stand in direct opposition to those structures.[2]

Beliefs and Rituals: Correlation

In order to understand the function of ritual within this
communitas in Christ, a closer look needs to be directed to what
these groups believed and how such beliefs correlate with specific patterns of worship. The particular beliefs and patterns of
life and action that go together to shape the life of a religious
group are nourished in forms of worship that correlate with
such beliefs, life patterns, and actions. Briefly, there is a direct
correlation between social experience and symbolization. The
more problematic issue is to determine which is cause and
which is effect.[3]

It seems likely that those marked by status inconsistency and
social mobility would be deeply attracted by the rituals and
symbols of Christianity. Among these, symbols of personal and
group transformation, together with rituals that expressed the

awareness of an evil world under God's judgment and grace, would be especially attractive to persons whose hopes and anxieties were shaped by holding an ambiguous place in the social order. On the other hand, it may have been more the case that the experience of alienation and loneliness that marked the lives of prominent members in the communities tended to reinforce precisely those paradoxical symbols which characterized Pauline belief.[4]

In a society that stressed position and proper order, status inconsistency brought with it a sense of anxiety and loneliness. To this, the intimacy of Christian community provided an alternative. The emotional language of family and affection, together with the notion of a personal and caring God, could elicit and sustain personal commitment between and among members. But most importantly, perhaps, the central image, the paradoxical and dialectical value projection of the Crucified-and-Risen-One, expressed a convincing picture of how things actually seemed to work in the world. There were four central beliefs at the crux of both social experience and symbolization within the Pauline Christian communities.[5]

First, there was belief in God as one. This was expressed in patterns of life and worship that enabled networks of local groups to express and receive their identity as a single assembly of God in the world. Unity was a pressing and abiding concern of leaders within the Pauline communities. In harmony with this goal of unity, life and worship within local communities were both exclusive and familial.

Second, God was believed to be both active and intimate. Rooted as they were in the intimacy of the local household assembly, patterns of life and worship were marked by a high level of personal commitment and a large measure of direct personal engagement.

Third, there is the eschatological worldview characteristic of the Pauline communities. These early Christians believed that the crucifixion and resurrection of Jesus had already brought about a change, indeed, a reversal, in the world order. Corresponding to this, they experienced a shift in the social place each person had experienced by conversion to the good news. This shift was also expressed in the rituals of the Pauline communities. In both baptism and eucharist divisions based on role and separations brought about by status were replaced by the *communitas*. The unity of brothers and sisters in the "new human" was understood to replace social systems that were operative before the advent of the Christ. These earlier social mechanisms had apparently crept into the Pauline communities and were shaping the contours of social behavior generated by those who purportedly had Christ as their inspiration. The old creation was determinating the new creation (1 Corinthians 11:17-34). But Paul insists that the old order was passing away, and the new order must be visible in the celebration of the Lord's Supper.

Fourth, there was the belief in the paradoxical and dialectical mystery of the cross and resurrection. These were members of a community that experienced social contradictions. In the Pauline *communitas*, persons of a wide mix shared in intimate personal fellowship which would normally be prohibited in society at large. And at the table of the Lord bread was broken and the cup shared between and among persons who, according to the rigid social stratification in the world of the Apostle Paul, were vastly unequal.

SOCIALIZATION INTO *COMMUNITAS*: THE LIFE AND LITURGY OF L'ARCHE

Though there are some similarities, there are also obvious differences between the Pauline communities and l'Arche. The communities of l'Arche of Jean Vanier nonetheless provide a useful reference for understanding the significance of Meeks' insights for contemporary Christian life and practice, because of the tremendous diversity of persons who are socialized into l'Arche. My aim is not to argue that l'Arche communities are addressing the same problems as the Pauline communities. Rather, my hope is to demonstrate that, even though the sociological method adopted by Meeks may be insufficient in itself as an explanation of ritual/sacramental efficacy, it is quite useful in helping to understand the role of ritual in socializing persons with vast differences into a community in Christ.

Vanier and l'Arche

Chapter 1 of this volume gives a short biography of Jean Vanier, the founder of l'Arche. It relates how this Canadian, former navy officer and professor, established at Trosly-Breuil, France, a home, called l'Arche, for the mentally handicapped.

From the seed sown at Trosly-Breuil in August 1964, l'Arche has grown to include over one hundred communities world-wide, representing well over two hundred family-like homes. Small in number and loose in structure, the communities of l'Arche are founded upon the belief in the uniqueness and sacredness of each person, whether handicapped or not. Motivated by the affirmation of the priority of the beatitudes in Christian and human living, the gifts of each person are to be nurtured and called forth with predilection for the poorest, weakest, and most wounded in community and society. The handicapped and their "assistants" (the nonhandicapped) live together in the spirit of the beatitudes.

Similarities between l'Arche and Pauline Communities

If I have understood Meeks' use of the term, many of the people in l'Arche may be understood in terms of status inconsistency. In society at large the mentally handicapped are simultaneously abhorred and respected. They are the product of "bad blood" according to some, and are the "beloved of God" in the minds of others. Once confined to asylums because confused with the mentally ill, or relegated to the role of village idiot, the mentally handicapped are often difficult to "place" or to classify, especially now that mainstreaming has more or less successfully opened the doors of institutions so that the mentally handicapped can "come and go as they please." One might liken the mentally handicapped to the freed slaves in the world of Paul. In Meeks' description, freed slaves developed a certain skill and financial security but were stigmatized by origin.

Status inconsistency is also descriptive of the assistants at l'Arche. Oftentimes with advanced degrees in medicine, philosophy, or education, they forfeit the privileges associated with their role, status, or career to live in community with the poor, the wounded, and the forgotten.

Within the community of l'Arche there is also a high degree of social mobility. Though Vanier's intention has been from the beginning to provide lifelong homes[6] so that the handicapped might grow in an environment of security and stability, both handicapped and nonhandicapped move from home to home, village to village, and in the case of the assistants, from country to country as needs arise.

There is also a noticeable parallel between the core beliefs expressed in the patterns of life and worship of the Pauline communities and those of l'Arche communities. To take but one example: belief in one God is expressed in patterns of life and worship wherein persons of various religious traditions live under the same roof, sharing life and sharing prayer as they do in the communities of l'Arche in India. One of the great challenges of l'Arche is to find forms of prayer and common worship that adequately express their belief in one God, while at the same time being appropriate expressions that respect religious and denominational differences.[7]

The Function of Ritual in l'Arche

At this point it may be useful to look more closely at the function of ritual in l'Arche communities. In doing so let us keep our attention fixed upon the wider implications of this study. Our own society is one in which many are marked by social mobility. On this point there seems to be little room for dispute. But I would also like to suggest that ours is a society and a church comprised of many persons characterized by status inconsistency as Meeks has described it. If this is true, one might ask what kind of ritual might serve our purposes of socialization better? More particularly, in light of the fact that l'Arche includes a great diversity of persons who are vastly unequal at least in terms of intellect, what are they doing to bring about socialization into a community of vision, hope, and promise of a new world order?

L'Arche is a community of self- and mutual-help. The awareness of need is strong, as is vulnerability. Woundedness and need for healing are deep. Hence pardon and celebration are leitmotifs of their life and liturgy. Brought together because of the hurts inflicted by society at large, those in l'Arche have found refuge, room for diversity and hope. Life in l'Arche is, from this perspective, counter-cultural. It is the social experience of alienation, suffering, and ostracization on the one hand, and refuge, welcome, and hope on the other hand that shapes the pattern of life and the specific beliefs expressed in worship. For example, we could look to the celebration of the eucharist in l'Arche communities that are specifically Christian. Those who are "socially outside" because of mental or physical handicap, and because of the psychic wound brought on by rejection and alienation, are "eucharistically inside," and thereby are given hope for healing. In the eucharist distinction between assistant and handicapped fades and a diversity of gifts flourishes and functions, from the greatest to the least. Though social status and stratification abide to some degree in the eucharistic celebrations of l'Arche, the eucharist nonetheless functions as a paradigm of communion and justice. Socialization takes place slowly and gradually rather than all at once as social experience is expressed and transformed through symbolization.

Because need, vulnerability, and woundedness are such a part of the social experience of so many in l'Arche, this colors their spirituality in large measure and needs to be expressed and transformed in prayer and worship.[8] The expression of these negative experiences is not found so much in the eucharist or other major religious rituals of the community. Rather, they are more likely to be expressed in minor rituals.[9] These take a variety of forms, most of which are domestic in orientation and tenor. Whereas it may be true that the eucharist is the heart and soul of l'Arche communities that are predominantly Christian, it is also true that the process of socialization into *communitas* occurs to no small degree in the minor rituals of the home. Evening prayer in the home provides occasion for intimate expression of personal prayer: a quarrel at work, feelings of abandonment by parents, an assistant's decision to marry which results in joy as well as sorrow on the part of those she will leave behind in the community. There are birthdays, name days, anniversaries, arrivals, regular departures, and frequent burials. Plaques and crosses in homes and workplaces mark the deaths of community members. All these minor rituals go together to shape the liturgy of life at l'Arche and contribute to the process of socialization of persons who occupy a very dubious place in society into a *communitas* in Christ. Because l'Arche is a community whose members have a profound sense of the negative factors in human life, these negative factors must be related in some fashion to the rituals that constitute community.

To the issue of social mobility it needs to be said that bonding between and among the members of l'Arche, and their sense of cohesion and unity, is strong despite the fact that communities are scattered throughout the world. This bonding is nourished and sustained in prayer and worship. But the bonding that occurs amidst this mobile community whose way of life is often described as "living with the provisional" and whose assistants may serve in France, Honduras, and the United States within a three-year period, is affective in nature. That is to say that they are rooted and bonded in what can only be called the spirit of l'Arche, not in any juridical, canonical, or parish structure. The rituals of the communities are recognizable throughout the world. Though they do vary according to local custom, their purpose is to bond persons of various languages and religious traditions into what has come to be called the family of l'Arche. The International Federation of l'Arche, which meets in a different country every four years or so, and which has no juridical powers whatever, provides occasion for ritualization of their common identity and solidarity.

A Challenge to l'Arche

L'Arche is not a finished product. As a result, it is fair to raise the question: how might the purposes of l'Arche be better served in ritual? The social experience of the l'Arche communities is marked by what might be called negative experiences in human life. The impact of these is expressed mostly in the minor rituals of the community. Herein the close connection between liturgy and spirituality is brought to the fore. But this connection, and the reciprocal relationship between the two, would be better served if there were more possibility in the community's major rituals, such as the eucharist, for naming and expressing the negative factors that have shaped their social experience, so that such negative experience might be more adequately integrated through public liturgical expression. The l'Arche communities need to seek new creative ways of expressing their belief that in God's future the strong, clever, and robust will be cast from their thrones and the poor and wounded will hold first place. This is expressed to some degree in the rituals of l'Arche, but needs to be more adequately proclaimed in its pattern of public worship.

Another area in which the purposes of Jean Vanier and l'Arche might better be served is seen in light of the ecumenical and interreligious character of many of the communities. The origins of l'Arche are within the Roman Catholic tradition. Its structures of symbolization have strongly influenced the spirituality and liturgy of the communities throughout the world. It remains an unfinished task for l'Arche communities to respond fully to the work of the Spirit in persons by cultivating forms of liturgy that more appropriately correlate with the belief in the oneness of God and the inherent sacredness and dignity of the human being by virtue of creation by God's hand, regardless of religious or denominational difference.

Beyond l'Arche

Several problems facing the contemporary churches are in no small measure brought on by particular manifestations of status inconsistency and social mobility. We might consider issues related to the changing role of women in church and society in light of the category of status inconsistency. Whatever argument one would care to advance in favor of or against the efforts of Christian feminists, their voices have made it quite clear that the fullness of the experience of women is not, and has not been, consistent with the status and roles assigned them. The confusion, disillusionment, and anger elicited by the women's movement is in no small measure due to the fact that, according to some, women have left their "place" and are "trying to fit into" other social structures—what some would insist is "a man's world." On the other hand, contemporary expressions of social mobility abound from urban regentrification to the traveling people in Ireland, and the homeless, street people in our own country.

In light of the position that many of the problems facing us might be understood in terms of status inconsistency and social mobility, the findings of Meeks and the practices at l'Arche offer useful insight. They partially answer the question: how can ritual better serve the process of socialization into *communitas* in Christ, given the vast diversity of persons in church and world?

IMPLICATIONS FOR THE
CONTEMPORARY CHURCHES

What form would ritual take if the problems of socialization facing the churches were to be adequately addressed and resolved ritually as they were in the Pauline communities and are, to some degree, in the present practice of l'Arche communities?

First, there needs to be a fuller recognition that the *communitas* in Christ stands in opposition to the prevailing social structures of "the world." Christian ritual is counter-cultural. Those forced to the margins of society because of race, class, sex, or economic standing should find in *communitas* a home of refuge, room for diversity, and a profound hope in a new order expressed in ritual. The problem with much contemporary ritual is that it mirrors the stratification of the world (e.g., its patriarchal base, the radical separation between clergy and laity) instead of expressing an alternative worldview. Precisely because of this, Christian ritual has become semantically empty for increasing numbers of Christian people, and has lost appeal to those who once looked to it as something providing cohesion, unity, and hope. For increasing numbers of Christians, particularly women, liturgy alienates and oppresses in much the same way that the social structures of the present order do. Ritual needs to regain its counter-culture bearings in light of the nature of the *communitas* to which Christians are called and committed; a community in which there is "neither slave nor free, Jew nor Greek, male nor female, but all are one in Christ Jesus" (Galatians 3:28).

Here it may be useful to point out that ritual/sacrament is to serve a critical function in relation to both culture and accepted, approved forms of worship. The transformation of both culture and operative forms of worship is enhanced rather than ruled out when greater consideration is given to this critical function. This shift in focus results in a view of sacrament and liturgy that is more apocalyptic than analogical, emphasizing the "not yet" over the "already," with attention to what is not given in sacrament as well as what is.[10]

Second, we live in a world in which there is little hope among the young. What grounds are there for hope in a century that has seen two world wars, tragedies of global significance, the attempted annihilation of an entire race of people, and the extermination of six million others? And what basis is there for hope in light of the possibility of the annihilation of the world as we know it through nuclear arms? Christians cannot pray with their backs turned toward these negative events. They must be given room in our assemblies. Christian ritualization that does not "name the negative" and our complicity in it, and does not express a vision of hope in light of these negative experiences, is inadequate.

Ritual serves the process of socializing people into a body that lives by the paradox of cross and resurrection. In much contemporary ritual there is a suppression of the negative. If there is not a more effective symbolization of the belief in resurrection *in* and *through* suffering, dying, and death (negative human experiences) rather than *around* or *beyond* these experiences, then Christian ritual and community offer no real alternative to the hopelessness and futurelessness characteristic of our age.

Third, and this derives from what is said immediately above, there needs to be more room in our assemblies for lamentation. Christian communities are not simply places for celebration. The vitality of the negative, focused on the mystery of the cross, must find expression in ritual and symbolization more than is managed at present. I am persuaded that there is no more apt place to begin than by retrieving lament as an appropriate form of public worship. Here we might envision ways in which liturgical readings, sermons, and eucharistic prayers might take more cognizance of the lamentation motifs in the psalms and in the Book of Lamentations.[11] Again, if Christian ritual is to socialize persons into *communitas* in Christ, then it needs to do so in such a way that the suppression of the negative and the denial of death characteristic of the present social order find a clear alternative that is at once realistic and hopeful. Lamentation is not endless moaning. It names the negative before God's face and calls for changing what can be changed. It also acknowledges what cannot be changed. Whatever hope is expressed rises up from this honest realization.

Finally, ritual should address affective needs for belonging and solidarity. Present approaches to ritual often appeal primarily to the intellect or the "cognitive" faculty. Ritual is viewed as teacher or pedagogical tool in a rather restricted sense. Christians are looked upon as those who believe the same things as these beliefs are expressed and projected in ritual. Further, our notions of belonging often cluster around the centrality of the geographical parish church. We belong to such and such a parish.

I submit, with all due respect to those whose valiant efforts are given to parish life and renewal, that the geographical parish church is no longer the center of belonging for increasing numbers of people. Here I am persuaded that the basic Christian communities model of South America and Latin America, no longer a stranger to our own culture, is becoming a locus for a sense of belonging and solidarity. These are small communities of self- and mutual-help, bonded together as a family by the spirit of the Gospel. The communities are small, intimate, personal. Bonding is of an affective rather than juridical or parochial sort. It remains to be seen what type of rituals will continue to emerge in order to bring about socialization into this expression of *communitas* in Christ. Whatever form they take, it seems clear that the prime concern will be to socialize persons into a *communitas* that stands in direct contradiction to the prevailing social stratification of the world. Perhaps it is this characteristic of ritual which needs to be most stressed and which provides the key to an explanation of the enormous growth and success of the basic Christian communities. And perhaps in this lies the reason for the suspicion that these "popular churches" are alternative churches. Their rituals socialize a diversity of persons into *communitas* in Christ more effectively than the "official," parochial churches manage to do.

* * * * * *

Present efforts toward a renewed understanding of the relationship between liturgy and life, worship and social experience, would do well to look more closely at social experience as this is expressed and transformed (or not) through symbolization. It is at this juncture where the Spirit's work in persons can be discerned. Increasing attention must also be given to alternative models for understanding sacramental/ritual efficacy, particularly those informed by the insights of social analysis. The construction of an intelligible theory of sacramental efficacy informed by sociological models is a task that awaits us in our common work. The insights of Wayne Meeks regarding how socialization into *communitas* in Christ took place in the social world of the Apostle Paul are helpful. The ritual and sacramental life of Jean Vanier and l'Arche provide a contemporary example of how such socialization into *communitas* occurs with greater or lesser success. But the unique and particular manifestations of status inconsistency and social mobility in our age require new ways of looking at the question of how ritual/

sacrament works (i.e., how it gives grace) and new forms of ritual which more adequately relate to contemporary modes of perceiving and being.

Notes

1. Wayne Meeks, *The First Urban Christians: The Social World of the Apostle Paul* (New Haven: Yale University Press, 1983).

2. John C. Haughey, "Eucharist at Corinth: You Are the Christ," in *Above Every Name*, ed. Thomas E. Clarke (New York: Paulist Press, 1980) 112.

3. Elsewhere I have maintained that the nature of the relationship between liturgy and spirituality is one of reciprocity and critical correlation; see Michael Downey, "Liturgie et spiritualité: une rélation réciproque et critique," *Liturgie* 52 (1985) 3-19; see also "Liturgy's Form," chapter 14 in the present volume.

4. Meeks, *First Urban Christians* 190-192.

5. Ibid.

6. Jean Vanier, "Lifelong Homes for the Adult Mentally Retarded" (mimeographed), 1966.

7. Thérèse Vanier, "A Struggle for Unity," in *The Challenge of l'Arche*, introd. and conclusion by Jean Vanier (Ottawa: Novalis, 1981) 135-148.

8. For an analysis of the spirituality of l'Arche, see Michael Downey, *A Blessed Weakness: The Spirit of Jean Vanier and l'Arche* (San Francisco: Harper & Row, 1986).

9. For his treatment of the importance of minor rituals, see Meeks, *First Urban Christians* 142ff.

10. For an appreciation of the critical function of liturgy and sacrament, see David N. Power, *Unsearchable Riches: The Symbolic Nature of Liturgy* (New York: Pueblo Publishing Co., 1984).

11. For more on lamentation, see Walter Brueggemann, "The Costly Loss of Lament," *Journal for the Study of the Old Testament* 36 (1986) 57-71.

EPILOGUE

19

Spirituality at the Juncture of Modernity and Postmodernity

I AM A "RELIC OF THE SIXTIES." AND I REMEMBER THE DAY THE SECOND Vatican Council began. Home from school because of illness (real or feigned I can't remember), I was watching, on the little black and white TV in our living room, hoards of mitered bishops enter Saint Peter's. It was one of those events so big that it was being telecast on all three channels. I was fascinated by it all. And I was delighted. Because even as a fourth grader, I loathed TV soap operas. As far as I was concerned, even a parade of bishops was better than "General Hospital."

What I remember most of all is people talking about the church finally addressing the concerns of people in the modern world. Only much later did I come to see that church leaders seem to have awakened to the demands of the modern world just as modernity itself was on the brink of collapse. This is not to diminish the inestimable contribution of the Second Vatican Council. It is only to say that, as in other epochs, at the very time when the church was attempting to come face to face with contemporary modes of perceiving and being, other forces in church and world were bringing about quite different currents and perspectives on human and Christian life.

Some thirty years after the council, "modernity" is increasingly judged to be an egregious aberration. "Postmodernity" refers to a rather all-pervasive sentiment that humanity must go beyond the modern. To what exactly? The answer is not clear. And so we stand at the juncture of modernity and postmodernity.[1] Even though we seem stalled at this intersection and unable to steer a course forward, it is becoming commonplace to describe our world as postmodern. And so perhaps it is more accurate to say that ours is neither a thoroughly modern nor altogether postmodern world. In my judgment, contemporary ways of perceiving and being are characterized by an uneven combination of features of premodern, modern, and postmodern sensibilities.[2]

The purpose of this final chapter is to give some indication of the features of these three sensibilities, attentive to the shifting understandings of the human person, of God, and of Christian spirituality emerging at the intersection of modernity and postmodernity. I am persuaded that what is called for at this point is the cultivation of deep reserves of hope in a hidden God of unfathomable mystery, rather than a return to the securities of a previous age. Or, worse, to appeal to a view of God that, for the most part, cannot be believed.

CONTRASTING VIEWS OF THE HUMAN

In common usage "modern" is synonymous with "contemporary." And so these days we say that modern technology makes possible instant communiques via FAX and next-day express mail. But the term "modern" is used now in a more restricted sense to refer to a particular historical period with its own characteristic worldview and ethos.

In its view of the human, the modern (Cartesian-Kantian) post-Enlightenment worldview emphasized individual subjectivity, interiority, and self-sustaining autonomy. This is quite a different view from those of earlier periods, referred to loosely here as the premodern. Prior to the Enlightenment and the onset of modernity, the human person was viewed as a more unified being whose meaning, purpose, and identity were understood to be discovered primarily in relation to others and God, as well as in the recognition of one's proper place in a clearly-ordered world of social and ecclesial arrangements. In a premodern worldview a sense of unity and coherence were quite strong. The enormous tragedies and sufferings afflicting persons and communities were more likely to be judged comprehensible in terms of God's providential plan for humanity, mere wrinkles in the unfolding of a divine tableau. Everything had its place, and everyone had a purpose in view of "the big picture."

More specifically, the human person was understood to be a unity. For example, Thomas Aquinas understood the human being to possess distinct capacities of intellect, will, and emotion. Happiness, as both gift and task, was realized in the proper exercise of these capacities and in their proper ordering to noble and higher ends. But these capacities were viewed as resting in a prior unity within the human being. They were not seen as separate faculties in contest with one another as in later views of the human, notably the faculty psychology of seventeenth-century France. At the risk of oversimplification, it can be put quite crisply: the premodern view of the human subject was more integrated and wholistic, appreciative of the importance of relationality and interdependence. This is true not only of the person vis-à-vis others, but also in terms of the various dimensions of the self.

With the advent of modernity's emphasis upon individuality, autonomy, and the superiority of reason, premodernity's more relational and wholistic matrix for understanding human being was eclipsed. At the juncture of modernity and post-modernity, it is precisely some of the central features of a premodern view of human personhood thus described that are needed as antidote to the egregious excesses of modernity's emphasis on autonomy and self-sufficiency. Modernity's bold and strident assertions of independence and autonomy are giving way to a postmodern sensibility which is awake to the realization that the human person is a relational being who exists toward others within a tradition or traditions.[3]

FEATURES OF THE POSTMODERN

The term "postmodern" is of recent origin and is quite ambiguous.[4] The adjective is used in a myriad of ways to describe and evaluate the current cultural, religious, and political climate as different from that of premodernity and modernity. As a distinctive worldview and sensibility, it is identifiable by way of contrast to modernity, modernism, or the modern. Modernity's bold claims for the idealist self-subsistent relational self and its view of history as inevitably progressive have been unsettled by the "terror of history" which interrupts and disorients, calling into question human conceptions of order, divine providence, indeed the very nature of God. David Power "names" the postmodern sensibility as one which refuses to deny the horrors and atrocities that have taken place in this century.[5]

More than anything else, it is the staggering horror of historical events that has shaken modernity. The atrocities of history unsettle the certitude of the "modern" sensibility and call into question modernity's ability to make good on its guarantees of order, cohesion, coherence in self, community, history, and world. Hiroshima and Auschwitz have done the most to make an ordered view of history no longer credible, and to put a bold question mark next to the very notion of divine providence. In our own day the mass genocide in Bosnia-Herzegovenia continues to make the order of history and of providence questionable for increasing numbers of believers. Convictions about order, unity, and coherence, once characteristic of the premodern sensibility, were carried over into modernity, even in its most atheistic and agnostic forms. But in modernity the premodern belief in order, unity, and progress according to a preordained divine plan was situated in the human rather than in God, in human reason rather than in God's providence. Nonetheless, the conviction about order, unity, and coherence remained strongly ingrained in the modern mindset and has exercised enormous influence in political and economic affairs. Modern theology emphasized the "turn to the subject," i.e., the individual human person whose ordered cognitive operations were understood to provide a basis for integration and unity in the self, as well as the seeds for the ideal human ordering of human relationships, communities, and societies.

Events stagger and startle, however. They shake up faith in a provident God bringing about a divinely-ordained order as well as belief in an ordered human freedom, capable of bettering the world. The violence inflicted upon innocent millions in the streets of "modern" cities, the massacre of whole races of people in different parts of the world, the bloodletting among the peoples of Rwanda and South Africa, the aggression of powerful nations against the poor and defenseless, the generations-old religious and cultural conflict in Northern Ireland, the horror of the AIDS epidemic, all these interrupt tightly-knit worldviews and neat-and-tidy systems of order, unity, and coherence. Would anyone dare suggest that such events belong in the order of providence? Yet at the intersection of modernity and postmodernity, even these horrors are often attributed to God's plan. It is heard far too often in college and university classrooms that God may have been trying to teach the Jews a lesson in and through the horrors of the Holocaust. Why? Since God (unquestionably viewed here as an absolute monarch) can do anything "he" wants, there *must* be a reason for everything that happens. But suffering, however repressed, eventually erupts to subvert the most basic and tightly-held modern belief that everything makes sense and fits into an ordered, coherent, unified purpose. Suffering and aguish defy modernity's most arrogant claim: Through adherence to the imperatives of rationality we can think our way through even this horror once again.

Though many of the interpretations of postmodernity are nihilistic, calling for complete "deconstruction," they nonetheless have important consequences for Christian spirituality. Other postmodern developments are more optimistic. These latter have been described as reconstructive or reenchanting.[6] Since Christian spirituality is concerned with the cultivation of the deepest reserves of human hope grounded in faith in the resurrection of Christ, even and especially when there seems to be no apparent reason for the hope, it is the more hopeful currents in postmodernism that merit attention. Some of these developments include the recognition that the altogether modern belief that history is necessarily progressive is itself an aberration, together with the awareness that many of the claims of the post-Enlightenment subject are far too audacious.

Not everything modernity prized is to be jettisoned. Its emphasis on human dignity and on human rights and liberties is to be safeguarded in the move from modernity to postmodernity. Likewise modernity's efforts to secure the equality of all persons in the pursuit of the common good. But postmodernism is alert to the egregious errors made through modernity's snubbing of religion and tradition (religious and otherwise), as well as by its adulation of the self-determined, autonomous, self-subsistent self. The response to these errors is postmodernism's critical yet appreciative awareness of the indispensability of relationality, interdependence, community, and traditions. There is often a great measure of humility in the postmodern period, a deeper awareness of the fact that our view of truth is necessarily partial, and that the promises of modernity and rationality gone unchecked in the technological age have failed to satisfy the deepest longings of the human heart. Nowhere is the audacity of modernity more apparent than in its pretensions about human transcendence, the superiority of spirit over matter and the body, as well as in its emphasis on divine transcendence to the point of eclipsing divine immanence.

Human persons are historical. Ineluctably in the mix of history, humans remain finite and fragile. Cognizant of this, the truth claims of postmodernity tend to be more partial. There seems a greater realization that any point of view is one view of a point. Discourse about God and God's activity in the world is more tentative. This does not imply that truth is relative, or that God is a matter of personal taste and pleasure. Rather it is to suggest that our rather tenuous grasp on truth is relative to the possibilities of our historical situation. Our apprehension of God and God's ways in the world is not to be gauged by Enlightenment canons of certitude, but rather in terms of the premodern sense of knowing and understanding.

The recognition that traditional human conceptions of order and providence are no longer plausible in light of the shock of history, together with the awareness that promises made by and to modernity's idealist self-subsistent self have failed to satisfy the deepest longings of the human heart does not inevitably entail abandoning faith in God. But it does entail the acceptance of a more fragile self and the loss of a familiar God image.

The interruptive character of history, the capacity of suffering to disorient and baffle, the discontinuities between expectation and event—all render human persons and history precincts of epiphany. But this is more likely to take the form of the episodic. The coherent narrative with beginning, middle, and end gives way to the epiphanies in Joyce, Proust, and Mann at the close of modernity. These writers still attempt to fashion a coherence in the narrative order. It is only with writers such as Beckett and Vico that temporality itself is ruptured altogether, and a mythic return to order is no longer acceptable. There is no big picture. Perhaps not even a collage. Just fragments.

Historical relativity is one of the hallmarks of the modern period, to be sure. That is to say that already in modernity it was recognized that perspectives are relative and limited by historical and cultural context. But modernity still affirmed that there was a "givenness" in the world, and that human beings could come to know this givenness, albeit in a partial and limited way. But in postmodern perspective, views of reality are themselves understood to be constructed. Human beings are makers and shapers of worlds of meaning and value.

In postmodern perspective the world is not understood as a coherent picture, but in terms of a multiplicity of constructs.[7] Universal norms and claims no longer persuade. Because of the perpetration of unspeakable evil through the laws and norms of cultures and societies, postmodernity is suspicious of any claim to objectivity and universality. A postmodern sensibility gives rise to the query: How can one claim that other countries in the world would be better off it they adhered to principles of American democracy? Or to the principles of Christianity?

Postmodern perspectives are suspicious of modernity's effort to construct the self-subsistent self. Such a goal is judged impossible and results in an artificial self which, in turn, constructs institutions and societies that are themselves artificial. As but one example, the contemporary college or university, with its proliferation of committees and departments all in service of a myriad of specializations, seems to have lost track of its central purpose: the education and formation of whole persons in service of the human community. A postmodern perspective recognizes the holistic nature of persons and societies. That is to say that the person is not purely, or even primarily, a rational being. Rather, the person is a being who desires wholeness while at the same time demanding respect for individual differences, historical specificity, and cultural particularity. In the perspective of modernity, wholeness and particularity seem ultimately irreconcilable. In postmodernity they are dialectically inseparable.

In sum, there are three hallmarks of a postmodern sensibility. First, since views of reality are not "given" but constructed, there is suspicion of all universal and normative claims, even and especially about God. This is especially due to the reality of historical evil. The interruptive character of history, the suffering and terror perpetrated by powerful elites and ideological victors, calls into question any and all claims to have a complete hold on the truth. Second, there is a suspicion of modernity's tendency toward compartmentalization and specialization. This is not only true of the institutions and societies given shape by modernity. It is also true of the human being who is not a composite of various components or faculties, the premier of which is reason narrowly understood. Rather, the person desires integration in relation to others in community and tradition. Third, there is the affirmation that particularity and wholeness are not irreconcilable but dialectically inseparable. Lamentably, modernity has made of them rivals and competitors.

THE ABSENT GOD

Whether it is based in revelation or in philosophical reflection, the image of God developed from the canons of the Enlightenment is no longer sustainable in view of the contemporary human experiences of interruption and disorientation central to a postmodern sensibility. The God of modernity who could be counted on to intervene on our behalf is absent. This God is thought to be *the* one God, the God of the Christian tradition, a Supreme Being who rules the world. With sphinx-like inscrutability, God exerts power as an absolute monarch. Power here is understood as the ability to do whatever one chooses, forcibly if necessary. Power controls, dominates, manipulates. Divine power is not to be questioned because, unlike other expressions of power, God's power is always exercised to achieve noble, even if incomprehensible, purposes. Whether through dominance or benevolence God is "in charge," intervening in human life and history in order to bring about worthy ends. In this view, God is altogether perfect, in a way that stands in sharp contrast to creatures. God creates and sustains the world, but is not in real relationship with it or with creatures, since real relationship would imply that God would be affected by human life and history. In this view, to be affected by the other implies change. And change implies imperfection. God's transcendence is stressed to the point of eclipsing immanence. And its counterpart in the human, the immaterial, or the spirit, is exalted at the expense of the body and matter. Both are denigrated.

At the crossroads of modernity and postmodernity, this understanding of God is beyond belief. Consequently, increasing numbers of people face a profound sense of loss of this familiar image of God. Together with this is the haunting wonder about where and how God is present in and to the world and to persons in the world. Along with this comes a deep uncertainty about one's place in the world, a place once assured in the tightly-knit worldviews and social arrangements of premodernity and modernity. In the ache of this loss, this sense of absence and disorientation brought on when one cleans house of all discredited and implausible conceptions of God, the question emerges as if for the first time: How can I speak the name of God in prayer?

Raising this question does not imply that there is no God. It is a question that must be raised in the experience of God's absence brought on by the crumbling of images, theories, and linguistic frameworks that have heretofore mediated the experience of God. It is precisely in the midst of such a collapse, in the ruins of a God image more idolatrous than theonomous, that one can "lean into" the experience of God known in the ache of absence, an absence which in itself is a mediation of presence. Here, at this juncture of knowing and unknowing, of light and dark, a dazzling darkness summons to see what is known in the unknowing.

This darkness is a moment of disclosure, and the experience of absence is a mode of presence. In the early moments of prayer we might first be inclined to search for signs of the unfolding preordained universal plan of salvation being enacted throughout a history in which "God writes straight with crooked lines." But in the deeper movements of prayer we can only squint to catch a glimpse of God's unfathomable mystery discerned in fragmentary acts of compassion, healing, hope, and justice in a world-become-shambles.[8]

In the encounter with God in the ache of absence, in the loss of what was thought to be known of God until now, what is called for is the cultivation of deep reserves of trust and hope, the strengthening of the conviction that even in this, God's unfathomable fidelity is found as both promise and presence. God is trustworthy not because "he" can be counted on to intervene in human affairs, but because of a promise of presence given and sustained in communities of remembrance, circles of memory and hope that urge us on even and especially when there seems no reason for the hope.

To refer to such a profound experience of loss as a "dark night of the soul" is to run the risk of minimizing it. For here the darkness is not just one experienced in the individual. And it is not simply a matter of one's life of prayer, one's "spiritual life." This loss of God affects the corporate life of a people of faith. It amounts to questioning most of what we have thought of God until now. And it demands that we allow God beyond all names and all tellings to be God. It requires that we allow God to come on God's own terms. Caught in this dialectic of presence and absence it is possible, perhaps for the first time, to experience the God whose power is the power of love and compassion, who invites and persuades to critical compassionate action and a mode of contemplation that does not grasp at images which obscure this incomprehensible gracious mystery. In a word it is to enter fully and completely into the apophatic way, the *via negativa*, knowing that our understanding of the very nature of God is at stake, and trusting that liberation from all images of God in order to participate in the life of the living God is the most compelling sign of God's presence and action in our world.

IMPLICATIONS FOR CHRISTIAN SPIRITUALITY

The implications of a postmodern sensibility for a specifically Christian spirituality are wide-ranging. Two of these are deserving of development here: a postmodern view of person as relational; and the interruptive and disorienting character of history.

Person as Relational

At the juncture of modernity and postmodernity there is the recognition that modernity's project of constructing the self-subsistent rational self was wrong-headed and artificial. Consequently there is greater attention given to other dimensions of the self in understandings of human personhood, especially relationality, community, and the necessity of traditions for human flourishing. On this score recent efforts to retrieve and reconceptualize the doctrine of the Trinity are most instructive.

Catherine Mowry LaCugna and Elizabeth A. Johnson among others have provided systematic theological reconceptualizations of the mystery of God that are attentive to the shortcomings of the concept of God developed by modernity.[9] For Catherine LaCugna, what has often been assumed to be the loftiest, most abstract and ethereal expression of the doctrine of God, the Trinitarian doctrine, is after all the most practical. Taken as the point of entry and destination of Christian life, the Trinity gives rise to an understanding of a spirituality whose keynotes are participation in communion of persons both human and divine, and the perfection of these relationships in self-donation, mutuality, and reciprocity. Because it is personal, relational, and communal, such a spirituality naturally connects with the ethical demands of Christian life in the Spirit, now viewed in terms of the flourishing of persons in loving communion rather than as individual sanctification achieved by a journey inward.

In this light all those dimensions of Christian life ordinarily associated with spirituality must be reconsidered.[10] As but one example, in classicist and premodern views, as well as in modernity, virginity and celibacy quickly developed as superior forms of life. Celibacy in particular was understood as a form of solitary life that precluded sexuality, marriage, and affective relationships. Virginity and celibacy were regarded as components of the authentic Christian life. Any survey of Christian history will show that spirituality of the laity was understood as derivative and lesser because of the priority given to virginity and celibacy, rooted in a particular understanding of God as immutable, impassible, essentially unrelated, self-existent, incorporeal. *Ascesis,* the exercise or discipline by which the Christian grows to full stature of life in Christ, was understood narrowly as mortification of the flesh. Rarely was it applied to other demanding aspects of the Christian life as such: for example, the rigorous sacrifices entailed in marital and family life, especially caring for one's children; the uncertainties of agrarian life and daily struggles for sustenance; complex decisions about the use and disposition of goods; the chaste exercise of sexuality for non-celibates; responsibility for the earth; the discipline of education and study; proper care and exercise of the body (nutrition, diet, balance of leisure and work); the tedium of too much work.

Informed by postmodern critiques of the self-made self, asceticism becomes less a matter of purification of oneself through the concentrated effort of the will, and more attentive to the purification of one's relationships and to the discipline of rightly-ordered relationships: being conformed to the person of Christ and being united in communion with God and others.

History as Interruptive

A postmodern sensibility calls for confidence in the episodic rather than in the orderly, in interruption instead of patterned providential predictability, and in a promise of presence rather than in divine intervention by either dominance or benevolence. Postmodernity's emphasis on interruption, disorientation, and discontinuity evoke the recognition that the God of the Hebrew and Christian Scriptures is not first and foremost a God of order and providence, but a God who is active in history and present to creation. This postmodern sensibility is not inevitably at odds with the Gospel of Jesus, who interrupted rather than fulfilled conventional certainties regarding God's plan of salvation for the chosen people. The promises offered by the Christ flew in the face of tightly-held expectations. Indeed his very coming and his cross were discontinuous with all that was judged to be God's way and work in the world.

An authentic Christian spirituality marked by the more hopeful and optimistic currents in postmodernity is willing to relinquish audacious claims about God's permissive will, a preordained order, and a benevolent providence that fly in the face of common sense and sober faith. It is willing to surrender to the unfathomable gracious mystery in the darkness which is in itself a disclosure. This Christian spirituality is buoyed up by the conviction that even and especially in the discontinuities and interruptions of human history, precisely in the events that boggle and baffle, God comes. Christ's constant coming amidst the episodic and interruptive gives rise to doxology which stumbles from the lips of those whose unknowing is the deepest kind of knowing.

The Riches of Loss

These changing currents and perspectives invite new experiences and expressions of prayer and worship. Above all, in both corporate worship and personal prayer the loss of the familiar image of God must be named for what it is. Next, the loss must be faced, and the absence of the familiar grieved. This requires a fuller recognition of the importance of lament in both prayer and worship.

Adequate worship requires lamenting the loss of these theories, frameworks, structures, indeed everything familiar, thought to mediate this divine presence.[11] To worship is to lean into the ache of absence rather than to retreat to the familiar patterns of giving lip-service to a God who once was counted on to intervene in human affairs. At the intersection of modernity and postmodernity, where are the churches in which can be heard voices raised to God in lamentation, weeping over the loss of what has been known of God until now?

Only when the heart knows the ache of absence do reserves of hope that dwell therein give rise to unrelenting thanksgiving. It is only in the ache of Christ's dying that life anew gives cause for doxology. Only when the depth of absence is lived long and lovingly can the heart awaken to Christ's constant coming. Stalled at the crossroads of modernity and postmodernity, it is a perfect act of praise and homage to call a halt to faith and yet believe that all is not chaos. And to give thanks and praise to the living God whose adventing is known even and especially in the shadow of the cross.

Notes

1. Elisabeth J. Lacelle suggests that we are "au carrefour," at the crossroads, of modernity and postmodernity; see her "Introduction: Postmodernité/Postmodernism," *Studies in Religion/Sciences Religieuses* 22:4 (1994) 405-416. See also *The Merton Annual*, vol. 6, ed. George Kilcourse (Collegeville: The Liturgical Press, 1994); several essays in this book take up the theme of spirituality at the juncture of modernity and postmodernity; especially helpful is Steven Payne, "'Although It Is Night': A Carmelite Perspective on Spirituality at the Juncture of Modernity and Postmodernity" (pp. 134-159).

2. This assessment was offered by David Tracy in his Cobb Lectures at Lexington Seminary, Lexington, Kentucky, Fall 1992.

3. Catherine Mowry LaCugna spells out a view of the human person as "theonomous," a position at once informed by premodern understandings of God and human nature as well as attentive to postmodern insight and sensibilities; see LaCugna, *God for Us: The Trinity and Christian Life* (San Francisco: Harper Collins, 1991), chapter

8, "Persons in Communion"; see also "Participation in Communion of Persons," chapter 6 in this volume.

4. For helpful descriptions of the postmodern, see Richard Kearney, *The Wake of the Imagination: Toward a Postmodern Culture* (Minneapolis: University of Minnesota Press, 1988) and David Ray Griffin, ed., *Spirituality and Society: Postmodern Perspectives* (Albany: State University of New York Press, 1988). See also D.R. Griffin, "Postmodern Theology for the Church," *Lexington Theological Quarterly* 28:3 (Fall 1993) 201-260.

5. See David N. Power, "Event Eventing," in Michael Downey and Richard Fragomeni, eds., *A Promise of Presence* (Washington, D.C.: The Pastoral Press, 1992) 271-299.

6. See David Ray Griffin, ed., *Sacred Interconnections: Postmodern Spirituality, Political Economy, and Art* (Albany: State University of New York Press, 1990), which represents the emergence of a reconstructive, reenchanting postmodernism.

7. Liliane Voye likens the present state of affairs to the view from the kaleidoscope; see her "La religion en postmodernité," *Studies in Religion/Sciences Religieuses* 22:4 (1994) 503-520.

8. See Constance Fitzgerald, "Impasse and Dark Night," in Tilden Edwards, ed., *Living with Apocalypse: Spiritual Resources for Social Compassion* (New York: Harper and Row, 1984) 93-116. For the image of ruins and shambles to describe features of the postmodern world, I am indebted to David N. Power. His own efforts to develop a theology of liturgy and sacrament in a postmodern world are seen in his "Event Eventing," in Downey and Fragomeni, eds., *A Promise of Presence*; for a fuller treatment, see David Power, *The Eucharistic Mystery: Revitalizing the Tradition* (New York: Crossroad, 1992).

9. See Elizabeth A. Johnson, *She Who Is: The Mystery of God in Feminist Theological Discourse* (New York: Crossroad, 1992) and LaCugna, *God for Us.*

10. Here I acknowledge my gratitude to Catherine LaCugna for her part in our joint effort to develop a contemporary Christian spirituality informed by the doctrine of the Trinity. For a fuller development of these and other features of Christian spirituality shaped by recent studies of the Trinity, see Catherine Mowry LaCugna and Michael Downey, "Trinitarian Spirituality," in *The New Dictionary of Catholic Spirituality*, ed. Michael Downey (Collegeville: The Liturgical Press/Glazier, 1993).

11. See Elizabeth A. Johnson, "Between the Times: Religious Life and the Postmodern Experience of God," *Review for Religious* 53:1 (January/February 1994) 6-28, who describes this loss of familiarities and securities and its impact on the present and future of institutional religious life.